THE RIPPLE EFFECT

The Ripple Effect

A Novel Exploring the Challenges and Triumphs of Running an Animal Shelter

MARCY ECKHARDT

Edition 1.2
Cover designed with input from Rochelle Smith
Cover features **Kele**, a Navajo Terrier

ISBN-13: 978-0615630151
ISBN-10: 0615630154

For the Women and Men who Work in Animal Shelters –

Thank You for What you Do Every Day, for Animals

Preface

"I'm sorry Shane I know you want more time, probably need more time, but I can't give it to you. Either you take the training and start performing the procedure or I hire someone who will. It's that simple," Payton Williams, Shelter Director and Shane's boss said to her.

It was anything but simple to Shane. She of course had considered euthanizing animals before taking the job. It was the animal shelter, that's what they did. But was it something she did? In the past few months she'd held the animals while someone else injected the drug. Was there really a difference?

Shane had only planned on staying at the job for a short time but she'd really started to like it. She didn't have much of a choice. She knew she'd be able to do it, be strong enough to do it. Kim, Jamie and Dee all did it. If they could do it and still be fine every day, so could she. But did she want to do it? For years she'd been trying to define herself, trying to find out where she fit into the world. Was Euthanasia Technician that place?

The only way to move up at the shelter, if she was planning on staying, was to become trained. And technically they euthanized a lot more old, sick and mean dogs and cats than anything else. Shane was okay with some of those being euthanized, especially if they were suffering.

"Fine. I'll do it," she told Payton. Not bothering to explain what she was feeling. After all, Shane figured it wouldn't have been a surprise to anyone that she didn't want the training. Why bother saying what everyone already knew. The strong remain silent, her father always said. How stupid she'd been to listen to his advice.

Chapter 1

Shane Hillard sat sideways in the rectangular dog run at Pinewoods Humane Society. Her butt was cold from the concrete and she could have done without the smell, but she felt oddly at ease. The room was quiet. The dogs had woken up briefly when she came in, but had already gone back to sleep. She had thirty more minutes before the rest of the staff got in.

Shane hadn't made it far on her morning rounds before stopping. The dog receiving and holding area, where she was sitting, was the second room she'd visited. Eleven runs lined each side, a four-foot concrete wall separating them. Chain-link fencing covered the twenty-two front gates, and extended above the concrete divider walls.

The thirty-six-year old Shelter Director only turned on one bank of lights when she entered the room. The florescent panels were seven feet over her head and cast a subtle glow down the long, wide aisle in the center. Shane walked slowly, glancing from side to side. She acknowledged any dogs she remembered from last week and checked the paperwork on anyone new.

All animals brought to the shelter spent their first few days in the receiving areas. The ones that were lost or in need of medical care stayed only briefly, while the others waited there until the state-mandated, three or five-day holding period was up. After that they belonged to the shelter, technically.

"Hey cutie," she said quietly to the black Lab mix who'd come in as a stray over the weekend.

Staring up at her, the young dog wagged his tail and let out a soft bark.

"Ssshhh," she said smiling, "not yet."

Shane stopped in front of any dogs she didn't recognize. Eager for affection, all but one tried to entice her to open their gate. She counted six new dogs since noon Friday, when she'd left for the weekend; four surrenders and two strays. She was half-way through the room when she saw the scared little one she was now sitting down next to.

At first she thought the kennel was empty and the paperwork on the gate belonged to someone else. But as she stopped to grab the intake forms she realized there was a full bowl of food and water. Knowing they wouldn't be in an empty run, she stared for a minute toward the shadowy back of the kennel.

After a bit, she saw the dog hiding in the far back corner. According to her intake paperwork, she was found tied to the front door on Saturday morning. Shane felt for the terrified animal and quietly called out to her, "hey there? You okay?" The dog, her head bowed, didn't move.

Shane knew in order to get a dog like this to come around she would have to start trusting people. Having a little extra time, Shane opened the gate and stepped inside. Not wanting to push the dog, and barely able to see how she was reacting, Shane moved slowly. Stopping only a few feet into the six foot run, she slid smoothly down the wall, across from the nervous animal. Once she got situated, Shane sat quietly, pretending to ignore her.

Only three-feet across, the run was too narrow to have her legs straight out in front of her. So Shane sat cross-legged, her long, thin body comfortable in the cramped quarters. She'd made it a habit of walking the kennels every morning but this was the first time she'd ever sat down in one. Listening, she could hear a dog farther down the row scratching at his ears then moaning in either aggravation or contentment. At least one litter of puppies was in the room. One after another, they woke up and began playing. Muted growls, soft whimpers and an occasional bark sounded from their kennel.

Uncrossing then re-crossing her legs, Shane pulled her lunch toward her. She'd spent the weekend with her nephew Jeremy at a baseball tournament in New Mexico. By the time they got back last night, it was too late to go to the grocery store. So she'd raided Jeremy's lunch supplies, which her sister always kept in the bottom drawer of the fridge. Pulling the pre-packaged container out of her backpack she looked at what she'd grabbed; Ham and Cheddar with Crackers.

Disgusting, she thought, wondering how her health-food-crazy sister could buy the stuff.

Shane pulled the glued plastic top off the container and pulled out a two-inch pinkish-purple disk. Turning the slimy substance over in her hand she realized she now didn't have anything to eat for lunch. Her stomach grumbled as if to confirm the thought.

They had stopped for a quick bite on their way home yesterday but it was late and Shane wanted to get Jeremy back. Not a morning person, the twelve-year old needed more than ten hours of sleep to function before summer school. When they had stopped at seven o'clock, they had three more hours to go. So she gulped down her dollar cheeseburger and slowly sipped the sixty-four-ounce caffeine filled soda.

Tearing the material identified as ham in half, Shane tried to move slowly. But it didn't seem to matter. The dog was terrified. Shane kept her eyes on the far wall as she gently tossed the half-circle toward the shaking animal. It landed an inch from her right paw but was enough to scare her even further. Ignoring the meat, the compact dog pulled herself deeper into the corner, as if she could become invisible.

"Sorry baby," Shane said quietly and moved another inch away.

The metal bowl with the dog's food from the day before hadn't been touched. Shane had pushed it out of the way earlier, but now looking at it she saw the canned food had dried and crusted overnight. Looking around, she realized the dog hadn't gone to the bathroom or touched her water either. Shane wondered if she'd moved at all.

The ventilation switched on, circulating clean air through the kennels. She always felt bad for the dogs that had to say in this room. Holding less than half the number of animals that were on the adoption floor, she originally thought it would be calmer. But in reality it was one of the most stressed rooms in the building. The majority of the dogs here were new to the shelter and unused to the routine, so they were louder and much more reactive. Two small windows, located on the outer wall barely let in any light. And without the acoustic panels the adoption room had, the concrete seemed to increase the volume when the dogs barked, instead of absorbing it.

Watching the poor dog sit there with her head bowed, reminded Shane of the weekend. Growing up back east, she had no idea how bad the dog and cat situation was in the west. The first time she drove to the Grand Canyon she couldn't believe how many stray dogs she saw on the way. Dogs along the highway, standing in desolate stretches of desert, and always at the gas stations. Many were sweet and eager for water, food or affection but some were feral and avoided humans. It reminded her of a third world country and broke her heart.

This past weekend, she saw dogs everywhere. In the parking lots, around the fast food restaurants, many even slept under the cars during the tournament. Most were bone thin and looked pathetic. Knowing the situation ahead of time Shane had brought two, forty-pound bags of dog food with her and fifteen gallons of water. She'd used it all before they left yesterday but couldn't help wondering if she had just delayed the dogs suffering for another week.

On their way out of town, Shane and Jeremy stopped at Burger King for a bite. Needing to use the facilities they ordered inside but planned to eat on the road. On their way out the door, Jeremy gave one chicken nugget away after another to the dogs that waited for them. Shane gave her cheeseburger to a pregnant black and white dog she saw lying under the bushes. As she headed through the drive-thru to reorder, Jeremy watched out the back of her truck as the dogs targeted the next tourist.

The size of West Virginia, the Navajo Nation is the largest Indian reservation in the country. Located mainly in northern Arizona, the Nation spreads across inhospitable and desolate desert lands. Barbed wire fencing and tumbleweeds were her only companion as she drove the barren stretches of highway. Small clusters of houses located about 20 miles apart were grouped near amazing rock formations. Shane loved exploring and climbing rocks. *A place like this could keep a kid busy for years,* she thought, envious that her backyard had been so boring.

Hogan's, small, one-room ceremonial buildings, often used for in-laws, could be found in every cluster of homes. The circular shaped buildings stood out among the rest and even in the twilight, Shane could see dogs wandering among them looking for food, water or a place to sleep for the night.

At first Shane couldn't understand the animal situation. She'd always assumed Native Americans treated their animals better than anyone else. Quickly she learned that wasn't the case. Many of the tribes that lived nearby had different views when it came to dogs and cats. Some only considered having an animal if they provided protection, but feared that protection was lost if the animal was allowed to come inside.

Ute tribes restrained their dogs on large bulky chains while Navajo's seem determined to avoid confining theirs. Daily, packs of dogs roam the streets of Navajo towns. So typical, they are virtually ignored by the townspeople. The dogs made their rounds between dumpsters, fast-food restaurants and along the highways.

Once complete, the group circled back to the neighborhood. As they padded across streets, one dog after another dropped out of the pack and returned home.

Shane knew she shouldn't feel bad, she was doing her part. For the last six months the shelter had taken in more than a hundred dogs from the Navajo Nation. But knowing that didn't change the way she felt. It was horrible seeing so many sick one's and she felt helpless leaving any of them there. In a way she was glad to be away from it.

Shane glanced down at the dog hiding under the bench. Her head was still bowed and she continued to ignore the artificial ham patty. But her shaking had calmed a bit. Shane hoped it was a good sign but didn't dare move.

Small, the dog looked like she weighed thirty-five-pounds or so. Her coat was short but thick. It was hard to tell, but Shane thought she looked to be mostly brown with some black markings. Her head was tiny, almost too small for her body and she stunk like garbage. Shane wished she could see her eyes, but the scared girl still hadn't looked up.

When they first started transferring in dogs from the Nation, the staff had guessed at the predominant breed. But like the one sitting next to her, it was nearly impossible.
Without human intervention, the dogs bred naturally. Jamie, one of the kennel supervisors, started calling them Navajo Pointers and it had stuck.

Reservation dogs, the term used for any stray dog coming in from northern New Mexico, Arizona, or Southern Utah were usually easy to spot. Thin with protruding rib and hip bones, the medium-sized dogs often had hair loss, worms and were covered in fleas. But they also had a unique ability to get along well with other dogs and affiliate quickly with people. These were the skills they honed living on the streets, begging for their daily meals from passing tourists.

Not this one, Shane thought. *She was scared. Maybe locked in a backyard all her life and now terrified of the world.* "You look more like a Navajo Terrier than a Pointer."

Shane tried again in her best happy but subdued voice. "Hey there baby, aren't you hungry? Don't you want a little to eat?" The small dog's tail thumped once on the concrete floor. *Well that's something,* Shane thought leaning back against the wall.

Looking around she realized how limited a dog's vision was in the runs. *No wonder they went spastic anytime someone walked down the corridor.* She could only see a couple feet on either side of the kennel and realized she'd jump, just like the dogs did, if someone came walking up the aisle. She heard the other dog moan again as he or she scratched at their ears.

After a few more minutes, Shane put her lunch back together and stood. She had a busy day and knew she needed to get started. The Board of Directors had held an emergency meeting on Friday night about the upcoming plan to go no-kill and Shane needed to find out what had happened.

The decision for the organization to change their name and philosophy to the current shelter trend had happened almost a year ago. The official vote was planned for next month, during the annual meeting with the membership.

Since Shane hadn't heard anything about it in close to a year, she figured it wasn't going to amount to much.

But an emergency meeting, on a Friday night, was a big deal. Nothing special had been going on at the shelter so she believed the rumors when she heard they would be discussing the change to no-kill. Shane didn't have anything against the change, but didn't understand why they needed it. The shelter was saving more animals than ever before.

As she stood, the scared dog pulled back farther under the bench but didn't look up. "Baby, you gotta chill a little bit. And you've got to eat something." Shane said quietly, pushing yesterday's food back in front of her. A few flies rose as the bowl slid across the floor but quickly settled back down onto the unappealing food. Shane tore up the ham and set it on top of the crust. Then moved to the gate, flipped up the latch, and let herself out, closing it securely behind her.

Someone switched on the second bank of lights. *Jamie must be in*, Shane thought. The rest of the dogs were waking up, stretching and shaking off the night. Though most of these dogs hadn't been at the shelter long, they quickly learned that morning brought breakfast. Shane walked down the remainder of the row trying to determine who had an ear issue.

Two runs from the end, she saw him. It was Jake, a beautiful German Shepherd, and a regular. Jake got picked-up at least twice a month by Animal Control. The staff joked that he spent as much time at the shelter as he did his own house.

He stood when he saw her so Shane opened his gate and slipped inside. The mammoth dog weighed over a hundred pounds, and was a love. As soon as the gate closed he leaned against her legs, eager for affection. Shane looked in each ear before rubbing them and telling him she'd take care of them later. He moaned and leaned against her for more. After another minute, she slipped out to continue her rounds.

A Cattle Dog mix at the end of the row performed a perfect downward-facing-dog yoga pose and yawned as she passed. Shane smiled slightly in response. "I know how you feel big guy, I could use a little exercise myself." Shane opened the door and headed out to the adoption floor.

Chapter 2

Pinewoods Humane Society or PHS, was like a thousand other privately funded Animal Shelters, loud and busy, with cracked concrete floors, posters of animals and people with animals, and a heavy smell of cleaning products emulating throughout the building. At least after eleven in the morning, before that it smelled like strong ammonia, unscoopable kitty litter and poop, lots of poop. It was something the visitors always commented on and the staff never seemed to notice.

The reception area was the heart of the shelter. The large room had a small seating area off to one side with a community bulletin board and free informational handouts. The horseshoe-shaped reception desk filled the space between the two sets of double-doors that led to the dog adoption area. The cattery, made almost entirely of windows, sat in the northeast corner of the room - providing entertainment for those needing to wait. A large staircase leading to the administration offices, circled upward to the balcony above.

"I'm sorry we don't have her yet." Shane held open the swinging doors as the woman with the missing Spaniel mix, followed her back to the lobby. "But don't give up hope. Spaniels are wonderful dogs. Sometimes someone picks them up and holds onto them for a couple of days before bringing them to us."

The petite, sixty-year old, well-dressed woman nodded but looked unconvinced. Hatch, her ten-year-old Spaniel had wandered away while she was gardening. Thinking he had curled up under a bush she didn't look for him immediately and was now beside herself worrying.

"The best thing you can do," Shane said, taking the Lost Dog Guide from one of the girls at the front desk and handing it to the woman, "is to not lose hope. Here's a listing of the other shelters near us. Some are far away but he could have gotten picked up and brought to another shelter, so it's important to look at every one."

Shane had hoped to get through her email by noon but with only a half an hour left she knew it was a lost cause. She'd spent the morning getting caught up on what happened over the weekend. Animal Control had been called out to check on a starving horse and found a barn full of cats, Kim one of the kennel supervisors had been rude to a customer and Shane had to call the woman back and apologize and then she spent over an hour on the phone with a man who called to surrender eight dogs and sixteen cats.

"We've got the lost report and I'll keep an eye out for him myself." Shane said, standing at the front door with the woman. As she turned to head back to her office she spotted Dee Nizhoni, the shelters Executive Director and her boss, on the landing above her.

"Got a minute?" Dee asked quietly. Though large, the rooms' acoustics were fantastic. Anything said at the front desk could be heard clearly upstairs in the administration offices. It wasn't until Shane learned that lesson the hard way that she wondered if the architect had done it on purpose.

"Sure," Shane said before looking back at the front desk, "I'll be upstairs."

Shane took the stairs two at a time until she was halfway up, then she slowed. The wide balcony and twenty-five-foot ceilings provided a great vantage point of both the reception desk and the mountains outside. To make the room more inviting and to capitalize on the magnificent views, much of the north wall was windows. The wide stone staircase circled to the balcony above the reception desk, providing a clear view of the lower Rockies. Shane slowed to enjoy it before continuing the rest of the way.

Growing up in the suburbs of Akron, Ohio Shane had never considered seeing something beautiful every day, especially at work. But after moving to Loma Bonita, Colorado three years ago she couldn't imagine living anywhere else. She had originally come out just to help her sister with Jeremy after his father, Dwight took off. But after a year she knew she wouldn't go back, couldn't go back. The mountains were a big part of it. But she also loved the wildlife and the dirt roads she was forced to drive on.

Never owning a four-wheel drive vehicle before moving to Colorado, Shane was excited to have a good reason to finally buy one. A month after arriving, she bought a used Jeep Grand Cherokee with 100,000 miles on it. Driving in the snow had never been an issue for her; she learned to drive in Ohio winters. Now she took pride in driving in the snow in a beefy truck.

Four-wheeling on Government run BLM land and in the mountains had become one of Shane's favorite pastimes. Piling her two dogs Henry and Juice, into her truck, Shane explored random roads, stumbled upon old mining towns and searched to see her first bear. After her first excursion, when she entered the Weminuche Wilderness to the west of Loma Bonita and six hours later emerged two hours east of town, she downloaded the latest GPS software and began studying local maps.

Back east there were few places so remote, so unregulated as to pose any real threat. But Shane quickly learned that a short drive in the wilderness here could leave her stranded, lost and with little chance for help. Now she knew the BLM roads around Loma Bonita as well as the paved town roads. Testing herself often, she tried to get lost but always ended up home before her sister called Search and Rescue.

The second floor of the shelter looked more like a typical office building than an Animal Shelter. The main corridor was four-foot wide and carpeted. Unlike downstairs, the posters here were expensive and framed and didn't include pleas to spay and neuter animals. Shane heard a litter of kittens crying as she walked down the hall.

Most of the doors were open so Shane peaked into the office shared by the Volunteer and Foster-home Coordinators. Neither were in but a three-tiered cat kennel sat against one wall. Two of the six kittens were playing while the others slept in a pile on top of one another.

Shane turned and continued walking to the end of the hallway. Dee's office door was open and Shane walked in. Dee Nizhoni had been with the shelter for more than ten years and Executive Director for the last three. The majority of her time was spent raising funds for the new building they hoped to have in the next few years but Shane and her still met weekly to discuss shelter operations.

Though none of the rooms on the second floor had windows, Dee's office was the most comfortable room Shane had ever been in. Intricate sand paintings hung on three walls, while the fourth was covered with a beautiful green, black and red Navajo rug. Six-foot wide and four-foot long, the rug hung sideways across the back wall. Shane had seen the rug for months before realizing the intricate design in the middle was in fact a large tree with roots, branches and leaves intertwining throughout the center area.

After an especially difficult week, Shane and Dee were up sitting in her office having a beer when Dee told her the story of how she had to make the rug as part of her womanhood ceremony.

"I was desperate to get away from the tribe," Dee began, surprising Shane who knew how much pride Dee had in her heritage. She commuted ninety minutes to work each day so she could live on the Nation and still work at the shelter.

"In my family the woman spun wool, that's what we did. We tended to the sheep and used the wool to make blankets, rugs, what-not, anything needed. It was never a question of whether we liked it or even if we were good at it. It's just what my family did. My best friend's family broke horses. They were the best at it. So if we ever needed a horse we called them, and if they ever needed a blanket, they called us."

"The hardest part for me was spinning and dying the wool. My sisters could do it with no problem, but for some reason I just couldn't do it," Dee had said. "But I wasn't allowed to go away to college without making my first rug. I was the fastest weaver in my family, so I traded with my sisters and cousins. I told them I would weave if they would spin and dye. My parents wouldn't have liked it, but it worked for us."

"Why this design?" Shane had asked.

"Because I'm stubborn," Dee replied, smiling, staring at the large tree. "My grandfather was old when I was little. He always called me "stubborn goat" because I always made things harder than they had to be. This design," she ran her hand over the enlarged tree, clearly visible once Shane realized what it was, "my grandfather created this. He always drew trees. Everywhere, in the dirt, on napkins in the diner, in dust on the hood of his truck. He loved trees."

"The key to being a strong tree, stubborn goat, he said when I was ten, is to make the roots bigger than the branches. Most people only draw what they see above ground, but that's not a tree. That's a part of the tree. The important part is hidden below the surface, and branches out far wider than any of the branches we can see."

"So instead of just making a rug, you made an especially difficult one?" Shane asked.

Dee smiled, "so it would seem. Once I decided what I was going to do, I wanted it to be perfect. So I had to work with my mom, my grandmother and my aunts. My grandmother died shortly after I finished. Now I cherish the time I was able to spend with her."

"Did your grandfather ever see it?"

Dee shook her head, "No. He had died a year before I started. But" she ran her fingers over the rug again, "I think a part of him is here with me, in this."

The rest of the office held similar tribal pieces. A leather lamp sat on one corner of the desk while on the other a six-inch long, clay tube held eagle feathers, fanning outwards. In front of the desk, an assortment of large and small plants circled a fountain that ran continuously.

Dee sat at her desk, looking at something on the computer. Like many Navajo's she wore her black hair straight down her back with simple bangs across her forehead. Her dark eyes complimented her skin tone but it was her prominent check bones and wide smile that made people constantly remark on how beautiful she was.

"How was your weekend?" Dee asked, turning away from the computer and gesturing to the chair next to her desk.

"Good, you know," Shane shrugged, sat down and picked up a pen. Lacing it over her first finger and under her middle one, she focused on it as she continued. "I hate seeing all those dogs. And trying to explain it to Jeremy was impossible."

"What did you say?" Dee asked, watching Shane.

"Just that we have different beliefs about animals and sometimes if people are struggling, it's hard for them to see another who's struggling." She dropped the pen, picked it up and set it back on Dee's desk. "Soooo, what happened at the meeting?"

Dee stared at Shane for a moment before beginning. "Judy Bishop's been appointed to the Board. She's heading the changeover to no-kill."

Shane stared back. Not a likely candidate for the board, it took her a second to register who Dee was talking about. When she did, she was shocked. "Judy? Always in here telling us how to do our jobs, Judy? Are you kidding me? She drives everyone insane." Shane couldn't believe it. Judy was a major pain in the ass volunteer and now given a position of authority, she'd be impossible.

Dee sat back in her chair, not looking any happier than Shane. "I know, she's a bit over the top."

"Over the top?" Shane repeated. "She's more than over the top. She's clueless and judgmental and a bitch most of the time."

"Apparently the Board doesn't think so. They wanted to bring in some new blood and she's been on them for years about this change."

"You can't tell me there wasn't someone better or less crazy. And why did they suddenly need to fill the seat now?

Most of the volunteers at the shelter were indistinguishable from the staff. They walked and bathed the animals, fostered, trained and helped clean up after them and they often answered the phones and helped with adoptions. But a couple volunteers, like Judy were difficult to deal with. Questioning every decision and process, they wore the staff down, assuming things wouldn't be done if they didn't do them themselves. Just last week a volunteer had laid down blankets in the middle of cleaning and Judy herself had been caught feeding animals that were on special diets.

Now in a position of power, Shane couldn't image how bad she'd be. "So why her? Why now?"

"They like her. She respects them. And apparently she knows no-kill. Said she's gone to some conferences and read some books and is the most knowledgeable to institute it here."

"Too bad she's completely ignorant about what we do and why." Shane tucked her hair behind her ear and felt her neck tightening up. "Seriously, she read some books and listened to someone speak and now she's an expert?"

"Yeah, so," Dee paused for a second, "she's going to be spending some time here, watching what you do and recommending changes that will need to be made so we can be aligned with no-kill."

"What kind of changes?" Shane sat up straighter, her heart racing. She'd been implementing changes since last year when she took over and they'd been doing great. *Why did we need this now?* "I don't even understand this no-kill stuff. Are there really going to be a lot of changes?"

"I have no idea," Dee shook her head slowly, "but I can see her being all over something like this. Be careful."

"Be careful?" Shane sat back heavily in her chair and rubbed the back of her neck.

"I don't know Shane. You know I'm not a fan of this whole thing. I have no idea what kinds of changes she could possibly want."

Always in-line with the Board, Shane was surprised when Dee told her she was opposed to the changeover. The first time they'd talked about it she hardly knew Dee and no-kill wasn't even being discussed.

Before being appointed to Shelter Director, Shane worked in the kennels and barely knew who Dee was. Every month the staff was forced to meet as a group with a psychologist. Dee was always in the meetings and seemed to have a knack for getting people to talk, but it wasn't until a few months later that Shane saw another side of her.

It had been a difficult time at the shelter. The staff was stressed, they were euthanizing a lot of animals and no one was happy about it. Shane would have found another job if she could have, but she was near Jeremy's school and she could drop him off in the mornings for her sister, so she gutted it out. The worse things got, the more often the psychologist was in and Shane soon found the meetings as uncomfortable as the job itself.

One day, Dee walked into Payton's office, the Shelter Director at the time, and announced another mandatory lunch meeting. After getting all the animals cleaned, Dee instructed them to get in their cars and follow her. Ten minutes later they were at the town's only sports bar.

Dee smiled broadly as they all looked at her. "What?" She asked innocently. After ordering a ton of food and giving each of them a roll of quarters to play darts, pool, or video games she explained, "we've been working our asses off. If we don't take care of ourselves, who will? And it's good for us to spend time together, having fun. Now go."

After a few rounds of pool and some really poor driving on a video game, Shane went back to the table. She thanked Dee for the lunch and the two of them got into a deep discussion about the shelter. The conversation was interesting to Shane. Dee had worked at a shelter for so long and had so many interesting experiences. Not long into their talk Dee brought up the no-kill movement and the negative impacts it was having on the sheltering industry.

"We were making real strides forward then everything became no-kill this and no-kill that. Our ad hoc sheltering community was suddenly attacked from within. For decades we worked individually, all struggling with similar issues. Then just as we were starting to come together as an industry; no-kill steps onto the stage and throws a wrench between us all."

"How?" Shane asked, surprised to hear there was unrest in the industry she worked in.

"By blaming the sheltering community for overpopulation, by saying all management in animal shelters needs to be fired and by outlandish claims like education to kids never proved worthwhile; no-kill disregards all the work that has been accomplished over the last three decades. The funny thing is no-kill wouldn't even exist if we hadn't gotten the numbers under control in the first place. Now the public thinks they're doing something right when they only support no-kill shelters, instead of realizing how many animals are getting left with even less than they had before. It's wrong and makes me sick to my stomach."

At the time Shane couldn't have cared less about the no-kill movement but she'd never had a real conversation with Dee before and was enjoying it. Thinking back, Shane wondered if that was when she had finally started feeling like she was part of the team.

The intercom buzzed, Dee clicked the speaker button. "Yes?"

"I'm sorry to disrupt you but we're buried down here," Kinsey, the front desk manager, sounded rushed.

"I'll be right down," Shane said, standing. "So other than crazy people being elected to positions of power, and unknown changes coming, anything else going on?"

"A couple of things in the works," Dee smiled at Shane's sarcasm. "Talk to Animal Control, they're investing a couple of cruelty complaints that may impact you."

"Yeah I heard about the cats," Shane said. When they were done, she headed back downstairs. Six people stood in line at the counter. Shane rounded the desk and asked Kinsey what she needed first.

Kinsey picked up the phone before turning to Shane. Her short, red hair was sweaty and plastered to her forehead. She made an exasperated look before cupping the phone, "I'd love to get that smell out of here, but maybe just get through some of these people?"

Shane nodded. She'd smelled the cat poop as soon as she had walked down the stairs. A tall, free-standing cat kennel was in the lobby with a litter of snowshoe kittens. The diarrhea smell was coming from it. Shane grabbed the phone, dialed the kennel and got Jamie on the second ring.

"Do me a quick favor, would you? Bring me up a small cat litter box with litter, for this kennel up front." Shane hung up after Jamie told her she'd be right up and walked back around the counter. She knew opening the kennel would be easy; the hard part was getting the litter box out without the animals following.

Luckily three of the four cream colored kittens were sleeping. The fourth was up on the second level of the kennel, eating. His dark ears and mask a striking contrast to his buff colored coat. Shane quickly opened the kennel, pulled out the litter box and walked over to the door marked exam. Opening the door, she slid the smelly box inside and turned back to the front desk smiling at Kinsey.

"Thank you!" Kinsey said, her hand on her heart. "Now can you grab Huck and Finn for me? These guys are adopting them."

Chapter 3

Ninety minutes later Shane was still helping at the front desk when she asked the next person in line if she could help them. The woman, in her mid-40's, was wearing a Denver Broncos baseball cap and carrying a box. She couldn't have been more than five-foot tall.

"It's my cat. I need you to help her." Setting the box on the counter, she reached to open the lid.

"Whoa," Shane said, stopping her. "Give me one second." The four-foot tall counter was great for filling out paperwork, but had its limitations in situations like this. Shane picked up the box and walked around to the seating area. Setting it down on one of the wooden benches, she motioned for the women to join her.

"What's the situation?" Shane asked. She hadn't grabbed surrender paperwork before sitting down, hoping she could avoid the situation. They didn't need another cat. It was June and they were overflowing with them. Chances were she was hurt. Lately more and more people were coming to the shelter because they couldn't afford emergency care for their pets.

Loma Bonita, Colorado was a small mountain town of 20,000 people, except during tourist season when it swelled to an oppressive 60,000. Not far from the New Mexico border, the town had an abundance of hot springs and one of the few large rivers left in the area; the Tamanatü River, but it was barely a blip on any map before the mid 1990's.

Paul Winterhawk, a local Ute Indian started inviting troubled kids to the area. Crossing tribal lines, Winterhawk reached out to Native American teens across the country. His ability to connect with them went deeper than just their heritage and his success quickly grew.

Now boasting a large school, ropes course, and outdoor adventure training facility, Winterhawk Academy had turned the sleepy town into a bustling tourist destination.
Tapping into the local resources Winerhawk used the hot springs and river to attract major names and celebrities.

From late March through early October fly-fishing tournaments, rodeos, and Winterhawk concerts brought tourists to the area. The locals, trying to get by as the cost of living skyrocketed around them, did their best to hold on. But with hay bales doubling in price and the decade long drought making even water costly, ranching and farming had become expensive livelihoods.

Veterinary fees rose along with the cost of living. Doctors, having implemented the latest diagnostic and treatment protocols had hoped to cash in on the costs. But just as their fees rose, the public's pocketbook constricted. Concern for the economy and the future caused people to reevaluate how much they were willing to pay for services. And the shelter was feeling the effects.

"She's got a broken leg," the women said sitting down next to Shane, the box in between them. She reached to unfold the flaps but Shane's hand was still across the top.

"One sec," Shane said holding the flaps in place. "How do you know she has a broken leg? Did you bring her to a vet?"

"Yeah of course. Cherry Creek, but they said it was going to be a thousand bucks plus more maybe. I don't have it. I love her. I've had her since I graduated from college but I just don't have a thousand bucks. That's a rent payment." Digging into her front pocket she pulled out a worn tissue and blew her nose. "She's just in so much pain. She's crying all the time. Please you've got to help her."

Shane sighed and nodded. "Did they take an x-ray?"

"Yes, they said it is compound break, whatever that is. But that she'd need a plate or a pin and then she'd have to go back for therapy for a couple of months."

"Therapy, eh?" Shane respected Veterinarians. They could save the lives of her favorite species and knew things she only dreamed of knowing. But stuff like this drove her crazy. She understood their fees even their desire to do therapy - it was that kind of hospital. But when people couldn't afford it, they should have referred them to a vet that could help. "When did it happen?"

"The day before yesterday."

Shane tried not to react but her face must have given her away.

"I brought her to the vet yesterday," the women said quickly. "But when I heard how much it was going to be I wanted to spend some time with her, to say good-bye. I didn't figure it would make a difference, since you'd probably just," she paused, "well you know."

"How old is she?" Shane asked, ignoring the comment.

"I got her when I graduated. So she's five, well five and a half actually."

Shane nodded, "well, let's see what we've got." She took a quick glance around. This was not an ideal place to do this, if the cat got out she'd be hard pressed to catch her. But not seeing any dogs she took a quick peek inside.

The cat, a short-haired calico wasn't trying to get out. She was lying at the bottom of the box. Shane opened the top completely to get a better look. Petite, maybe six or seven pounds the cat was mostly white with large orange and black patches.

Shane reached in and petted the small girl. As she did she lifted the cats lip and checked her gum color, it was pink and moist. Then Shane ran her hand over the cats head and stopped behind it. Pinching the skin together, Shane moved it back and forth between her fingers, checking her hydration status.

"She looks good," she said to the women. "How did it happen?" Shane had already considered that she'd been hit by a car but then dismissed it. The cats coat looked great, she didn't have asphalt or debris in it like she would have if she'd been hit. But if a kid had done it to her, Shane needed to know.

"I stepped on her," the woman's already red checks, brightened as she focused her attention on the cat. "It wasn't my fault. Well of course it was my fault, but she's always under foot. And I was coming down off my step stool. It's impossible to reach the cupboards over my refrigerator without it. And I stepped backwards and the next thing I know she's screaming and I'm falling. It was just lucky I caught myself or we'd both have broken legs.

Shane could hear the cat purring. "Is she spayed?"

"Oh, no I just didn't see any reason. She never goes outside."

Shane had heard enough, "we can't treat your cat."

The woman nodded still focusing on the purring animal. Tears flowed down her face.

"But I can treat her if she's our cat. So this is what I can do. If you'll surrender her over to us, I'll get her leg fixed and you can adopt her back next week. But I'm gonna spay her as well. Do you have any money at all?"

"You'd do that? You'd fix her leg? I thought for sure you'd put her down." It was the first time she met Shane's eyes.

"Yeah," Shane said. "No offense, but I don't want her. I have more than enough cats and couldn't get a six year old with a broken leg adopted if I tried. And we're not in the business of putting animals down. You could have done that at Cherry Creek if you wanted to. We are however, in the business of lifelong homes and if you're committed to her, which it seems like you are, then we'll do what we can to get her back to you."

"But why can't you just fix her? Why do I have to surrender her to you?" She had stopped crying.

"The vets in town aren't happy that we have a medical clinic, so my Board of Directors wants to take it slow. But there's no reason she should have to suffer or be away from you." Shane reached back into the box and scratched behind the cat's ears and under her chin. Half of her face was orange the other half black, while her chin and around her small, pink nose was completely white. "What's her name?"

"Mosi," the woman said, smiling for the first time.

"Mosi, eh?" Shane smiled.

"It means "cat" in Navajo," the woman explained, unnecessarily.

After finishing up, the Bronco's fan hugged Shane tightly, thanking her over and over.

Shane smiled. When she first started at the shelter, she was uncomfortable hugging strangers. Now she initiated many of the embraces. Not knowing if it was because she was getting older or because of what she'd experienced, she now found them oddly comforting. Embracing woman gave her a way to show her support without having to say anything.

Shane felt good about her decision. "So, we'll get her records and hopefully be able to see that x-ray. We'll do the surgery as soon as possible, no later than Wednesday. And she'll probably be able to go home next Monday. Our vet will take a look at her later today. Why don't you call tomorrow and I'll let you know what's going on."

~

Four hours later Shane walked back to the medical area to check on Mosi.

"What do you think?" Dee asked, catching up with Shane as she walked through the kennel doors.

The dog adoption area, typically called the kennel, split the building in half, making it impossible to get from the front to the back of the building without going through the dog area, unless you went upstairs. The dogs reacted anytime someone came into the kennel but quickly quieted down once they realized it wasn't someone new.

"The guy says he's got some time," Shane said, shrugging. "We'll do what we can." They were talking about the man with all the dogs and cats that Shane had talked to that morning. He'd been diagnosed with a heart condition and needed to move to a lower elevation. "He needs to sell his house so we may have a while. I'm gonna drive over there and see what we're dealing with."

Dee nodded, "good idea."

They walked out through the kennel and down the back hall. Labeled doors lined each side of the hallway: Dog Holding, Dog Isolation, Storage.

Once the doors to the kennels swung closed they could hear Jamie in Dog Isolation, singing. Jamie Lewis a kennel supervisor, was one of Shane's favorites. She'd been at the shelter for years but had never wanted to do anything but work in the kennel. Now she was invaluable.

Most people quickly grew tired of the kennel. It was the most physical job at the shelter and one of the dirtiest. Kennel workers spent their days cleaning up after the animals, dealing with the public and hauling laundry, dog food and the dogs themselves. It was the job with the highest turnover and both Shane and Dee knew how rare it was to have someone like Jamie who loved it.

Jamie's voice sounded loudly through the closed door. As they got closer, Shane could hear the words clearly, "if you're going through hell, keep on going, don't slow down, if you're scared don't show it, you might get out before the devil even knows you're there."

Not wanting Dee to comment about Jamie wearing her iPod again, Shane quickly began talking. "Yeah, he's got eight dogs and sixteen cats. But who knows how many of them are adoptable."

"Yeah," Jamie screamed out. "If you're going through hell, keep on moving, face that fire, walk right through it, you might get out, before the devil even knows you're there."

She really didn't have a good voice, Shane thought for the thousandth time. Though it never stopped her from belting out any song she loved. Shane was actually a little envious of Jamie. Loving to sing herself, she confined her singing to the car and shower knowing how bad her voice was.

Luckily the medical suite was at the end of the hall and they were spared the next refrain. The medical area had been added onto the shelter the year before and now provided crucial additional space and a low-cost spay/neuter clinic for the public. A separate entrance to the medical area would be finished by the winter. Until then everyone used the front desk, which made it more hectic than usual, especially at the end of the day.

As they walked into the three-room suite they saw Dr. Hunter, the shelters Veterinarian, in the surgical bay working on an animal. Ginny, the shelter's Veterinary Technician was in the far room in front of a microscope. She turned when the door opened.

"Hey Ginny, just checking on that cat from earlier today. Did the doc get a chance to take a look at her?" Shane asked as she walked over to the kennels where Mosi was now set up. A large, thick towel had been put over the bottom of the two-foot by three-foot enclosure. A litter pan with short sides was in the back and a short, plastic double food bowl near the front with food and water. Mosi laid in the middle, watching everything going on.

Ginny, nodded but rolled her eyes and looked to her left. Just as Shane was about to ask her what was up, Judy Bishop the new Board member came out from around the corner. Shane felt her blood pressure rise but forced herself not to glance at Dee, behind her.

Judy Bishop stood 5'9" and weighed 120 pounds. If she'd been blessed with a pretty face she could have been a model. Unfortunately she had sunken eyes, a large nose and crooked teeth. She cared enough about appearances to carry around her own lint brush but not enough to wear something other than fur-capturing cardigans.

But it was her hair that gave the staff something to talk about. Not seeming to care what she looked like, Judy didn't style her hair, didn't even comb it. Every time she came to the shelter it was different. Shane figured she showered at night and went to bed with wet hair but couldn't understand why she didn't look in the mirror in the morning. Today she had a large flat spot on the right side of her head. The short greying brown hair around it looked matted and tangled. The other side sported two wings; one over her ear and the other sticking straight out the back.

"Hi there ladies, how are you today?" Judy asked, looking as happy as Shane had ever seen her.

"Judy," Dee said, without smiling. "It's good to see you in here so quickly. I was telling Shane earlier that you were appointed to the Board and would be spending time here, learning how and why we do things."

"Something like that." Judy said as she walked toward the kennel area where Shane was standing, petting the now purring cat. "We get to spend lots of time together now, Shane. And you'll have to tell me why you make the decisions you do."

"Judy," Shane said, closing the kennel door and facing her, "I have no problem explaining to you why we do what we do, I do however, have a problem arguing with you. If you could listen to me and try to understand what I'm saying, that'd be great, but you usually challenge me."

"Hardly," Judy said, looking away.

Shane walked over to the surgical bay, rolling her eyes at Dee as she did.

"Hey Doc," Shane said quietly, hoping to keep the conversation between the two of them.

Dr. Hunter had been at the shelter eight months and got along great with everyone. Having run his own clinic for thirty years, he was a tremendous asset. But surgery came first and Shane knew he wouldn't answer her until he was done.

Having completed the spay, he was now closing the dog up. Shane watched as he pulled the suture material through the two flaps of skin, tightened it, tied a knot and cut off the remainder. Knowing the doc liked the animals to breathe straight oxygen before waking up; Shane asked if he'd like her to turn off the gas.

Nodding, he continued with the sutures, quickly completing eight more. The black lab was lying on her back, her front legs crossed over her chest and held in place with two short pieces of rope. The constant beeping of the machine reading the dogs heartbeat was the only sound until Dr. Hunter removed the drape covering the dogs stomach and wiped the area with a piece of gauze. "Ginny, I'm done in here." He called out, standing up and removing his gloves.

Pulling a paper towel off the roll, he rubbed a sheet over his nearly bald head. "Sweet cat," he said pulling out Mosi's chart and his notes. "I haven't seen an x-ray but if it's as bad as the notes indicate, I think we should take the leg."

"How about repairing it?" Shane asked. She knew amputation was an option but she wanted to consider fixing it if possible.

"I can't do it," Dr. Hunter said, "not here. Maybe when I had my hospital but we just don't have the equipment. It's a pretty bad break. I'd recommend amputating even if I was still at my own clinic. She's a solid cat, she'll do just fine."

"Yeah, I was just hoping there would be a way to save it."

"Even if we did the surgery, there's no guarantee. If the owner doesn't keep her confined or if she tries to jump or if the dog chases her or if a hundred things happen she could have problems forever. And pain forever."

"Okay," Shane nodded. "Can you do it tomorrow?"

"Sure, I don't think we're too busy. Ginny, can you check?"

Ginny had carried the medium sized dog to a kennel and was back in the surgical bay cleaning the table.

"Don't do anything until I talk to you." Shane said. "I need to talk to the owner first."

"Owner? The cat's got an owner?" Judy asked, coming up behind Shane.

"Not an owner. The women who surrendered him," *Shit,* Shane thought. She'd been helping people get emergency medical care for their pets for close to a year using the unorthodox approach. Not sure the Board would allow it, she hadn't brought it up. She figured Dee was well aware of it, she knew everything going on at the shelter, but now the Board would know too. *Damn.*

"Why would you waste your time telling her?" Judy asked. "She gave up all rights to the cat when she gave him to us."

"She gave up her cat because she didn't want her in pain, not because she didn't love her. I want her to have this cat back when it's all done, so yeah I want her to know what's going on."

"She gave her up, why would you give her back to her? She obviously doesn't love her that much if she can give her up." Judy countered.

"Obviously, huh? Some people would say the opposite. That she loved her cat more than most of us because she put the cats needs first. It's not for me to judge how much she loves her cat. I have 132 cats up for adoption right now, I don't want or need another. Plus this way I can get her spayed as well."

"If you didn't want to adopt it out, you shouldn't have taken it in in the first place," Judy said.

"I should have let the cat suffer?" Shane asked looking around the room for support. Dee's eyes were fixed on Judy, but her expression was blank. Shane had endured the intimidating Navajo stare herself before and was glad it wasn't fixed on her.

"It's her responsibility. If she can't afford the cat then she shouldn't have one. You shouldn't give it back to her and you certainly shouldn't call her to discuss the animal's treatment! Jesus are you this lenient with everyone?"

Shane could feel herself losing her patience so she took a deep breath. "So your argument is that if the woman can't afford emergency care for her pet than she shouldn't have her?"

"Yeah," Judy said.

"You should work in a vet hospital," Shane remarked sarcastically. "Here at the Animal Shelter our primary commitment is to lifelong homes. If that's a good home, with a tight bond you're damn right I'm not going to break it. Veterinary prices change every day. They've gone through the roof in town. I guess we could do an audit every time the vets raise their prices and go around taking animals from homes that can no longer afford them? How about that?"

"Hardly," Judy mumbled.

"Do you know how much we make an hour here? In your scenario not one person that works here would be able to have a pet because none of us can afford local veterinary or emergency care."

Shane continued, "and what happens when a new vet comes into town and opens up a low-cost clinic. Can all of us then have your blessing to have pets because we can afford their care through that one particular place? Pet owning is not just for the rich; everyone deserves a pet and I want everyone, actually I need everyone that wants one, to have one."

"If she can't afford its care, then she shouldn't have it. It's that simple," Judy repeated.

"Simple, eh? So simple to you is us holding a cat that won't be up for adoption for months?"

"She can go up for adoption, if anything she'll get adopted quicker because someone will feel sorry for her."

"That's not how we do adoptions and there's no way I'm going to put a new amputee in a strange house. You're also forgetting that we have 132 other cats that need to be adopted before her. So I guess simple to you is taking up a medical foster home for a cat that may or may not get adopted in the next year while ignoring the fact that there's someone who loves her dearly, wants her back and is now in her debt because she caused the injury." Shane was already tired of Judy. The annual meeting was six weeks away. The thought of dealing with her for six more weeks made Shane's jaw tighten.

"It costs money to have an animal. It's not a right, it's a privilege and if they can't pay for that privilege then someone needs to look out for that animal's best interest. Why should they have an animal if they can't take care of them when they get hurt?"

Jesus does she think the same thing about kids? Shane wondered, shocked at how black and white Judy was being. "Your right it does cost money to have an animal, but there is not one level of care. Look at it this way, if people can't afford to stay at the Hilton, they have choices they can stay at a Super 8 or at a campground, they don't need to pay top dollar if they don't want to. The same has to be true for veterinary care. Right now we have a town with veterinary offices similar to Hilton's. High-priced, lots of value, lots of care and concern – that's all great and good but some people just can't afford that level of care. Those people don't deserve to lose their beloved pet because we don't have an affordable veterinary hospital."

Shane hurried to finish before Judy interrupted her. "A Super 8 provides a basic room with a lock on the door and a bathroom. That's enough. We're a basic clinic which means we won't do surgery on the leg, but we will amputate it. The cat will get along just fine and the cost will be a lot less. This is not a one-size-fits-all world, you know. We need choices, people are demanding them. And if the vets aren't going to provide them, then we have to. And if I have to utilize a 'pay what you can afford' formula from time to time to maintain a lifelong home for a cat – then you're damn right I'm gonna do that." Shane turned back to the Doctor, "thanks Doc, I'll let you know," she turned to leave.

Chapter 4

"Shane what do you want to do with that scared little thing in receiving." Jamie asked walking through Shane's office at the end of the day. "She hasn't even been checked in yet."

Shane knew who she was talking about, it was the same dog she had sat with that morning. "Just leave her for now. You'd have to use a catch pole to get her out, and I don't want to put her through that."

Each animal that stayed overnight at the shelter was checked into the organization. It involved giving them a basic physical exam, checking them for a microchip, naming them, taking a picture, and getting vaccines into them. Typically done before the end of each day, the nameless one in Holding had now been there for two days without being checked in.

"I'm going to move Jake then. He's barking like hell and scaring the shit out of her."

Shane smiled. Jamie could always find a reason to handle any large dog that came into the building, she was nuts about them.

"I don't know where you're going to put him. Isolation's full. Hey speaking of Iso," Shane said. "Dee and I were serenaded by you when we were in the back hall earlier."

Jamie's eyes grew wide, "I wasn't wearing it, just singing. I swear Shane."

Shane nodded, smiling and followed her out to the front desk. "It sounded like a good song."

Jamie turned to say something but was interrupted by Judy coming out of the cat adoption area.

"You're offering two-for-one cats?" Judy said, from across the front lobby.

Damn, Shane thought, hoping she'd left. Ignoring the interruption, she turned back to Jamie to finish their conversation, but before she could, Judy spoke up again.

"I'm wondering if you've really thought that through. We need people to value animals, people value what they pay for. If you go around giving away kittens like they aren't even worth the hundred-dollar adoption fee, what does that say about them?"

"Excuse me," Shane said to Jamie before turning back to Judy. "I'll be with you in a second." Then turning back to Jamie she asked, "has she eaten anything?" referring back to the scared dog in receiving.

Jamie shook her head.

"Let's give her another day or two and then decide."

Nodding, Jamie walked over to the computer, singing the Sesame Street theme song as she walked, "Can you tell me how to get, how to get to Sesame Street?"

"Now," Shane began, turning toward Judy, "You don't understand why we're offering two-for-one cats, right?"

"I want to know if you've considered the impact you're having."

Shane had to give Judy credit for standing her ground. Never one to buck authority, she typically gave the Board of Directors a wide berth but Judy was another story. Since Judy began volunteering six months ago, she'd been second-guessing every policy, procedure and decision made at the shelter. Before now, Shane would have dismissed her question and let someone else answer it, but now that Judy was on the Board, she had no choice.

Shane picked up the phone and dialed Lily, the foster home coordinator's extension. "Lily, it's Shane, I'm at the front desk. Do you mind if I put you on speaker?" A second later Shane clicked the speaker button and set down the handset. "Lily how many cats do we have in foster right now?"

"Sixty-four."

"And are you aware of any new one's coming to the shelter."

"Yes, Shane you know this. We have four more litters scheduled to come in by Wednesday, but right now we're averaging about two unscheduled litters a day."

"And how fast are they moving Lil?"

"About four to six a day."

"Four to six kittens, not four to six litters, right."

"Right."

"Okay, thanks Lily." Shane turned to Judy, "The reason I have two-for-one cats is because I have 132 cats currently up for adoption. As you heard, we're averaging eight to ten coming in a day and we're only adopting four to six. Do the math."

"That's not the point. Don't you see that you devalue animals when you make them free like that? They get vaccines and they're altered, that's got to be worth something."

Shane knew the key to winning an argument was to not get emotional. Her dad always said, "If you feel emotions coming on, shut your mouth. The strong remain silent," Shane repeated his favorite mantra over in her head.

She took a deep breath then began. "They do get vaccines and wormed *and* they're altered *and* they have microchips implanted in them. It costs us twenty-eight dollars to take in a cat and give it all this and it costs us an additional twenty-three dollars a day to care for them until they're adopted. We have 132 cats up for adoption. If things continue, we're going to have double that by the annual meeting.

"When you don't make people pay for things they don't value them," Judy repeated without as much force.

"Sure, and if there are too many of something, people don't value it either. People can get cats from anywhere; the paper, a friend, by opening their back door and putting down a bowl of food. There are so many cats around that people consider them disposable. Right now I want every new kitten to come from us, that way they're altered, it's the only way we're ever going to get ahead. When we get their numbers in check, we can worry about the nice-to-have's like charging full price for every cat."

"Well then you need more foster homes." Judy said.

"Shane, Brenda's on line one." Jamie said quietly. "She wants to bring some dogs up from New Mexico."

"Can you take a message?" Shane snapped. She needed to get away from Judy.

"We'll finish this conversation later." Judy called out after her.

Shane wondered what else there was to say, but followed her dad's advice and kept her mouth shut. Sighing, she realized she was going to have to watch her back.

Without knowing exactly where she was going, Shane found herself standing in front of the scared little dog's kennel. She looked like she hadn't moved. Pushing open the gate, Shane moved slowly, hoping not to scare her.

Sitting down, Shane leaned back with her head against the cool concrete and focused on her breathing. Deep breath in, hold for as long as possible, long breath out. Her sister was the one that got her into breathing deeply and now she did it all the time. Last year, Sheila, Shane's older sister and roommate was on a yoga kick. Every morning she'd wake Shane up at five a.m. to do a half-hour of stretching. Shane would never have agreed except she'd lost a bet and had no choice. After the four weeks were up Shane gladly gave up the practice and enjoyed the extra half-hour of sleep.

But not long after she quit she realized she missed the deep breathing exercises. It was the one part of the routine she enjoyed – and it seemed to help with the headaches she'd always been plagued with. So she started making herself breathe deeply throughout the day and anytime she was dealing with issues. It still amazed her how much it helped.

The kennel looked the same as it had when she was there that morning, except the food had been changed. But the bowl was still full, as was the water. The dog hadn't gone to the bathroom and from the look of it, hadn't moved at all. Still crammed under the platform the poor thing looked uncomfortable. Half sitting, half standing her head hung low as much out of necessity as out of desire.

"Hey girl, is your day going as bad as mine?"

The dog's tail thumped once on the concrete.

Shane smiled, "I'm sorry. You've got to be miserable. Here I am feeling sorry for myself and you haven't gone to the bathroom in two days. I couldn't do it sister, I'm constantly pee'ing." The small dog shifted slightly and Shane noticed the color of her toe nails was inverted on her two front feet. On her right foot her toe nails were black, white, black and black from the outside in. On her other foot they were white, black, white, white.

Shane leaned back again. She was going to have to find a way to deal with Judy, otherwise it was going to be a long couple of weeks. *What did two-for-one cats have to do with no-kill, anyway?*

She had a couple calls she needed to get back to before the end of the day. But she was glad she'd come back to sit with the little dog. She was feeling better already.

Chapter 5

The following day Shane's head was pounding. For lunch she downed three extra-strength Excedrin's with as much Gatorade as she could stand, then sat in her office with the lights off. After rubbing the back of her neck, Shane closed her eyes and rested her head in her hands. Slowly the pounding turned to pressure. She imagined the vise her dad had, when she was a kid. It was attached to his workbench in the basement. Shane's head centered firmly between the jaws – every movement causing them to crank down a notch tighter.

Shane's head had never really been in a vise, it just felt like it. She'd had bad headaches since she was a kid, but lately they'd gotten much worse. Taking sometimes as many as nine extra strength Excedrin's a day, she knew she was probably screwing up her body but it was the only way she could function. Someday, when she got insurance, she'd go see a doctor. For now, she was just glad this one seemed to be responding to the drugs.

A quiet knock sounded on the door before it opened.

"Shane, I'm sorry to bother you." Laura said, as she peaked in the door. "We're slammed up here, Kinsey asked me to ask you if you could give us a hand?"

"Yeah, of course." Shane said wondering how long she'd been out. After wiping her mouth and rubbing her eyes she glanced toward Laura. "Yeah, of course. I'll be right out." She blinked a couple times, no black spots. *Yes! Thank god for drugs,* she thought standing slowly to let the blood reach her head.

Stepping through the door closest to her, Shane wished she could wear sunglasses on a day like this. The bright, Colorado sun poured in through the front windows and made her shield her eyes. Feeling weak and disconnected, she leaned against the counter. *A couple more hours,* she thought. *Just let me get through the rest of this day and I promise I'll sleep from the moment I get home.*

Laura was at the tag machine working on an engraving, her long, thick wavy hair held in numerous ties down her back. Kinsey Baer, the front desk manager, held the phone in one hand while directing a young woman to the kennels with her other. *Deep breaths,* Shane reminded herself.

"What can I do?" She asked Kinsey. Kinsey, like just about everyone, had started in the kennel but quickly realized she was much more suited to the reception area. When she pitched the idea to Dee and Shane, almost a year ago, she showed a mismanaged, thrown-together area desperate for her organizational skills. And she was right.

After only three months in the position, Dee and Shane both agreed the front desk had never been so well run. Kinsey swore she would increase the number of lost animals returned to their owners, which she did, but she had done so much more than that.

The number of dramas they experienced was cut in half the first month she took over. By the third month Shane was actively listening to her to see why. Kinsey greeted people by name and thanked them when they volunteered. But the biggest difference Shane found, was that she listened. Even when the people were crazy, wrong, or over the top she let them talk. Shane didn't do that. Trying to avoid dramas at all costs, she cut-in when someone started ranting or just shut them out. With Kinsey they never seemed to get to the ranting stage.

Kinsey nodded to the older couple sitting by the window. Mr. and Mrs. Markovitz are all set, they're just waiting for Mattie. Can you take care of it? As soon as I'm done with this," she held up the receiver, "I have to take lunch."

"Yeah, of course," Shane said before realizing who she had said, "Mattie? Really?"

"Yeah, great, huh?" Kinsey said smiling before bringing the receive back up. "Sorry to keep you holding."

Mattie, a Shepherd mix was a beautiful, stately old dog who'd been at the shelter for months. Shane picked up Mattie's paperwork to see what they were waiting for.

"Doc's pulling blood," Kinsey whispered.

"It should be just a second," Shane told the elderly couple. Mattie was one of their longest residents; her being adopted was great news. Shane stretched her jaw and moved her neck around, *better*. Her head felt like it was beginning to clear.

"Did you find what you were looking for?"

Shane felt the hairs on the back of her stand up.

Judy followed a couple as they came out of the dog adoption area, repeating herself to get their attention. "Did you find what you were looking for?"

When did she get here? Shane thought, looking up at the clock and realizing she'd been out for her entire lunch break.

"No, not today. We'll be back though." The couple was in often, and Shane smiled at them.

"Are you sure?" Judy called, "we've got some great dogs back there."

Shane rolled her eyes and picked up the receiver to find out what was up with Mattie. As the extension rang she listened as Laura answered the phone.

"Good afternoon, Pinewoods Humane Society, this is Laura, may I help you?"

Shane loved newbie's. They were happy to answer the phone and always so nice to people. Laura Patrick had only been working at the shelter for a couple of weeks but she was a superstar. She had spent most of her time in the kennel up until now, but Shane needed someone else trained at the front desk. *Finally*, Shane thought, *I'm getting a great staff.*

"Um, yes ma'am." Laura rolled her chair over to the computer and clicked on the lost and found tab. "Okay, he's a Sheltie, a thoroughbred? A purebred, you mean. Okay. Uh-huh, how old? Okay."

No answer in back. *What the hell?* Shane thought setting the phone down and looking up at the Markovitz's.

Mr. & Mrs. Markovitz sat watching the activity at the front desk. In her seventy's, Mrs. Markovitz sat with her hands folded over the small bag she held in her lap. Her legs, crossed at the ankles were pulled under her. Mr. Markovitz had on a long-sleeved white shirt with black buttons and jeans cinched high on his belly. They looked like the typical eccentric couple you'd see in town, him, an old cowboy and her with money from back east.

What was taking so long? Shane wondered, as Kinsey waved goodbye for lunch. "Pinewoods Humane Society, can I help you?" Shane said, answering the phone.

"Yeah I just found a dog. Looks like a small Lassie, or something," the caller said.

Shane tapped Laura on the shoulder and whispered, "Is that still the lost Sheltie?"

Laura nodded.

"Sir, can you hold on one second? We have the owner of the dog on the other line." Shane put the call on hold for Laura and turned toward the woman who had just walked in and was now standing at the counter.

"Yes I, um, I need to turn in my dog. I can't keep him anymore." The young woman glanced only briefly at Shane, but it was long enough for Shane to see the deep bags under the woman's eyes.

"Okay," Shane said. "What's going on?"

After a few moments the woman's kids, not tall enough to see over the counter, headed over to the bench area to play. The woman didn't seem to notice as they wandered away. She looked upset to Shane. Not the type of upset when people had to give up a pet. *This was different*, Shane thought. The woman seemed numb, hollow in a way. She reminded Shane of how she felt after euthanizing animals; like she'd checked her emotions at the door and was running on auto-pilot. Shane wanted to ask her if she was okay but didn't think it would be appropriate. She smiled sympathetically instead.

Just then Jamie's voice sounded over the intercom, "Shane, to the kennel, Shane to the kennel." *What the hell?* Shane thought. *She knows there's no way I can get back there until Kinsey gets back from lunch.* She handed the woman a clip board with a surrender form and asked her to fill it out while dialing the extension to the kennel.

"Um, okay, let me see." Laura said, covering the mouthpiece, "Shane, can I give them each other's phone number?"

Shane looked over and realized Laura was completing a found report. "Oh shit, I'm sorry. Yeah, just ask the woman if you can give the guy her number, and vice versa and let them figure the rest out." When Jamie finally answered the phone, Shane asked her what was up.

"You gotta get back here. This chick is trying to get people to adopt Dalton, and he's nuts."

"What? Who?" Shane asked. Jamie sounded genuinely upset which wasn't like her.

"That Board chick that looks like big bird. She's driving me crazy, Shane! Asking me all sorts of questions, I'm behind as hell back here. And now she's trying to talk people into Dalton. Shane, he's a mess."

"Shit, you're right. I saw him this morning and meant to tell you to take him off the floor. As soon as they're gone, bring him back to Holding, would you?"

"Yeah, but what am I supposed to do with her? She keeps opening the kennels and pulling out the dogs. It's bullshit Shane. I can't work like this. I'm trying to get everyone rotated and she's moving them, during rotation!"

"Okay, I'll get her up here. Oh and do me a favor and get some food together for Mattie, would you? She's going home." Shane didn't wait for her response but clicked the phone to the intercom and requested Judy to come up front.

"Shane, Brenda's on line one," Laura said, putting down the receiver.

Sighing, Shane knew Brenda wanted to transfer dogs in and Shane wasn't ready to make that decision. "Okay," she said to Laura before reaching for the completed surrender form from the woman. Her kids had discovered the cat room and were covering the window with fingerprints.

"She's in New Mexico and wants to know how much space we have." Laura set the receiver down.

"Of course she does." Shane said knowing if she didn't talk to her she'd bring them up anyway. "Okay, I'll talk to her. Tell her to hold, would you?" Shane looked over the dog surrender paperwork. Shepherd mix, no accidents in the house, hasn't bitten.

"So he's nineteen-months old?" Shane asked.

"Uh-huh." The woman said with no more attention to Shane than her kids.

"And you're giving him up because," Shane paused waiting to see if she would answer, when she didn't, Shane read what she had written, "he's gotten too big." Shane looked up at the woman, hoping she'd provide a little more explanation.

"It's just too much with the kids. I, I, it's just too much." She gestured toward the boys who had started chasing each another between the cattery and the front door.

Shane nodded, *what was the point?* The woman looked like she had enough to worry about. "I just need you to sign here and then you can bring him in."

"Can you call me if, you know, if you have to put him down."

"Would you take him back?" Shane asked. Everyone asked to be called but no one ever came in when they actually did. And this woman looked like she'd be grateful when the dog had a safe place to go to. *Maybe one less thing for her to worry about,* Shane was grateful she could provide that at least.

"Well," she shook her head. "No, not us. But maybe there's somebody." She watched as her kids crawled under and over the wooden benches.

Shane knew she'd never see her again. "Yeah, sure. I'll call if we have to put him down. But you should know that we don't euthanize healthy, adoptable dogs, only if there's an issue." The phone rang again.

Laura reached for it but Shane told her to go get the dog from the woman's car while she answered the phone. Shane watched the woman as she gathered up her kids and followed Little Laura out the front door. *I forget how good my life is,* Shane reminded herself.

"You called?" Judy said, coming through the swinging doors a minute later. She seemed very comfortable for only being on the Board a couple of days.

Reaching up, Shane massaged her neck. "Yeah, I need to talk to you but I can't do it here. I'll be free in about ten minutes, I'll talk to you then."

Judy didn't say a word. But when she turned back toward the kennels, Shane quickly added, "And don't go back into the kennels until I speak with you."

Turning back with a sigh, Judy stared at Shane for a minute then headed upstairs.

Shane decided the doc must have gotten hung up with something else, and picked up the intercom to remind him. She dialed the general extension and tried to find some energy. "Great news everybody, Mattie is getting adopted. I repeat Mattie is getting adopted. Please bring Mattie to the front."

Just as she hung up, Laura came back in with a large, jet black Shepherd. It took everything she had to hold him near her as a volunteer, walked by with one of the dogs coming in from a walk.

"What's with that?" Laura asked, referring to the hollering coming from the back.

"Oh I just announced Mattie's going home."

"That's cool." Laura said, smiling and looking at the older couple. "She's a great dog, you're really going to love her."

"I'm sure we will, young lady," the woman replied, unfolding and refolding her large ankles. "Are you going to miss her?"

Laura shrugged, "I guess, but knowing she's in a home is so much better than seeing her here every day. She's a great dog. And a lonely heart. We always get excited when a lonely heart goes home."

"A lonely heart?" The woman frowned and looked at her husband.

"Oh, oh no, that's what we call the dogs that have been here more than forty-five days," Laura explained.

"Laura," Shane said. "Bring him around, would you?" The young girl still had the Shepherd and Shane wanted him away from the front when Mattie arrived.

"Is it true?" Betty, the volunteer asked Mrs. Markovitz. She had just returned from dropping the dog she had been walking off in his kennel. "Are you adopting Mattie?" Betty had been walking dogs at the shelter for years. Always bonding with the long-timers she knew Mattie well. It didn't surprise Shane that she wanted to check the people out herself.

Mattie had been a difficult dog to adopt. She was one of those dogs that would only work in a particular type of home. Severely overweight when she came in, she had been diagnosed with a full-blown case of pancreatitis. It had taken months to get her to shed the weight. But her personality was awesome. And luckily they didn't have many seniors when she came in. Now it was 248 days later. Mattie had lost forty-four pounds and her pancreatitis was under control. At nine-years-old she didn't need or want long walks, just a soft bed and a little loving.

"Oh you're just going to love her. We all do." Betty continued.

The door from the kennels slammed open. Jamie walked through carrying a twenty-pound bag of dog food over one shoulder and Mattie's leash in her other hand, singing. "Yeah, it's time to move on, time to get going, what lies ahead I have no way of knowing, but under my feet baby, grass is growing, yeah it's time to move on, it's time to get going."

Tom Petty was Jamie's favorite song to sing whenever long-termers were going home. Finally hearing all the words, Shane liked the song but would have rather had Tom Petty singing it. She walked around the counter and grabbed Mattie's leash from Jamie.

"Which car is yours?" Jamie asked Mr. Markovitz, gesturing to the bag of food she was carrying "And I'll put this in there."

"The green Chevy, right there in front" he said pointing to the large vehicle in the handicapped spot.

Though grey-faced, Mattie was a majestic looking dog. At one time she was all brown with black on her ears and above her eyes. Now her muzzle and legs were completely grey. But she was a sweetheart, an eighty-five pound lapdog.

"Remember," Shane said, "Mattie is on a special diet. That bag should last you a good couple of weeks maybe even a month. She needs to eat this kind of food the rest of her life, you won't be able to buy it in stores, you have to get it from us or your Veterinarian. Okay?"

"Okay." The man nodded as Mattie circled and sat against his leg. He patted and stroked the top of her head.

Still a big, solid dog, Mattie rested her head comfortably on Mr. Markovitz's leg. Always a lady, she waited patiently for her walks, treats and food and never once went to the bathroom in her kennel. Even at her age, her eyes were still animated, though a bit cloudy.

Her original family had surrendered her after being told that she suffered from pancreatitis. They were convinced that the cost of caring for her would be too high and wouldn't be talked out of it by anyone at the shelter.

Betty had been hovering over Mattie but moved aside when Jamie came back in. Jamie, one of the kennel supervisors, sat down in front of the large dog. "Goodbye beautiful." Jamie said, stroking Mattie's chest. Mattie hooked her arm across Jamie's forearm, as if she were going to miss her as well. "You be a good girl and these nice people will take great care of you. She loves to be scratched behind her ears." Jamie showed Mr. Markovitz. "Or right here." She rubbed the dog's broad chest with her hand and Mattie's back leg twitched as if she was being tickled. Jamie stopped and lowered her head to the dogs. She spoke quietly to her then stood and turned and quickly walked back through the double doors.

Mr. and Mrs. Markovitz stood to leave as Jackie, another volunteer came back from dropping off the dog she'd been walking and said her good-bye's. "Mattie, how great you're getting a home! You be a good girl now." The heavyset woman turned to the adopters "She's a great dog you know, she's never once gone to the bathroom in her kennel while she's been here."

Mr. Markovitz nodded to her. *They looked exhausted,* Shane thought. *Best to get the three of them moving.* She said her goodbye's and swallowed the typical questions that always roared up after caring for an animal for so long. Will they know when she needs to go out? Will they lock her in a laundry room? Will they make sure she has a bed for her sore elbows? Will they love her? Shane followed them silently and helped Mattie into their car.

Chapter 6

"First impressions?" Shane asked Little Laura after Mr. and Mrs. Markovitz had left. She was referring to the large Shepherd mix Laura was still holding behind the front desk.

"Strong. Solid," Laura said looking at the dog. "No fear. Maybe even a bit intimidating." Sitting, she rolled her chair to the side to get a better look.

She was right, the dog was a bit intimidating. All black, his coat was shiny, thick and in good shape. His ears were different than most Shepherds though. They were angled inward, towards the middle of his head. And he didn't have the triangular face, typical of the breed. But it was his posture, his demeanor that showed what he was thinking. He sat alert, his weight on his front legs, his ears erect. Shane couldn't see any white around his eyes but they were focused on the front door or windows, so it was hard to tell.

"Any issues when you took him out of the car?"

"No, he didn't even look back. Just came right along with me as though it was the most normal thing to do."

"What does that tell you?"

"Um, let's see," Laura hesitated. Shane bit her tongue to give her time to figure it out. "He's not bonded to his family?"

"Are you asking me or telling me?"

"I'm telling you," Laura smiled, she'd heard the question before. "He didn't seem to care that they drove off. My dog, that's at my parent's house, would have gone crazy if someone tried to take her out of my car."

Shane nodded, "and now? What do you see now?"

"The same, I guess. He doesn't seem to care about us at all." She ran a hand down his back. The dog didn't seem to notice. "He's not relaxed, maybe, stoic?" When Laura first brought him around the desk the dog had walked next to her. After a quick, cursory look around, he planted himself; front legs apart, ears forward. Ignoring them, he hadn't moved, just focused on the front windows.

"Aloof," Shane agreed, looking back at the surrender paperwork.

"Yeah, exactly."

"Reason for surrender," Shane read, "too big. I'd say it's more likely that he's not a family dog. Look at him, he's a guarder. He doesn't want companionship, he wants to oversee something. Be responsible. Not hang out with kids." After a minute she added, "It's probably a good thing she brought him in."

"Oh, look at you gorgeous. You're beautiful." Judy came up behind the large dog, leaned over and put her arms around his neck.

Shane held her breath. If it was anyone else she'd warn them off but Judy would never listen to her. Though after a second, Judy did pull away and stand up. Shane wondered if she had heard a growl or just realized how stiff he was.

"You're handsome, so strong and tough, look at you. Do you need a home?" Judy looked at Shane. "What's his name?"

"Hogg." Laura responded.

The dog didn't move under Judy's praise. He didn't open his mouth, relax his jaw, shift his weight or respond in any way. *He was going to be a tough one,* Shane thought rubbing her neck again.

"Laura, bring him back to receiving, would you? His name is really Hogg?" She shouldn't have been surprised, but still.

"They even spelled it for me," she called over her shoulder, holding up two fingers, "Hogg with two g's."

"Hello, Hello." Kinsey called, just back from lunch. She propped the door to Shane's office open and moved the chair Laura had been using back under the counter. "Anything exciting happen while I was gone?"

"Just Mattie leaving," Shane said. "Hey I'm going to steal Little Laura for a bit this afternoon but let her do as much as possible, would you? I'd like to get her trained up here ASAP."

"Sure thing. She's great, huh?" Kinsey said lining the clipboards up and putting the pens back in the cup. Kinsey was a stickler for how the front desk was set up. She spent as much time making sure newbie's knew where everything went as she did making sure they knew what to do. It annoyed Shane. Luckily they had come to an unspoken agreement where Shane tried her best to respect Kinsey's system and Kinsey stopped giving her shit about it.

"You going to lunch?" Kinsey asked.

"I took it at my desk. How is it out?"

"Beautiful, you gotta get out there. Hey take that pathetic little thing in receiving out, would you? Jamie says you're fond of her." Kinsey smiled as she picked up the ringing phone.

"I don't know about that, but I am determined to get her to eat." Shane motioned for Judy, who had just come back downstairs, to follow her into her office.

"Brenda's on line one," Kinsey called out just as Shane was closing the door.

"Oh shit, I left her on hold," Shane said referring to Brenda Bowen, the volunteer that was a sucker for hard luck cases. She'd have the place full of sick and maimed dogs if she had her way. Her current crusade had her rescuing dogs from overpopulated areas and relocating them to one's with more resources.

"This will just take a second," Shane said picking up the phone. "Brenda, its Shane. What's up?"

"Shane, listen I'm down here at Los Mochis and they have a litter of Pomeranians and two young Hound mixes. All of them seem pretty healthy. Can I bring them up?"

Shane knew talking to Brenda required translation, like reading advertisements for dogs. When an ad described a dog as very intelligent, it meant hard to manage. When they described him as mischievous like a puppy, it meant he's never been trained. In Brenda's case, six dogs translated to ten, pretty healthy meant they had something, but it was probably treatable. Unfortunately, Brenda's idea of treatable and Shane's weren't always the same. Of course Brenda didn't have eighty other dogs to worry about.

"Where are you?" Shane asked, shifting the papers off her keyboard and bringing her computer back to life.

"Los Mochis Animal Services."

Shane pulled up their website. A Southern New Mexico town, Los Mochis had its share of poverty, crime and animal neglect. Too far south to be included in the national transfer programs, they were on their own to handle the excess animals in their area. But the website was through the city government and didn't show the available animals, so Shane switched to Petfinder to search for the dogs there.

Judy moved the pile of papers off the extra chair, wiped the seat and sat down.

"How old did you say the Pom's were?"

"Oh they're young, like maybe five, six months."

"Closer to a year, you mean." Shane clicked on the animals pictures and scrolled down the page.

"Yeah that's what they're guessing, but I'd say they're a lot younger than that. Plus they're small dogs, they're really tiny, Shane, and we don't get a lot up there."

"Young Pomeranian's and no one's adopting them. What's wrong? And be straight with me. We still have those two from Utah you brought in. I can't take anyone else that can't be adopted right away."

"There's nothing wrong with them. They just have goopy eyes and some discharge from their cute little noses."

"Uh-huh." Judy was intently scanning the shelves behind Shane, *looking for ammunition,* Shane assumed. "And what's wrong with the others?" She sighed, *why did Brenda always do this to me?*

"The same, nothing major."

"So you want to bring six or more, sick dogs up here, with god knows what? What about the ones that are already here?" *Shit,* Shane thought, *Judy has got to be loving this. What was I thinking letting her eavesdrop?*

"Oh c'mon Shane, it's never like that. And they're Pom's Shane, c'mon they're adorable, like little cotton balls. As soon as they're healthy they'll go in a minute. And the Hounds are so sweet, and there's so many of them here, this'll be their only chance. C'mon Shane, Please."

What the hell? Shane thought. She knew how bad it was down there but they were getting short on room for dogs. "Brenda, go ahead and adopt them if you want. But *you* have to foster them. You get them healthy and when they're ready, I'll find homes for them. And I'll even let you use the clinic to diagnose them and we'll cover their meds. But, I'm warning you right now, if any of them have parvo, ring worm or some other contagious disease and you bring it into this building, it's the last dog you'll ever bring here. Do you understand?"

"Oh, thank you, thank you, thank you. You won't regret it, Shane."

"Make sure I don't. Bring them in between ten and eleven tomorrow and we'll check them out." Shane hung up the phone, swallowed down some warm grape Gatorade and turned toward Judy.

"What was that about?" Judy asked.

Ignoring her, Shane began what she had gone over in her head, "Judy, we have protocol here. It's what helps us be able to care for this many animals successfully. You cannot come in here and break that protocol."

"Excuse me?" She laughed, "you're going to lecture me?"

Shane felt her blood pressure rise. She took a breath and swallowed her automatic reaction. "If you would like to handle the dogs, or work with adopters, then you need to take the time to be trained. You cannot just open doors and let people in with the dogs. It's not safe, and it's not allowed."

"You listen to me miss—"

Shane held up her hand and spoke as loud as her head would allow, "and you wash between every animal you touch. Once you complete volunteer orientation then you can walk the dogs. If you'd like to progress further in handling the animals then you'll need to work with Madge to be certified. Just like everyone else. Being on the Board isn't a free pass to do whatever you want." Shane's head felt like it was throbbing with every beat of her heart.

Standing suddenly, Judy fired back, "We'll see about that. You think you're a good manager? You think you know what you're doing? You have no idea. What's wrong with me introducing dogs to people? They're a lot more likely to adopt them if they've interacted with them."

"They can interact with any dog they'd like, they just need to come up to the front desk so we're aware of it."

"Controlling it, you mean. Admit it. You're just a control freak who runs around this place doing anything she wants."

"What would you have done if Dalton bit one of those kids? Or if Betsy walked by with Aldo when you had his kennel open? What would you have done? I can tell you what Dalton would have done. He would do whatever it took to get around you and anybody else in his way to get to Aldo. Then he would have killed him. And you would have just stood there."

"Killed him!" She laughed again, "don't be so dramatic."

Shane could feel her checks burn and a lump form in her throat. The vice on her head felt so tight she closed her eyes. Biting the side of her mouth alleviated the tears but didn't provide her with anything smart to say.

Judy continued, "I let them pet the dogs, so what. They're probably out there right now with him, I did that dog a favor. I'm not trying to hurt animals, you know. I love them, it's the reason why I'm here, I want to get every one of them adopted."

"Your way." Shane said, wondering if she should her tell her they were putting Dalton down later that day.

"My way, your way, who cares? Why does it have to be one or the other? Let's just get that dog in a home."

"Listen, our goal is to get every animal into a loving home. In order to do that we have to keep them healthy. You have the luxury of only thinking about one dog, I'm concerned with eighty and the other eighty that will be here next month and the following month. I need you to abide by the protocols we have in place. You love animals so much, then understand that the protocols are what keeps them alive and available for adoption. Why don't you consider that for a minute?"

There was a soft knock on the door.

"Yeah" Shane hollered, before immediately regretted it as the pain in her head exploded.

The handle turned tentatively, it had to be Laura. "Shane, I'm sorry to bother you but there's a couple up here wanting more information on Dalton. Kinsey told me to come get you."

Shane shook her head and stood. Dalton had been at PHS for four months and no one had looked at him once. A black and tan, short-haired cattle dog, he hadn't bonded with anyone. Now, circling constantly in his kennel, he ignored the volunteers who brought him out for a walk and had completely disconnected himself from the rest of the world. The day before Jamie reported he was starting to be aggressive to male dogs. They'd already lost him and Shane knew the only things she could do was put him down. *I should have done it already.*

"Let's go," Shane gestured for Judy to follow.

"Ah, this is great. My first adoption, and Dalton of all dogs." Judy clapped her hands together.

Shane rolled her eyes to Kinsey who smiled sympathetically back. "Laura," Shane turned to the young girl who had sat back down. "I want you to listen to this." She walked around the front desk and guided the waiting family to the bench area.

"Hi, I'm Shane Hillard, the Director here. I hear you're interested in getting a dog." Judy and Laura came up alongside of her.

"Yeah, we want a puppy!" The little girl shouted. She looked about eight years old, a little younger than Shane's nephew, Jeremy. The parents looked like nice, grounded people that cared for their kids and would be a great home for any dog. A puppy would be perfect for them.

Smiling at the young girl, Shane asked the parents what kind of dog they were interested in.

"A family pet." The woman put her hands on her daughter's shoulders. "You know, one that can go out in the yard, but also play in the house. One that will play with the kids and won't run away if the gate gets left open."

"And what kind of dogs do you like?" Shane knelt down in front of the kids.

"Big! Like that one." The little girl pointed to Dewey, the forty-five-pound Border Collie/Shepherd mix on his way in from a walk.

"That's what you like? You like long hair like that?"

"Yeah, and he smiles."

"You're right, he does smile." Shane stood up. "Dewey, who just came in is a great dog, and we have a couple of others that would be perfect in your home. And guess what?" She asked, looking at the kids again.

"What?" they both hollered.

"We've got some puppies coming in in just a few days." Shane looked up at the parents. "We're you thinking about a puppy or an adult dog?"

"No, no a puppy would be fine. Ah," the woman hesitated, "What about that, one?" she directed her question to Judy.

"Dalton, they like Dalton." Judy took a step forward.

"I'm sorry, Dalton's not a family pet. He's a solid, strong dog that's been here a while. He's the kind of dog that would only work in a very specific type of home. He's not good with kids or cats or even livestock. He wouldn't make a good pet."

"What?" Judy came up behind Shane.

"Later," Shane said quickly to Judy before turning back to the family. "Check our website on Friday and Saturday to see what we have available. It's updated as soon as new dogs come in. The first litter that I'm aware of is coming in on Saturday, but at this point they can come in anytime."

"Do you know anybody else that may have one?"

"Plenty, but the only ones I'd recommend is Clover Valley or Durango. They have great assessment programs, and provide all the same things we do; altering, vaccines, and microchips."

"Oh great, that's great. Thank you." The family left, without so much as a backward glance.

"What the hell was that?" Judy was pissed. "You just denied them because you're mad at me. You do realize that, right?"

"I didn't deny them. They look like a fantastic family."

"Then why didn't you give them that dog? You dismissed them, told them to go somewhere else."

"How is it that they heard me and you didn't?" Shane asked. "Dalton would never have lasted in that home, and that wouldn't have done anyone any good." She turned her back to Judy, hoping to make her disappear. She needed some fresh air.

"Laura, do me a favor. Make yourself a note to call Mr. Markovitz in four weeks and check and see how the food for Mattie is holding up, okay?"

"Sure, Shane." Laura reached for a pen.

"Kinsey I want to do the follow-up call for Mattie myself tomorrow. If I don't do it by four o'clock, would you remind me?"

"Of course."

"And let Lily know Brenda's gonna be fostering two litters starting tomorrow, probably ten puppies. I'm taking a break." Shane headed out back hoping for a few minutes of peace.

Chapter 7

Two hours later Shane was getting some much needed fresh air. Driving the shelter truck, she and Little Laura were headed to meet the man with eight dogs and sixteen cats. With both windows down, the wind whipped through the truck making it impossible to talk. Shane didn't mind, she was enjoying the fresh air.

The man lived in Pubela, one of the small towns south of Loma Bonita. Just east of Morelia, the town didn't even have a post office. A run of covered horse stalls next to a community water station marked its border. Shane slowed to turn off the paved highway and onto the dirt road marked CO Hwy 67.

God, I love living out here, she thought admiring the views. Driving south, the mountains were behind her, but the wide open fields made it possible to see as far south as New Mexico and as far west as Utah. Smoke from the oil stacks in New Mexico made them easy to spot. But Shane could also see The Sleeping Ute, the mountain range located just inside the Colorado border to the west.

Last year, when her mom came out to pick up Jeremy, she said the land was barren. "How can you live here, it's so brown." But Shane loved it. The trees were a lot smaller than the one's back home but the Aspen's with their white bark and two-toned leaves and the short, stocky Pinon Pines with their twisted and intertwining branches were great in their own way.

Every morning Shane walked her dogs on the land next to Sheila's house. Owned by a man who hadn't been to the area in more than ten years, Shane got his address from her sister and wrote him a letter. She asked if she could walk her dogs on his land in exchange for keeping it clear and clean. To her surprise she received a quick and positive reply.

"Young lady, as an avid dog lover myself I am glad to hear you make it a priority to get your beloved pets the exercise they need. Feel free to use the land and enjoy it. I, unfortunately have not been able to for quite some time and I'm afraid it has fallen in disrepair."

Now Shane, and her dogs, Henry and Juice knew his land well. With her nephews help, she'd cleared a path through the oak brush and lined it with rocks. Dotted with yucca plants and sage brush, Shane spent hours walking around, sitting on the edge of the arroyo's, and watching Juice and Henry run between prairie dog holes.

Pulling up to an intersection, Shane slowed the truck down. She was looking for County Road 68 and glanced at the sign to her right, County Road 62. As she accelerated, she noticed the hay fields all around her had already had their first cutting. Five-foot round rolls of hay sat on their sides, marking the different quadrants of the fields. In a few days they'd be picked up and brought to one central area where they would be held under a cover until needed or sold.

"So why are we coming out here?" Laura asked now that it was possible to talk. "Not that I don't appreciate the afternoon drive."

"This guy has a bunch of dogs and cats that he wants to give to us. We've got some time since he needs to sell his house, so I want to check out the animals."

"Do you do this a lot?" Laura asked.

"No," Shane laughed. "It's the first time we've ever done it. But it's a perfect scenario." She turned onto the dirt road. "He needs to find homes for his pets. There's no way I can take all his animals in at one time but I could take a couple and once they're adopted take a couple more."

Seeing the address she was looking for on the silver mailbox, Shane slowed and turned in the dirt driveway. A fence blocked her progress and Laura hoped out of the truck to open it. As she did, Shane glanced around. Fifty feet in front of her, on either side of the driveway was a row of old cars and trucks. Acting as both a privacy wall and a noise barrier, the cars were in different states of disrepair. Hoods seemed to be missing off all of them. One old partridge-family-looking bus had all its windows broken and the tires had been removed off all the vehicles. Shane saw them lining the roof of the single-wide trailer that sat farther back off the road.

Laura walked the fence open and Shane slowly pulled forward until she was parallel to the row of cars. Just past the cars, to Shane's left six, chain-link dog pens sat side by side in two rows. Each approximately thirty-foot square, all except one had a homemade dog house. The last one had the cab of a truck perched on hay bales. Each pen housed one dog. The owner had said they were Great Pyrenees but they looked more like Pyrenees Anatolian Shepherd mixes to Shane. Popular in this part of the county, the large dogs had the long white Pyrenees coats but square heads and dark ears like Anatolians.

Getting out of the truck, Shane glanced back at the line of cars. Unbelievable, she thought looking around. *I could have driven past this place a hundred times without ever seeing the dogs. They wouldn't be able to see anything either,* Shane realized and wondered what they did to keep themselves sane.

Barking since she'd pulled in, she watched them as they reacted to her presence. Some stood and jumped with each bark, others stood the entire time with their feet up on the fence. They looked to be more than five foot tall when they did it. A loud whistle sounded and Shane saw a man coming out of the house. Pulling the door closed behind him, the man whistled a second time and the dogs paused long enough to look his way.

"Mr. McCay," Shane called out walking toward him. Laura had caught up with her and the two of them walked up the driveway. The junk wasn't confined to the row of cars. A second, narrower row of junk sat on the other side of the pens, between the dogs and the house. Shane saw an old stove, barrels filled with empty beer bottles, and stacks and stacks of plastic cat litter containers. One inside another, each stack was at least twenty containers tall. *He's not going to be selling this house anytime soon*, Shane thought, wondering if he'd bring the trash to the dump or just bury it, like so many people seem to do.

Merlin McCay approached Shane, his hands deep in the pockets of his jean jacket. "Nice to meet you ma'am. I appreciate you comin' out here."

"Don't mention it." Shane said relieved he didn't want to shake hands. Obviously a bachelor, Mr. McCay didn't look like he saw a shower very often. His long, scruffy, white beard had turned yellow from cigarette smoke years before and was now speckled with pieces of food. His jean jacket, buttoned up to his throat, was filthy. And he smelled. Even upwind, Shane could detect a mixture of cat pee and cigarette smoke.

The elderly man wore his long, white hair in a ponytail under a sweat-stained cowboy hat. His 1980's shaded tear-drop glasses, skinny jeans and rattlesnake-skin boots made Shane wonder if he still saw himself as a hippy. Shane had met plenty of others like him since she'd moved to the area. Old guys who let themselves go, collected a yard full of junk and became crazy hermits. She was glad she'd brought Little Laura along with her.

"Nice piece of land you got here," Shane said, hoping to hear more about how long she had to move the animals.

"Yeah. It's only forty acres, but it does the job."

"Yeah?" Shane glanced around. Away from the house, dogs and garbage the land was clear. She could see his fence line to the south and west. And to the north he had a clear shot of the mountains. "It's beautiful. I'm sorry you have to sell it."

"Ah, yeah, it's my heart. Doc says I need more oxygen than we have here. So I gotta move."

"Where you heading?" Shane asked.

Loma Bonita sat at an elevation of 7,300 feet. Shane rarely noticed the thin air, except when someone came in from out of town. Otherwise healthy, in-shape people got winded and struggled due to it. When Shane was out of town, she didn't notice the increased oxygen, but she did have extra energy and it seemed like she didn't need to sleep as much.

"Phoenix. My daughters are there and I'm ready for less snow."

Shane nodded, "are you planning to bring any with you?" She asked, gesturing to the dogs.

"Just Peaches, she's in the house. Well let's get started," He said walking over to the first enclosure. "Over here, this here is Penny. Penny's a good dog."

"How old is she?" Shane asked taking a picture of the large dog with her phone. The dog's eyes were brown and gold and she stared directly at Shane.

"Six. She was born here but then got bought by the Millers over on 61, you know them?"

"No," Shane said, reaching through the four-foot square openings in Penny's fence. Penny leaned against her hand, enjoying the attention.

The giant dog was filthy. Her coat should have been white but years of living in dirt made it look more grey then white. Shane rubbed under the matts on the dog's neck and behind her ears.

"Okay so the story with Penny. She got adopted, you see? Then all of a sudden she ended up back here," He paused then continued, "you see? Not sure what happened there. Miller had her, I don't know what he did to her but she won't go near a car at all anymore. Sad," he said shaking his head and walking toward the next pen.

Identical in looks and size to Penny, PooBear was her litter mate and stayed in the pen beside hers. As sweet and dirty as Penny, PooBear was also a love. Shane bent to give him some affection after taking his picture. "Do they ever interact with each other?"

"They haven't been out of these pens in years." Merlin said, his hand grasping his beard over and over again.

Shane could tell he was telling the truth. Not just from how starved for affection the dogs were but also from the condition of the gates. Bungeed together at some point long ago, the chords were filthy and weathered. Grass had grown up and through the bottom rungs of the gates and locked them in place.

A hole had been cut in the fence above two five gallon buckets which were buried half up in dirt. Green water sat in one bucket. Grass and small sticks floated across the top, Shane looked away, disgusted. The food bucket was just as filthy. Dry kibble sat in the bottom, flies and small gnats buzzed around it.

"PooBear here, I don't know what they did to her. But she was gone for three weeks and came back and killed the goat she'd grown up with, see?"

"What?" Shane asked a bit lost.

"Them people who had her. Had her for three weeks and when she come back she tore that goat apart. They'd grown up together, them two. Wasn't right for her to attack her like that. I seen it myself, the morning after she got back. The pen was a bloody mess and there was Honey the goat, ripped in half, see?"

Shane didn't see, and didn't want to. Glancing at Laura she asked Merlin, "so you've kept him locked up ever since?"

"Yep. Couldn't trust him."

Unfortunately, Shane knew she might not be able to either. Large dogs often got adopted out to the county rather than in town. One's that killed goats were not easy to adopt. They walked through the rest of the dogs outside. Shane glanced at Laura a few times as Merlin told a similar hard-luck story for every dog there.

"This here is Red," Merlin said, gesturing to the seventh dog that was tied up next to the trailer. An old refrigerator with the door removed was turned on its side and used as Red's dog house. After seeing Merlin stop outside of the area Red could reach, Shane realized he hadn't petted any of the dogs.

Red, who was actually black, was attached to the house by a six foot chain. Looking more like a Newfoundland than any of the others, the large dog whined at Shane as she approached. He'd gotten his chain stuck under an old tire and now only had a couple feet to move. Shane walked over slowly and pulled the tangled chain out from under the heavy tire. The huge dog jumped on her in gratitude.

"Whoa," she said, taking a step back to steady herself. "What's his story?"

"Oh poor Red, he was a passed-over puppy."

The way he said it made Shane feel like she should know what it meant, but considering that every dog on his property had some sort of pitiful story that blamed one neighbor or another she couldn't imagine what passed over meant.

"Two people came by, see?" Merlin began, still pulling at his beard. "Both of 'em came by to buy puppies, see? And neither took him. Neither of them, see? So he's got him some issues."

He's not the only one, Shane thought. The dogs were going to be difficult to adopt out. All needed to be groomed and housetrained. They'd have to be taught to walk on a leash and go up and down stairs. *Son-of-a-bitch.*

After spending a few minutes giving Red some much needed love Shane asked about the cats.

"Yeah, you want to see 'em? They're all in the house."

Modular and mobile homes were popular in this region of the country. Before moving out here her mom had told her, "don't you end up in a trailer Shane Alexander Hillard." Back east no one she knew had mobile homes or modular one's but here, everyone did. Including her sister. Her sister's large modular was one of the few that was on a foundation. With peaked ceilings, granite counter tops and hardwood floors it was a great house and one her mom never seemed to comment on it.

But Merlin's trailer was old, so old it only had one small window on the front wall of the fifty-foot unit. Diarrhea brown, the outer wall panels looked like they were barely holding on. Shane, with Laura behind her, began to follow Merlin up the wooden steps. Feeling them shake under the weight, Shane paused until Merlin got a foot in the house. The wood stairs and porch had long ago disconnected from the house and Shane held onto the railing as she took the first step.

As Shane placed her foot on the second stair a wave of moist, smelly air assaulted her. Ammonia, the overwhelming smell of cat pee stung her eyes. Like a bag of potato chips that swells at the high altitude then bursts open at the slightest touch, the fumes in Merlin's house had burst outward when he'd open the door, rocking both Shane and Laura backwards.

Shane stood, grasping the railing for a moment until her eyes cleared. *This was not going to be pretty.* She glanced back at Laura then continued up the few stairs to the small porch and through the doorway. As Shane took a tentative step inside she sunk into the carpet. A shiver went up her back and she tried not to think of why it felt like she was standing on four rugs piled on top of each other.

A narrow hallway ran to the right, lined with old dark paneling. Directly across from the door was a room filled with piles of stuff, all covered with tarps. The place was filthy and smelled even worse.

Shane couldn't tell if they were empty or full but twenty or so kitty litter buckets lined the hallway. Her eye's had stopped burning but were still watering. There wasn't a cat around but it didn't matter. She'd have to evaluate the cats once they came in.

"So what happened, see, was I was married to a woman, a woman I was guardian of. You see life wasn't good to her and I took her in but in Colorado you're married to someone without even knowing it. You know that?"

He seemed to be waiting for an answer. Shane figured he was talking about common-law marriage but was having a hard time concentrating. Her eyes were beginning to adjust to the dim light and she was looking around. Everything was filthy. The light switch was almost black and the door jam, a charcoal gray. "Uh-huh."

"Well she died and the anarchy went all to hell."

Anarchy? Shane glanced at Laura who was looking down the long hallway. The look on her face showed she was as disgusted as Shane.

"You see, right after she died, the dog at the top died too. Then I brought Peaches in the house. She was living outside and was the youngest of them all. And it all went to hell."

"Oh, hierarchy, you mean," Shane said, relieved. She finally understood what he was talking about. "You brought the youngest dog in to live in the house? I bet everyone got upset. You brought the dog from the bottom of the pack up to top tier status."

"Yeah, anarchy, that's what I said. Peaches, see? She was the lowest on the totem pole, then came in to live with me and everything went to hell. Now the other dogs hate her."

"I bet," Shane said. She'd seen enough and needed to get back outside. The smell was making her remember she'd had a killer headache just a couple of hours ago and she didn't want it to come back.

"Mr. McCay, we have everything we need. As we talked about, these dogs are going to take some time to place. So once I have an opening I'll give you a call. I'd like to start with Red." Shane would have taken the dog in that day if she'd had any room. Living on the end of a chain was a miserable existence for a dog. "Let's get him in there. Once he gets adopted we'll bring in another. Does that work for you?"

"Yes ma'am, that'll be just fine. I thank you kindly for your help."

"Don't mention it," Shane said eager to be outside.

Chapter 8

It seemed quieter than usual in the kennel the following morning. Jake was still there but his ears were obviously feeling better. Mo and Kimmy, the stray cattle dogs that came in together had been moved to the adoption floor and the puppies were out in foster. None of the animals there today seemed to care when Shane walked in and sat down a few minutes earlier.

The dog sitting next to her shifted the weight on her front feet. Shane looked at her for a long minute, "today baby. I'm sorry but I'm not doing you any favors after today. You've got to be suffering." Shane had taken up her usual place in the kennel, halfway between the gate and the dog.

The poor thing still hadn't gone to the bathroom but since she wouldn't come out from under the platform, her kennel hadn't been hosed down. Hair bunnies stuck to the concrete floor in different spots. A number had found their way into the crack that ran next to the separator wall. Shane had been trying to find something, anything that would seal the cracks in the floor, but everything dissolved with the constant cleaning, bleach, and high-pressure water. She looked in and shook her head, *disgusting,* she thought. Impossible to clean, the staff used the pressure sprayers to force out the accumulated hair, treats, and debris, which just eroded the remaining concrete even faster. I *suppose I should get something in there, even if it did break down. Maybe it would slow the erosion.*

Already closer to the little girl than ever before, Shane decided to press her luck. She shimmied herself slowly across the floor until she was up against the platform, next to the terrified animal. The dog pulled back as far into the tight corner as possible. Shane knew she was pushing the limits. Dogs, like people, always had the choice; fight or flight. It was obvious to Shane that this dog would choose avoidance rather than fight, but now Shane was dangerously removing that option from the equation. If the dog was going to bite her, it would be now, and it'd be Shane's fault.

Using her foot, Shane pulled the plastic bag with her lunch in it, closer. She grabbed out her sandwich and the can of cat food, hoping it'd be enough to temp her. The pop of the cat food lid quieted the deep breathing around the room. Shane froze, waiting for the dogs to go back to sleep. After a moment the steady breathing resumed.

Shane started bringing her lunch after Christmas last year when she realized how much she was spending every month buying take-out. She wouldn't have cared, not having much to spend her money on, but her Christmas present to Sheila was to pay for Jeremy's sports, for an entire year. At the time she couldn't think of anything to get her and Sheila was always complaining about how much it cost him to play football, soccer and baseball. So Shane had told her she'd pay for his sports for one year. She had no idea at the time that it was going to be so expensive.

The dog moved, shifting her weight again. "How you doing today, baby?" Shane asked hoping to encourage more. The dog didn't stand a chance if she couldn't relax a bit. Slowly, she was coming out of her shell. Yesterday she actually looked up when Shane was leaving. Today she was curled in a little ball on her blanket when Shane walked up. But her progress had been less than stellar and she still hadn't eaten or gone to the bathroom.

She was actually kinda cute, Shane thought. Her brown and black coat was pretty typical but it was her face that stood out. She had a light, tan mask that came to peaks above each of her dark eyes. Her nose reminded Shane of one you'd see on a Teddy Bear, small and black, and perfectly proportioned to her muzzle. She had small folded ears which sat high on her head. If she'd ever relax they'd probably look great with the rest of her face. But she was a bit disproportionate; her body seeming bigger than her small head. And her big belly looked wormy. "Here you go baby." Shane held the cat food under the dog's nose.

Shane hadn't pushed her this far before but time was ticking. The dog had been in the shelter for four days. After three days she was legally theirs and they needed to assess what kind of a pet she'd be. She still hadn't gone to the bathroom and Shane wondered if she was so potty trained that she wouldn't go inside. She needed to get a leash around her neck just to give her a chance to walk around. *God she was pathetic.*

After a minute of nothing, Shane put the can back down unwrapped her sandwich and pulled off a corner off. The piece she had had a good amount of cream cheese on it. She never realized the pleasure she got in eating junk food for lunch until she started bringing lunch from home. Suddenly, lunch was no longer something to look forward to but something to endure. One day eating peanut butter and jelly for the third day she decided she'd had enough. Shane wrote down everything she loved eating when she was a kid and committed to having decent lunches from then on.

Today it was her childhood favorite; cream cheese and pickles. Made just like it was when she was a kid with big hunks of dill pickles and enough juice to make even the plain cream cheese have flavor. Her mouth watered just thinking about it.

"Alright sister. Enough of this. I know you're hungry. You have to be hungry." Shane held the corner of her lunch toward the black, little nose and slowly moved her hand closer, then closer still. Nothing. She scooped out some of the cream cheese and spread it quickly across the top of the dog's nose then across the top of her foot. Once she had the taste of it, Shane hoped, she wouldn't be able to resist.

At first the dog didn't move. But after a minute, a thin line of drool formed on one side of her mouth. After a few seconds it reached its way to the floor. Shane held her breath. After another long minute, the small dog licked her nose.

Shane held out another piece of her sandwich. Watching, she could see the dogs nose moving slightly. After a couple of sniffs she leaned forward and gently took the piece of bread out of Shane's hand.

Shane let out the breath she'd been holding. *Finally*, she thought, relieved. Picking back up the can of cat food, she held it under the dog's nose. Shane watched as the she first smelled the food then slowly took a tentative lick. "Jeezo girl you've got to be starving. Stop being so shy and eat."

As if she heard her, the dog's desire seemed to increase. The more she ate, the faster she got. By the time she'd cleaned out the can of cat food, she was partially standing.

Shane had turned sideways to be able to hold the can for the dog. Now that she was facing her, she saw how cute she was. Small brown eyes were lined with the same dark brown her ears were lined with.

She pulled the dogs food from yesterday over and put it in front of the now standing animal. Shane wondered if the dog would come out from under the platform if she moved away but wasn't sure she wanted to take the chance yet. They'd made good progress and she didn't want to jeopardize it.

The dog didn't seem as excited about the kibble/canned food mixture as she did about the cat food, but bent to eat it anyway. Shane added the remaining corners of her sandwich to make the mixture more enticing and the hungry dog finished it in minutes.

Once done, Shane slid around to the side, determined to get the dog out for a walk. Pulling a nylon, braided slip lead out from her pocket, Shane looped one end. Not wanting to scare the dog, she didn't want to throw it. But if the small animal ducked back under the platform, Shane would be hard pressed to get it around her.

She held the leash toward the dog, letting her smell it. The dog wasn't interested, so Shane slowly lifted it higher and in one smooth movement, lassoed it around her neck.

The dog froze. Her front legs were half bent, her head straight out in front of her. Shane didn't pull but tightened up the lead and let it sit around her neck. Realizing this might not be as easy as she was hoping, Shane stood and gave the leash a soft tug. The dog didn't move. Shane repeated it, again nothing. This time Shane tugged a little stronger and held it for an additional couple of seconds.

Suddenly the dog took a step forward, then another. Shane reached to open the kennel while the tentative animal stuck out her front legs, bowed deeply and reached forward in a deep stretch. Afterwards, she shook from head to toe.

Shane smiled, thinking how good that must have felt after all these days. The dogs may scare the hell out of her, but Shane knew it was worth it if she could get her outside for a few minutes.

Twenty minutes later, Shane was still outside with the cute little girl. She'd gone to the bathroom three times and was now waiting for Shane who had stopped to talk with Jamie as she pulled in. Sitting down with her head tilted up toward the sun, the dog reminded Shane of the old RCA dog. Looking at her sideways, her tall, rounded shoulders and small folded ears looked just like the old advertisement.

Chapter 9

On Thursday morning Shane cleaned dog kennels with Margo, one of the new hires. She had assigned Jamie to cats, since Laura was out that morning and Kim was at the psychiatrists. Only eighteen years old, Margo was slow and spent as much time playing with the dogs as cleaning. By eleven o'clock Shane was soaked, exhausted and frustrated. And she still had to clean-up Dog Isolation.

Dog Isolation held any aggressive or questionable dogs as well as those that came in for bite holds. State law required that any dog that broke skin when they bit someone had to go on a ten-day rabies quarantine. Often the area was empty, or used for overflow, but today, and for the last two weeks, three 120-pound Mastiffs were in residence. Their heads were huge, as big as basketballs, but with short noses and penetrating eyes. More stocky than tall, they were intimidating. Their barks shook the shelter right down to its foundation, and Shane as well.

When she first saw them she was overwhelmed by their size. Of course Jamie wasn't. "The bigger the better," she always said. Jamie had been down on the ground playing and rough-housing with them as soon as they got there.

All three were from the same owner, a family living just north of the town. One of their chickens had been found torn to pieces and the wife insisted the dogs come to the shelter. They had twin, two-year old boys and she didn't want to take any chances. Shane agreed to hold them for a ten-day rabies hold, even though a slaughtered chicken wasn't typically a sign of rabies. The husband was in love with his dogs and they would be difficult to split up. So when he came in and begged her to let them stay an extra couple of days so he could finish a large enclosure in his yard, she agreed.

Today, Brutus, the dark brown male was out of sorts. The smell had hit Shane when she opened the door to feed them earlier. Cringing, she squeezed her eyes shut and took shallow breaths, trying to avoid the taste.

"That's disgusting." Margo said, holding the bottom of her scrub shirt over her face.

Looking in, Shane saw that the entire kennel was covered in diarrhea. Brown spots dotted the floor, walls, and even the gate. Not having any place to put him, Shane left him there and fed the remaining two.

She couldn't imagine eating with that smell but they didn't seem to mind. Cleo, short for Cleopatra, the matriarch of the family, wrinkled her nose a bit more than usual but after a minute she gulped her food just as quickly as her other offspring; Amadeus.

It was after eleven when Shane got back to Isolation. Pulling Brutus out, she walked him to the tub. After giving him a bath Shane tackled his kennel. It wasn't as bad as she had originally thought. At least it didn't seem so after pulling out his bed, blankets, bowls, and Kong's, which were all disgusting. The dog had a ridiculous amount of blankets. She pulled out a large trash bag and tossed them all into it. Once the run was sprayed and scrubbed down she let the cleaner sit while she pulled Cleo out of her run and did the same thing. They needed to get these guys out of there. *What's today?* Shane wondered. *Thursday, good, I'll give him a call and see what's up.*

The runs in Iso were self-contained units each elevated over the floor a few inches. Made out of metal instead of concrete, the floors had four narrow triangle indentations running from each corner to the center drain. Since they were impossible to dry using the squeegee, Shane used towels, wiping down the walls, floor and dog beds. Amadeus was a puppy, a 100-pound puppy, but still a puppy. Instead of tying him up or letting him walk loose, like Cleo, Shane put him in her kennel and cleaned his. She would have loved to play with him but she didn't have time.

Tying the garbage bag with Brutus's bedding, she threw it in the back hall. Then carried the towels, bowls and toys to the prep room. Opening the door she saw Margo sitting on the floor with one of the puppies.

"What are you doing?" Shane asked trying to keep her temper in check. "Did you put beds down? Have you filled waters? Is Holding done?"

"No. I was taking a break." Margo avoided looking up at Shane.

"Now's not the time."

As she stood Margo mumbled, "is it so much to ask to be able to play with the dogs once in a while?"

"You can play with them all you want once the work is done. It's after eleven, we're open. Every dog in the building needs to have bedding, toys, treats, and a full water bowl. Put the puppy back and make it happen. Now." The towels in the dryer were still wet so Shane turned it back on for forty-five more minutes. "Then do the laundry," she called back to Margo before heading up front.

"Did something happen with the Mastiff's yesterday?" Shane asked Kinsey when she got to the front desk.

"Jesus, what happened to you? You look like shit." Kinsey said, looking up from the filing cabinet.

"Thanks." Shane said, trying to flatten down her hair. "That's what happens when you clean by yourself."

"Not that I'm aware of." Kinsey answered, "what's up?"

"Brutus had blow-out diarrhea last night."

"Stress? Oh wait," Kinsey thought for a minute, "Judy had them out yesterday. I meant to tell you and forgot all about it."

"She did?" Shane shook her head. That was probably it. Stress colitis, was common at the shelter. *Though why Judy was handling dogs that weren't theirs was another matter entirely,* Shane thought. "Is Kim back yet?"

As if on cue Kim, the Senior Kennel Supervisor, came into Shane's office from the kennel.

"How was the dentist?" Shane asked her.

"Don't ask." Kim leveled her with a look. Going to the shrink wasn't Kim's idea and she still resented being handled. Wearing the same thing she wore every day; white sneakers, cheap dark blue jeans and a t-shirt, Kim dropped her wallet, keys and lunch in the bottom drawer of the small desk in Shane's office.

Using the Dentist as the reason why Kim was out every Thursday for ninety minutes wasn't fooling anyone but they were all smart enough not to mention it.

"Little behind today or what?" Kim asked, slipping a scrub shirt over her head.

"Yeah, she's worthless." Shane motioned back toward the kennel. "Hey, Brutus had blow-out diarrhea this morning. Anything happen that I don't know about?"

"Brutus? Shit. No, but no one's got water in the back. Let me just get Adoption and Holding set up and I'll get back there and check on him."

"His records look good." Kinsey said, handing Shane Brutus's medical records before turning to the short, stocky man that had just approached the desk.

"Yeah, someone said you had my dog here," the man said.

"Okay," Kinsey said smiling. "What kind of dog do you have?"

"A brown one. A Pit."

"I'll bring him back," Shane said knowing there was no one else to do it. There was only one Pit Bull in receiving, for a change. He was a cute, young puppy with a long tail and square head. *It would suck if this was his owner,* Shane thought, walking to the front.

Seeing if the animal was at the shelter was the first step when someone lost their pet. Once identified, the owners could then complete the paperwork and pay their fines with the front desk or Animal Control.

"How long have you been missing your dog?" Shane asked as her sneakers, still soaked from cleaning, squished with every step. They walked through the Adoption area and into Holding.

"I dunno, couple days." He shouted over the dogs. The man's hair had been shaved short. He wore an old white t-shirt with a line of holes across the bottom. Stretched over his round belly it highlighted the dark green tattoo ink that covered both his arms completely. He walked with his hands over his ears.

"Down here," Shane gestured, knowing he'd never be able to hear her. Surprisingly they only had two Pits in the entire building, both mixes. Truly, a beautiful brindle girl on the adoption floor, and the little one in receiving. Shane stopped in front of the kennel and turned toward the man.

The dog was mostly white but had big brown spots all over his body. H stood up on the fence, his tail wagging wildly. "Guess he recognizes you." She said, when the man reached her.

Barely six months old, the dog initially joined the others in the chorus, but quieted down when he saw his owner. Obviously happy, the dog circled a couple of times, whined then jumped up on the front gate again.

The man stood staring at the young puppy. After a few moments he leaned down and hollered, "What were you thinking? I told you not to leave the yard." Leaning farther in toward the submissive animal, he shouted even louder, "Didn't I? Didn't I?"

Shane jumped when the man raised his voice and the dogs around them reacted immediately; barking and jumping up on the kennel gates. Feeling protective Shane placed a hand on the gate of the puppy's kennel and tried to insert herself between the dog and the man. The puppy dropped down onto his stomach and rolled over. His tail still wagged but not with the same enthusiasm.

"Get up, you wuss. Stand-up when I talk to you." The pissed-off man kicked the gate. The chain-link, attached to the thick metal framing around the door, bowed inward where his boot had struck it. He reached up and fumbled with the latch.

"You can't do that sir." Shane took another step, inserting herself completely between the man and the young dog. The dogs were going crazy and she knew he would never be able to hear her.

"Get out of my way." He hollered, still trying to figure out the latch guard.

Damn, he had bad breath. "You can't take him out yet," Shane moved his hand aside and covered the latch with hers. "We need you to fill out some paperwork." She braced her arm, hoping he wouldn't challenge her. She knew she wouldn't stand a chance against him, he weighed a hundred pounds more than her, but she wasn't going to let him just take the dog.

The puppy, still on his back with his legs spread wide, watched as the man hesitated then dropped his hand and turned back the way they had come.

"It's okay baby." Shane told the puppy, though she couldn't guarantee it, considering.

She followed the man back to the front desk, "the white and brown in receiving, #1502 is his." She told Kinsey while rolling her eyes.

"Everything alright?" Kinsey asked, poking her head into Shane's office after asking the man to fill out the Return-to-Owner paperwork.

Shane was still shaking, "Oh, he's an asshole, kicked the gate right in front of me. Sucks the poor things gotta go back to him."

Kinsey smiled sympathetically before turning back to complete the paperwork for the dogs release.

Chapter 10

An hour later, Kim, Jamie and Little Laura were finishing up their meatball subs in the office while Kinsey and Shane watched the front desk. With only a few people in the building, the five of them were enjoying a rare moment when they could all sit down together.

"Why is it," Laura asked tentatively, "that some people are so dead set on one type of dog, while others don't seem to care at all?"

"Because they saw it on TV, or in a movie." Kim said, matter-of-factly. Sitting back in her chair, she wiped her hand across her mouth then wiped it on her jeans before taking a drink of soda.

"Is that it?" Laura asked.

"Yeah, course it is. They saw a Cocker or Dalmatian in a movie and had to have one," Kim continued, even though she had just taken another bite of her sub. "Course few of 'em knew what they were gettin'."

"I don't know," Jamie said making a face at Kim's mouth full of food. "I can't say I've seen too many movies with Rottie's or Dobie's that I liked but I just love the breeds. I think it's like comfort food. I love meatloaf because it reminds me of being a kid and being part of a family and good home cooked food and all that. Well Rottie's and Dobie's are the same thing. We had both growing up, mostly Rottie's but my uncle had Dobie's. Every 4th of July we'd all get together, cook up a huge drum of corn chowder and watch everyone's dogs play. They're comfort food to me."

"Meatloaf, huh?" Shane smiled. "What about you Kins, why do you think it is?"

"I've always thought it was more like your first love. I mean you always remember your first love and they always have a place in your heart. I have five dogs at home, four are mixed breeds that I connected with but one is a Portuguese Water Spaniel. We had one when I was in high school and that dog helped me make a lot of important decisions. They're my first love and I think I'll always have one around. But a Portuguese mix would be just as good."

"So what does that say about those of us who aren't drawn to a particular breed? Who get dogs just because of the connection?" Shane asked, standing in the doorway.

"You're fucked," Kim said, spaghetti sauce on her chin. "Think about it, you have no allegiance."

"Don't listen to her, you're just not picky, like the rest of us." Kinsey said.

"Bullshit, you don't love them as much." Kim said, smiling slightly.

"Well it's not like I'm not partial. I'm not into small dogs and I'm not into the northern working breeds. But give me a good Shepherd mix, Lab mix or a Hound mix and I'm down." Shane was thrilled they were having a conversation that had something to do with their jobs. "But it doesn't have to be a purebred. I could care less about that. And I don't care if Poodles are great dogs, I'd never have a Doodle anything. It just sounds stupid."

"Maybe it's because you're a loner." Jamie said crumpling up the wrapper from her sandwich and tossing it into the garbage.

"Maybe," Shane said, surprised by the comment. *Is that what they all think of me?*

~

"Hey Cody," Shane said to the Jake's owner, standing at the front counter at four that afternoon. His German Shepherd had been in Holding since the weekend, even though Kinsey had been calling him for days. *Nice of him to finally show up,* Shane thought. She'd cleaned the dog's ears and visited with him every day, but she knew he was miserable there.

Headed into her office to return some calls, Shane knew Cody would be upset about his bill so she left her door open. But just as she sat down, the opposite door, that led to the Adoption area, opened and Judy stuck her head in.

"Good," she said. "I'm glad you're here. Can you come out and look at this kennel?"

Shane sighed, *now what?* She followed her to the end of the first row of kennels, rounded the corner and walked half-way down the next aisle to a kennel holding only one dog: Maggie, a ninety-two pound yellow Lab.

"Would you just look at that? It looks like someone has been massacred in there."

Shane smiled despite herself. *It did look pretty bad.* Maggie wagged her tail constantly. She'd been at the shelter for two weeks and had beat her tail on the concrete wall so much a sore had formed on the end of it. This was the first time it had opened up, but it did mean they needed to move her to one of the wider runs. *Shoot,* Shane thought, *who can I move?*

"It's from her tail." Not finding a leash in her pocket Shane grabbed a slip lead from the supply at the end of the row and opened the latch on Maggie's kennel.

"Well I know it's from her tail. That's not the point, why is she here like this?"

Shane looped the leash around the dog's head before she bounded out of the kennel. *Where else would she be*? Shane shook her head not able to think of anything clever to say between the barking dogs.

Happy tail, a condition caused when dogs beat their tails on the concrete walls of the kennel, looked much worse than it was. A simple wound on the end of the dog's tail, once it opened it bled anytime the dog's tail wagged. Unfortunately, like with Maggie, blood was often sprayed everywhere; throughout the kennel, across the floor, in the water bowl and often even out into the walkway. The first time Shane saw it she was as surprised as Judy.

The trickiest part of the condition was treating it. Keeping the bandage on and an infection out was difficult in the same setting that caused it in the first place. *Maggie was a good girl though,* Shane thought, *we could keep her behind the front desk until it got better.*

She walked the dog down the back hall to the medical suite. As they walked, Maggie's tail decorated the walls and floor with splotches of blood. At one point Shane tried to hold it, to keep it from swinging but that just got Maggie more excited and she stopped, circled and wanted to play.

Shane was thinking about Judy's comments a few minutes later as she cleaned up the blood trail. *What the hell,* she thought. *What did she expect in a situation like this? What else could we have done? It hadn't happened before now. It's not like we're going to take an animal out of circulation because they might end up getting a sore on their tail.*

"Shane to the front please, Shane to the front." Laura's voice didn't sound good and Shane thought she heard someone yelling in the background. Picking up the towels she'd used to clean, she dropped them in the prep room before heading up to the front desk.

When she got there she saw Cody, Jake's owner, standing at the counter looking like he was about to kill someone. Judy was standing next to him. Shane wondered briefly if that's how she looked when Judy was next to her.

"What's up?" Shane asked as Laura turned around, rolled her eyes and moved over so Shane could step forward.

"I can't believe you fucking neutered my dog. How dare you! How dare you! You bitches, you've been wanting to do this forever, haven't you?"

Shane was confused. She didn't see Kinsey but Kim looked like she was going to blow, no wonder Laura sounded so upset.

"Unbelievable you cut my dog. You cut on my dog without my permission. I can't believe you! You bitches, who the hell do you think you are?"

As Shane looked around for answers, Kim shot back. "I can't believe you let your unneutered dog walk around the neighborhood!" Kim's face was as red as Cody's. "Ever hear of a little thing called overpopulation? People like you are the reason this place exists."

God damn it, Shane thought, *why did there always have to be so much drama?* "Kim!" Shane said, leveling her with a look before turning back to Cody. "Cody, we didn't neuter your dog. Your dog's been here a hundred times and we've never neutered him. Why do you think we'd do it now?"

"Bullshit. This woman said you did." He pointed to Judy who was now busying herself petting a dog.

"And you believed her?" Shane asked. "Cody, this is not your first time here. Jake's never gone home neutered on any of his other overnights, so why would he now? Trust me, your boy is still intact."

"Good." He said glaring at Kim.

"Judy, Kim, my office, now." Shane turned towards Laura, "Are you okay with a Return-to-Owner?"

She nodded, "Animal Control's on their way."

"Great, we'll be in the office," Shane said closing the door behind them.

"What the hell was that?" She asked Judy.

"Me? What about her?"

"I asked you. Did you tell him his dog had been neutered?"

"He said it'd been here four or five days so I told him we'd probably already went ahead and neutered him and put him up for adoption."

"You didn't even check first," Kim said. "We all know that dog, he's been here a hundred times. We'd never neuter him or check him in or put him up for adoption. Why don't you get your facts straight before talking to the public?"

"So sorry that I told a customer the truth. And if that dog's been here that much then he should be neutered or given away to someone else. It's obvious his owner can't take care of him."

"Yeah, that's what we're going to do, take his dog from him. That's really good customer service." Kim said, biting her nails.

"I thought the third time they came through they had to be altered? Don't you abide by the laws?" Judy shot back.

"We do, when they exist. But that's not a law in Colorado." Shane replied, "and if we went around neutering people's animals against their wishes we'd become pretty unpopular pretty fast. And you," she said looking at Kim, "what the hell was that? I know we all know Cody, but other people out there don't know that and they think we'll act the same way to them."

"You hollered the word fuck in front of all those people," Judy added.

Kim, who'd been leaning against the opposite desk with her arms crossed, stood and pulled her scrub shirt up over her chest and pointed to the t-shirt she had on underneath. The large, bold letters read; I AM NOT A PEOPLE PERSON!

"C'mon Shane, that was ridiculous." She said pulling her shirt back down. "Like we'd ever neuter his dog? And him screaming at us like that, like we don't know his dog is responsible for half those puppies we get from that neighborhood? That just ain't right. He knows better."

"You killed somebody's dog last year. Why's it so hard to believe you'd neutered someone's dog now?" Judy said staring directly at Kim.

The air felt like it got sucked out of the room. Shane couldn't believe Judy had just said that. She looked at Kim wondering how she'd react.

"You bitch, you don't know anything." Kim hollered, all humor gone from her face. She pulled open the door and walked out into the kennels.

"What?" Judy asked, faking innocence, "it's the truth."

"No it's not. And Kim's right, you don't have any idea what happened to that dog."

"Well then tell me. Tell me, how it was that you killed someone's dog. Dee says you're invaluable, how is it that someone so invaluable could kill an owned dog? I got news for you girl, times are changing, and you excusing bad behavior," she gestured to the door Kim left through, "and sloppy practices, are coming to an end." Judy left through the same door Kim did.

Shane could hear her dad's voice in her head as she blinked back tears. *No emotions. Be strong. Swallow them, choke on them, but don't show them.* She sat down heavily in her chair holding her head in her hands. *The strong remain silent,* she knew, *I just don't know how much longer I can stay strong.*

Chapter 11

A week later Kim, Jamie and Shane stood in the holding area looking at Gigit. Still not wanting to name her, Shane had gone to calling her the silly name until she could decide what to do with her.

"She'll eat, sure, but she doesn't show well." Kim had already disregarded her as a hopeless case and turned to move on. "I don't know what you see in her, Shane."

"I know," Shane said, watching the now happy little girl. Partial to big dogs, Shane was as surprised as anyone that she'd become as involved as she had. With so many dogs coming through, many only staying hours or days, the staff didn't get close to a lot of them. Jamie did, especially if they were over seventy-five-pounds or stayed for a while. But on occasion a dog would come through and connect with one of them in a special way. Those were the ones they got caught up with.

But Shane didn't feel that with Gigit. She liked her and really enjoyed seeing her come out of her shell. But she didn't feel that connection, that bond she had felt with both Juice and Henry, making her adopt them. The little dog was growing on her, but Shane's only interest was in building her confidence and giving her a chance at a new home.

She was getting a little better, Shane thought, as the dog wagged her tail quickly from side to side, trying to get Shane to open the gate. Pawing at the ground, as if she just needed to reach a little closer, she looked adorable. But unfortunately she still only acted this way when Shane was around. If she kept getting better she'd have a chance. Shane just didn't know if they had the time to wait.

Once a week Shane, Jamie and Kim walked the kennels together. Each of them did it every day, but after realizing they each held key information, Shane recommended they do it together. Kim never wanted to participate and often found a reason not to join, but today Shane tracked her down.

Three months ago Shane had overheard Kim make a comment about one of the dogs they had. A large, Rhodesian Ridgeback mix, the dog was a beautiful, solid animal. There wasn't a playful bone in his body, but he was a love. He'd been there six weeks when Shane overheard Kim mention that Betty the volunteer said she knew the dog. Kim hadn't taken her seriously. She didn't take any volunteers seriously, especially Betty who said she knew a lot of the dogs.

Shane may not have taken her seriously either but Sheriff, as they were calling him, resembled a dog Shane had checked in on her first day. He was a sweet, young Ridgeback, full of the usual puppy playfulness and fun. He'd been adopted quickly. Shane couldn't believe that it could be the same dog. He looked older than two years, a lot older.

The adoption took place before they got the new software. Since none of their previous records were carried forward, finding the owner would have meant digging through boxes of old records. After hearing Kim's comment, Shane talked to Betty. They compared notes and realized it was indeed the same dog. After leaving numerous unreturned messages with the family and factoring in that the dog had been purposely abandoned, they decided he was better off at the shelter. But the lesson was enough to make Shane walk the kennels weekly with the supervisors.

Jamie, who worked the kennels the most, had something to say about all the dogs. Kim and Shane only added information if they saw or had experienced something. Jamie could read dogs well but she excused a lot of bad behaviors. Shane and Kim had to constantly remind her to stop encouraging dogs to jump up.

They moved down to the next kennel, it was Hogg. The large, black Shepherd mix surrendered last week.

"Why is he still in here?" Shane asked.

"I can't get a bead on him," Jamie said, not opening the kennel door or kneeling down. "At times he'll lean into me, but even when he does," she paused, "it's like, I don't know, manipulative, in a way."

"Yeah I agree," Kim said. "I don't trust him at all."

Shane looked at the erect dog. His tall ears sat so high on his head, when something caught his attention they actually touched. She had never seen a Shepherd like him before and didn't like the look. His ears looked like they had been docked; the outside of each was perfectly straight and looked like they'd been cut to angle inward. A typical Shepherd had large, wide ears, which offset their long noses. With the points of his ears angling inward instead of outward, it was hard to define his face. "I haven't seen him growl or lift his lip." Shane said, watching the serious dog watch them.

"You're not gonna get any warnin' with him." Kim had turned to continue down the aisle but turned back to look at him again. "He's one of them that's fine till he blows. And when he does," she looked at Shane, "he'll slap nine kinds of shit out of you."

Jamie, defender of all large dogs, remained oddly quiet. Shane looked back at the unmoving dog before turning to catch up with the others.

"What the hell? What is she doing back here?" Kim asked a minute later, standing in front of the run with Onyx inside. The two-year-old black and white, Border Collie/Lab mix had been adopted two days ago and returned the day before.

"Didn't come when she was called," Jamie said sarcastically.

"What?" Kim snapped.

"Oh," Jamie waved her hand, "the woman said there was no bond. She called her at the dog park and Onyx didn't even blink. Said she's always felt a bond with her other dogs."

"Are you fucking kidding me?" Kim turned towards Shane.

Shane shrugged. Not being there the day before she had no idea if it was the reason or not. Unfortunately, it wasn't the first time she'd heard it. "Think of it as a good thing. Onyx is a great dog, she needs a better home than that one."

"Losers." Kim said before turning to the next dog.

Fifteen minutes later they were done. Shane headed up front to call Durango and Boulder to see if they could do some swaps. Having too many Shepherd mixes and older dogs, Shane needed some alternatives. Swapping animals between shelters gave those that were lingering a new group of potential adopters. *The catch was that they usually swapped an old dog for an old dog, but who knows*, Shane thought. *Maybe I should volunteer to take a Pit off their hands.*

Seeing the front desk was enjoying a moment of quiet Shane asked Kinsey to call Dalmatian rescue for the stray in back.

"Sure, but they never have any room."

"I know. And I think we can move him anyway, but just in case."

"You got it. What about that Shepherd back there, should I call rescue for him?"

"He's not a purebred." Shane said knowing she was asking about Hogg. They'd had a glut of Shepherd mixes but most of them were on the floor and most were mixed with Rottie's, Labs, Aussie's or Border Collies. Hogg, though not purebred, looked the part more than anyone else. Even Bowser, whose markings resembled a Shepherd's the most, had folded ears and a curled tail.

Hogg looked like a Shepherd but his size didn't match. And his muscular shoulders and short curled tail looked more like a Husky's than a Shepherd's.

"That big, black one in back?" Judy asked, coming down from upstairs.

"But do me a favor and check with Lily," Shane continued, ignoring Judy for the moment. "See if we can move one or two of those seniors that are on the floor into foster homes for a couple of weeks."

"Anyone in particular?"

"Let Kim and Jamie decide, but I'd recommend Leroy or Sassy for starters."

Older dogs were great to have in the shelter. The volunteers came out by the dozens to walk and pamper them. They also had a calming influence. Not as quick to jump at every passerby, the elderly dogs barked less often and seldom went to the bathroom in their kennels. But the shelter wasn't good for them.

They seemed to fade faster than the younger ones in the environment. And having a glut of them on the adoption floor made potential adopters feel bad. The fewer they had, the faster they were adopted. The more they had, the slower they were adopted. It was just another kennel mystery to Shane.

"I think that dog in back is a purebred." Judy said for the second time.

"He's not, believe me." Shane said over her shoulder as she walked into her office.

"So if he's not a purebred, he can't go to a rescue?" Judy asked, following her.

"Not a purebred rescue, and that's the only one I'd send him to." Years ago the term rescue referred only to purebred rescues. Typically run by breeders, they were a good outlet for purebred dogs but were often limited on available space. Over the last ten years the term "rescue" had grown to include small, private entities and limited-admission Animal Shelters, those that got their animals from other organizations, not the public.

"Well what about a general rescue or a shelter that accepts transfers."

Shane looked at Kim, who was sitting at her desk, "A no-kill shelter, you mean?"

"Exactly, they take in dogs from other shelters."

"He'd never pass the screening and I wouldn't allow it."

"You wouldn't allow him to be transferred? What do you want to do? And don't say kill him because there's nothing wrong with that dog."

"Judy," Shane snapped back. "We use the word euthanize here. Considering how close we live to places that do indeed kill the animals in ways you don't want to hear about, you should understand and respect the difference."

"That dog hates people." Kim said, not looking up from the catalog she was thumbing through. "Here. Here it is Shane." She handed over the book and pointed to the EZ Nabber they'd been discussing.

"He's just been moved between a lot of homes. He needs time to bond," Judy said.

It was hard for Shane not to smile once she made eye contact with Kim. *The dog had spent his whole life with the same family, but of course what did they know?*

~

Two hours later Shane was paged to Dee's office. Preferring to be around the animals, the Director usually came down if she needed to talk to Shane. Not knowing what she wanted, Shane did a quick tally of everyone before heading upstairs.

The administration offices, boardroom and a fully-stocked kitchen were all located on the second floor. The kitchen had a large fridge, working microwave, tables, chairs and magazines. The kennel staff, as Shane and her staff were called, had been encouraged to eat their lunches in it and occasionally did, but usually ended up in Shane's office or outside.

She walked down to Dee's office and saw Judy standing against the far wall. *What the hell? No emotions,* she reminded herself but her hands still began to sweat.

"Shane, thanks for coming up." Dee stood, piercing her with a direct stare and gesturing to the empty chair.

Shane sat sideways so Judy wasn't behind her. "What's up?"

"Shane, Judy has some concerns about one of the dogs downstairs. A Shepherd named Hogg. Is that really his name?"

"She does, huh?" Shane turned to look toward her. "And what is Judy's concern?"

The room was quiet. Judy looked toward Dee then took a step forward.

"Well first this condescending attitude you always have with me. I'm not just a volunteer anymore, I'm on the Board of Directors and I expect some respect. Second, the fact that you won't consider transferring a dog out of the facility. And third, that this is endemic of a much bigger problem."

"And would that problem happen to be me?" Shane asked, feeling the sting of being called out on her attitude.

Judy looked at Dee again.

"Look Shane," Dee said. "You know I'd never step on your toes. I just thought this would be a good opportunity to explain to Judy the other factors you have to take into account when evaluating dogs."

Shane wiped her hands on her jeans. *Deep breaths* she reminded herself. She couldn't believe this.

"Shane?" Dee repeated.

"Well if you want to know why I'm condescending," Shane said to Judy, "it's because you have no idea what you're talking about. You've never worked in a shelter, you've never managed 200 animals at the same time, not to mention a staff and a half-a-million dollar budget. How about you go do that for a while then come here and tell me how to run this shelter." She turned back toward Dee her voice now shaky, "What do you want to know?"

"Can you tell *me* about the dog?"

"Well, let's see. He's nineteen-months-old, all black, Shepherd mix. He's aloof, distant. Doesn't connect with anyone, not even Jamie." Shane knew Dee didn't deserve the attitude but she couldn't help it.

"Okay," Dee looked confused. "Judy I don't understand, this sounds like a no brainer. He's an adolescent – strike one. Dogs between sixteen months and four years are our most common here. And unfortunately they don't usually move quickly. Black dogs are difficult to move – strike two. And probably half of our kennel population is Shepherd mixes – strike three. Add to that that he's not a nice, loving dog that would make a good family pet, and you see Shane's made the right call by recommending not to transfer him. Why go to bat for this one?"

"For the record, this is not my first time working in a shelter. I've been volunteering for years at shelters in California and Nevada. And I know more than you think I do. Maybe I don't have your "experience" as you put it, but I've got my own. I lost my dog because of an Animal Shelter and I'll be damned if I let that happen to another person. I like this dog. He's strong, he's solid. He'd make a great watch dog."

"We don't adopt out watch dogs. We adopt companion animals, family pets," Shane said wondering what had happened to Judy's dog.

"So you can't make an exception?" Judy turned to Dee. "You see this is exactly my point. When you use euthanasia as a solution, you rely on it too much. This is obviously a dog that hasn't seen a lot of compassion in his life. Maybe he just needs some time and someone to care about him?"

"Who said anything about euthanasia? I haven't decided to euthanize him, we're evaluating him. And so far, we have very few answers except that he scares the hell out of us and doesn't seem to have an affectionate bone in his body."

"And if it turns out that he would be a good watch dog, would you still be opposed transferring him?"

Look who's talking about condescending, Shane thought. "Did it ever occur to you that we may know what we're talking about? That not all dogs are perfect? Remember when I said you have the luxury of only concerning yourself with one dog – I don't have that. I have to make sure we are still here for the dog that needs us in two months or two years."

"I think more likely, you're just quick to give up. You can't blame that on the dog."

"Give up? That's what you think we do? That's why we have dogs in this building that have been here over 200 days because we give up?" *The nerve of this woman,* Shane was pissed.

"Maybe not on the ones you like. What about that little dog in receiving. She doesn't "show well" as you put it, but she's still here."

"You're right she is." Shane's heart raced at the thought of Gigit being compared to Hogg. "She's adoptable, if I can get her over her terror, she's worth spending time on. Hogg," She looked over at Dee, shaking her head. *God I hate that name,* "he's not. I can't adopt that dog out in good conscious – not yet, he's a ticking time bomb."

"You don't know that. That little dog could bite just as easily."

"No she wouldn't. I've pushed her boundaries plenty and she's never shown an aggressive side. But the Shepherd. Jesus, Jamie who rolls around on the floor with those Mastiffs, isn't comfortable around him. I can't think of one home he'd be suited for."

"And you wouldn't even consider changing the rules for just this dog? If I find a salvage yard or someplace he can guard, would you consider letting him go over killing him?"

"What kind of life is that for a dog?" Shane asked. "Do you know how they train guard dogs?"

"At least it's a life. Which is more than you're offering him." She turned back to Dee. "Let me try. What do you have to lose?"

"So you're saying life above all else." Shane added, "no matter if he suffers in his new life, at least your conscience will be clear? Shouldn't it be about what's best for the dog?"

Dee looked between Shane and Judy.

Judy walked up to Dee's desk. "Three years ago I took a vacation. I left my seven year old Dachshund with my friend while I was away. He escaped from her yard and was picked up by Animal Control. By the time I got back a week later, he was gone. They had euthanized him. My baby, killed alone. And why? Because they use euthanasia. Don't you see, when it's available to workers they'll use it. That's why it's so important that we stop having it available. Let me see if I can find a place to take him, at least give me a chance to place him."

Shane knew she was reading that dog correctly but couldn't say specifically how she knew. She agreed with Kim and Jamie, she didn't trust the dog. "If he bites anyone it's going to be on our head," she reminded them.

"Alright," Dee held up her hand. "Let me have the night to decide and I'll speak with you both in the morning."

Chapter 12

At ten the next morning when Dee called down to ask Shane to join her in her office, Shane was still talking to Dave and Debbie Whooton, tourists visiting from Phoenix.

"I can't believe it," Debbie repeated for the hundredth time. I can't believe after all that, that we really found him. I was starting to wonder if we ever would."

The couple, still soaked from the all night search for their dog, was standing in the lobby with their black Lab, Hank. Yesterday afternoon they had left Hank in their mobile home at the campground while they went into town for dinner. While they were gone a severe thunderstorm rolled through the area. Upon returning, they opened the door to their trailer. When they did, they were nearly knocked over by Hank who rushed out.

"He never even stopped when we called him," the woman was in tears when Shane first met her that morning. "He's never taken off from us before. And of course it was because of the thunder but we didn't know."

The couple had left six messages on the shelters voice mail, begging for help with their lost dog. Shane knew that losing a dog in a strange town would be heartbreaking and she felt for them. Though tucked up next to town, the campground they were staying at fed into a remote ravine. Shane had been in search parties before for dogs lost in the area and knew how difficult it could be.

"We've spent the night out looking for him but we haven't seen him once." The woman sobbed into the phone. "There's nothing but woods behind the campground, he's got to be out there somewhere. But I don't understand why he's not coming to my calls." Shane knew that searching for the dog at night in the rain on unknown terrain was pointless, but didn't say anything. *The couple was distraught, they probably needed the activity to keep them sane.*

The long ravine snaked north from the campground for miles. Covered in thick Oak brush, the sides were difficult, sometimes impossible to traverse. Shane didn't think she'd need to. After talking to the woman that morning she'd piled Little Laura and Snickers in her truck.

"Are we bringing Snickers so he can go for a walk?" Laura asked, excited to be released from morning cleaning duty.

"Yes and no. At the very least, it'll be a nice treat for him but I think he can help."

"Help with the search?" Laura looked at the sixty-five pound Golden mix who was laying in the backseat with his head down on his paws.

"Maybe. I can't say I've tried it before but dogs are the quickest way to get other dogs to do anything. It's true." Shane said seeing Laura's look.

Once they walked through the campground, Shane asked Laura to hold Snickers leash. Studying the ground, Shane found Hanks trail, lost it then found it again. The rain throughout the night helped but the couple's footprints didn't. Once she was sure the dog hadn't doubled back, Shane took Snickers off the leash. She figured they'd be able to find the dog if he was still in the ravine. If he'd gone back out, it would have been another story but she didn't see any footprints heading back.

The path was pretty trashed. Walking at night, in the mud, using only flashlights the couple had torn it up pretty bad, but every once in a while Shane caught a clear footprint. Measuring Snickers print against it, she could tell the dog was a little bigger than the Golden. Looking at the indentation Shane wondered if he didn't have a broken toenail on his right foot. It never seemed visible with the rest of his imprint.

With only two trails through the ravine, one doubling as a dry creek bed, Shane figured they just needed to go in farther to find the scared dog. Running as he had in a blind panic, he would have followed the easiest route. But once he calmed down or ran out of adrenaline, he'd find someplace to hide. That was when she'd need Snickers.

After another half hour, Snickers began dancing on the trial. His nose in the air, he ran to the right and left trying to find the scent he had picked up.

"Hank!" The couple screamed. Dragging behind, the couple was exhausted from their night of searching. But as soon as they saw Snickers getting excited they seemed to wake up and get their second wind.

A minute later Snickers ran to Shane's left, through a thick patch of Oak brush. Everyone followed and watched as Snickers ran around a pile of dirt to a rusty, old fifty-five gallon drum lying on its side. Sitting down in front of the opening, the pretty dog held his paw in the air, as if to shake hands with whoever was inside. Debbie and Dave, still hollering Hank's name, ran to the empty barrel and sat down next to Snickers.

"Hank!" Debbie cried, looking into the small den. Happy, relieved, and exhausted the couple reached in to leash the hiding dog. Hank bounded out of the barrel and into Dave's arms. Jumping all over his parents, the dog cried, barked and whined all while covering them with kisses.

By the time they'd gotten back to the campground Shane thought she was carrying ten extra pounds of weight on each foot. The mud, a thick, clay mixture had encapsulated her hiking boots completely. She and Laura used the curb to clean them before getting into the truck. Snickers was a mess too. When they got back Laura brought him directly to the backroom for a bath.

"You guys were so great. I don't think we would have gone that far back. And we would have walked right by him if it hadn't been for Snickers. Thank you so much."

"You're welcome," Shane said again. "We're just so glad we could help." She turned to head up to Dee's office. Even with wet shoes she was feeling pretty good. *Way to go Snickers.*

Hearing the call come into the front desk, Shane knew Dee was waiting for her. She assumed they would talk first then have Judy join them, so she was surprised to see Judy already there, along with Paul and Kylee from the Board of Directors. This was not what she was expecting. Shane's heart began to race and she wiped her damp hands on her jeans before taking a spot against the bookcase.

"Thanks for coming up Shane," Dee smiled at Shane before beginning. "Let's get to it, shall we. To re-cap, yesterday afternoon I was approached by Judy Bishop, a member of the Board who asked me to intervene in the management of the shelter. Now as Paul, Judy and I discussed last night, it is not the boards place to micromanage daily operations here, but I've been assured that this is not that, but instead an opportunity."

"Because there is going to be a vote before the membership at the annual meeting next month, the Board would like to use this opportunity to show the staff that there are alternatives to euthanizing. I believe the exact wording was," she looked down at a scrap of paper in front of her, "as a test-drive to implement a no-kill philosophy." Dee slowly read each word.

Shane could see Judy nodding out of the corner of her eye. *What did she have to gain in this?* Shane tried to distract herself by looking at Dee's artwork. A sand painting just over Dee's right shoulder had two vases on it, one lying on its side. The design painted on the vases matched the lampshade on Dee's desk, Shane had never noticed that before.

"For the record," Dee continued, "I would like to repeat how opposed to this idea I am. I went down and sat with that dog last night. He is not a friendly dog, nor a dog that many people would consider adopting. I don't disagree with your argument that every life is precious. But I believe we have a responsibility to look out for dogs, all dogs. And adopting a potentially unsafe dog or transferring one, and thus making it someone else's problem, is putting that dog's life above the humans it's going to come into contact with."

Shane couldn't believe it. They were going to transfer Hogg. Even though both of them have said not to do it, they were going to do it anyway. "Unbelievable," Shane mumbled, let out a loud sigh then refocused on Dee.

"We have a responsibility to animals, all animals." Dee continued, ignoring Shane's interruption. "Which means when we meet and encounter a dog that could do serious damage to the reputation of all dogs, it is our responsibility to ensure that doesn't happen. Because this dog can inflict serious harm if he so chooses and because there are clear indicators showing us that this can happen, I strongly recommend not transferring him. But realizing the decisions has already been made, I strongly recommend only transferring him to a good shelter or rescue, one with a strong insurance policy and one smart enough not to put him into a novice (or probably any) home."

Bravo! Shane thought. She wished she could make an argument like that. She hoped it got through and turned to look at the Board members.

Paul looked at Kylee briefly then spoke, "Well as you just said Dee, it is a potential threat, not a guaranteed one. It's your observation and that of your staff," he nodded in Shane's direction but didn't look at her. "But as this has happened right on the eve of our upcoming vote, it seems like it's an omen. And I think it's a perfect way to showcase alternatives to euthanasia."

"We have alternatives to euthanasia," Shane said, not able to hold her tongue any longer. "And we do transfer to other shelters and rescues, a lot. But not this dog." She shook her head.

Paul smiled briefly then continued. "As I said, your observation is noted. Judy will arrange for a suitable transfer." He looked at Judy, "Judy work with Dee to ensure the transfer will keep us clear of all liability." Then he clapped his hands together, "oh and speaking of the annual meeting and our change to no-kill,"

Shane could feel the muscles around her clenched jaw, straining. *My observation is noted. What the hell was that? That dog is dangerous, and that's just my observation! After watching and caring for a couple thousand dogs, I'd better be able to tell a dangerous dog from a frightened one. And to blow off Dee?* Shane looked up at her again. She looked tired. In her mid-fifties Dee had that beautiful complexion of her Navajo ancestors, but today she had dark circles under her eyes.

Paul continued, "I'm sure you're both as excited as we are that we're finally making this move. I hope you'll take some time to talk to the troops about the benefits this can bring us. We need to get everyone onboard to show a cohesive front to the membership. Shane," he paused, "will you do that? Explain to the staff the benefits of being no-kill and ensure they know we'll need their support at the meeting next month?"

"Sure," Shane said in the most monotone voice she'd heard come out of her mouth in a while. "Um, can you tell me what those benefits are?"

Paul looked so shocked at her question that Shane tried to take it back. "I mean, is there something specific you'd like us to focus on?" She made a face at Dee before looking back at Paul.

After he told Shane that he would get back to her, Shane asked if they were done.

"Yes, but keep him in back for now, would you?" Dee said looking directly at her.

"Whatever you say." Shane said, tapping the doorframe on her way out. Pausing at the top of the stairs she hovered between Dee's office and the landing. She needed a minute and walked into the kitchen to splash some cold water on her face.

What the hell was happening here? Shane wondered. *Why would they go to these lengths to save this dog? Of all dogs? Is this what no-kill means?* "Jeezo," she said out loud. *They could have transferred Shirley or Wingnut or a bunch of others before this one. What the hell?*

She blotted the water off her face with a paper towel and took a deep breath. *Do I care?* She held her hands under the cold water trying to control her emotions. The Board members passed the room and headed down the stairs. *I took this job because I go with the flow. I don't give a damn.* She turned off the water and dried her hands. "They tell me what to do and I do it. So what the hell am I so upset about?" *Dad was right, I should have just kept my mouth shut.*

She'd never seen the Board not support Dee's judgment before, and wondered if that was upsetting her as much as Paul dismissing her views. Shane headed back downstairs.

Dee, having walked downstairs with the Board a minute earlier was standing at the front desk. She smiled sympathetically at Shane as she walked up. "I was just explaining to everyone that the Board is going to use Hogg as an example to see if they can move a potentially unadoptable dog. They say this will help them make the decision on whether to change over."

"What do you think about this, Shane?" Jamie asked, looking serious for a change.

All eyes had been on her since she got to the bottom of the stairs so she knew her face must still be red. "I think he needs a new name. Jamie when you check him in, change it to Harley, would you? I hate the name Hogg, and Harley will be easy to remember. I also want his microchip tracked. I want to know if he shows up at a shelter down the road. Kinsey, will you figure out how to do that?"

"Of course," they both said.

"Great, I'm gonna take an early lunch, Kim can you cover for me?" She hoped no one would follow her, she needed to grab a couple of uninterrupted minutes of silence in her car.

"You know how I came to terms with this last night?" Dee said, as Shane walked away. "I compared it to a cat that we adopt out as a mouser. Think about it, if we get a cat back two times or more, and we have room, we hold onto them and adopt them as mousers. Technically we adopt out only companion animals as pets, but we've chosen to adopt some cats out as mousers because that's what they want to do. Maybe we'll get lucky and this dog will end up in the city somewhere protecting a junk yard or warehouse, it seems like it'd be the perfect job for him."

"Yeah, but chances are a cat's not going to take a chunk out of your leg." Shane heard Kim say just before the swinging doors closed behind her.

Chapter 13

The next afternoon was another beautiful day. The temperature in the mid-80's and the afternoon storm clouds were just beginning to form over the mountains. Shane walked out the back door of the shelter and turned into the breeze. Closing her eyes, she listened to the leaves of the Aspen tree's rustling above her. A moment later her shoulders relaxed and she moved her head from right to left, trying to loosen up the muscles in her neck. A pull on the leash she was holding brought her back and she smiled at the small dog.

Shane had brought Gigit out with her. She was doing really well, at least with Shane. She loved Shane. Every time she saw Shane move, she'd thump her tail on the floor, excitedly. Shane enjoyed the attention but wasn't having any luck transferring it to anyone else.

They walked around the cremator toward the small patio under the cottonwood tree. Two picnic tables were set in an "L" shape. Five gallon buckets, filled with sand and cigarette butts sat on either end. Jamie and Little Laura sat at opposite sides of one table. Taking any opportunity to get the shy, little dog to interact with someone other than herself, Shane had gone looking for the girls. She hoped if the dog spent some time with them she would relax a bit, like she did with Shane. Shane also wanted to find out how they were feeling after the situation with Hogg or Harley.

After yesterday's decision to transfer the dog, the afternoon had turned out relatively quiet. Everyone left her alone for a change. She used the time to find a grant for more emergency funds. It was just the distraction she needed. She should have been in her office finishing it but she needed a break. And of course she thought it was good for Gigit to get out.

"Yeah it won't be long now," Shane heard Jamie say to Laura as she walked up, "a lot have already switched over. It'll be interesting to see what changes." Jamie flicked the ash of her cigarette.

Laura smiled as Shane sat down next to her, up-wind of Jamie's cigarette smoke. "How you doin' Shane?" They were the only two that worked in the kennel that didn't smoke.

"Good Laura. How 'bout you?" Shane guided Gigit's leash around the end of the bench. When the terrified little dog first came out of her kennel everyone wanted to touch her. Unfortunately, every time they did she'd cower between Shane's legs or under a chair. So now they ignored her, watching and waiting for her to gain some confidence.

"Enjoying the sun," Laura said tipping her face farther-up towards it and pushing her sunglasses up on her head.

It did feel good, Shane had to admit. Her sister had told her before she moved to Colorado that she'd better own an expensive pair of sunglasses. It didn't take long to realize why. Back east they could go months without seeing the sun in the winter, but not in Colorado. Here it was sunny 300 days a year. Even in January the sun was warm on her face and Shane loved it.

"So is it true?" Jamie asked.

"Is what true?" Shane took a deep breath as the muscles in her face and jaw relaxed. Gigit assumed her typical ready-to-bolt position, lying parallel to Shane. Hovering on all fours, the young dog tried to watch everything going on.

"Are we going no-kill?"

"No question." Shane answered, her face still tipped up to the sun.

"Ripples," Jamie said, lighting another cigarette off her first one.

"Ripples," Shane agreed.

Before Shane was appointed Shelter Director, a girl named Payton Williams had the job. Shane always thought her heart was in the right place but she made decisions without thinking through the consequences. One time after a particularly sticky situation, Dee brought the entire staff to the science lab at the local college. She had arranged a presentation in their water lab.

Using the smallest of connections, the instructor showed how the effects in one tank, affected the environment and animals in another. Causing even slight ripples in one area, affected all the pools. By measuring minute movements in the water, the professor showed that the ripples were still affecting it, even after the water looked calm.

Dee used the trip to show how one bad situation could affect the organizations reputation for years. Using the two white boards in the guy's classroom Dee put the words "Lost Dog" on one board. "Let's say we miss a lost dog report. We get the dog in, don't check the book and adopt him out." On the other board she began writing from the lower left hand corner diagonally upward, "Family with lost pet."

"So this family has a bad experience with us, and they tell their friends. The woman talks about it with her girlfriends over lunch, the guy mentions it to his buddy's over a beer after work and the kids of course talk about it at school and online." As she talked, Dee made arrows from the original family. At the end of each she drew a circle. In the first she wrote "girlfriends" the next "buddy's" until she had four circles. Off each of these circles she wrote, family, girlfriends, buddies, again. "Think of how often you repeat a story you've heard. Especially something juicy like the shelter adopting a dog they don't realize is lost. Every one of these people who hears it, will tell others that they know. And they'll tell others and so on and so on."

"Maybe they won't tell them right away, but at some point later, someone in their life, maybe someone at work or at church brings up something about the shelter. Their response is going to be based on this story. And it's going to be negative."

The Ripple Effect, as the instructor called it, created an intense discussion which resonated with everyone it seemed except Payton. By the next day Jamie had incorporated the term "Ripples" into her language and they'd been hearing it ever since.

"Can I ask," Laura put her sunglasses back on and looked across the table, "what happened? I mean, all I know is what I heard on the news."

"You mean you don't believe everything you read in the papers?" Jamie said, pulling her chair closer to the table. It had been almost a year since it happened, but Jamie still jumped at the chance to tell her version of the story. "Payton, the Shelter Director at the time was old school. Like Kim, but worse. She had this gigantic chip on her shoulder, man she could be a bitch." Jamie brought her cigarette to her mouth.

"The dog was an owner surrender," Shane said, trying to keep Jamie on track.

"Yeah, yeah," Jamie continued. "You see this woman brings in this Husky. Big old dog, lived outside his whole life, hadn't been to a vet in years, teeth rotting out of his head. One of those guys that's been thrown in the backyard and forgotten."

"He was pretty pitiful," Shane agreed. "Blue, they called him, because of his eyes."

"Anyway, he's surrendered to us," Jamie continues, "can't take care of him, divorce, moving, the usual. We take him in and have him in Holding for four days. We didn't have anything open on the floor and even if we did, I can't imagine we'd put him out there."

"It was the end of summer and we were busting at the seams." Shane said.

"It's true, I'd never seen so many puppies as we got last year," Jamie agreed more to Shane than Laura. "Hopefully that won't happen again this year. Anyway," she turned back to Laura. "Animal Control busts a house out on the mesa. They had twenty-five dogs; mostly wolf-hybrids but some Huskies and Malamutes too. And Payton freaks out. We didn't have one kennel open and we're of course getting ten or so in a day. Not even half that are moving out of here. The fact that we were about to have a bunch of dogs coming in, put her over the top. She euthanized him. Him and six others."

"Which was business as usual at the time," Shane added quickly, "and wouldn't have been a big deal, except -"

"Except the ex-husband." Jamie continued blowing out the cigarette smoke she'd just inhaled. "Apparently the dog was supposed to be his, the wife took it one night and he'd been looking for it ever since, so he said."

"Did he file a lost report?" Laura asked.

Shane shook her head as Jamie answered, "Nope, but he said he came to the kennel a couple of times to look and never saw him."

"He was in the back," Laura finished the thought, realizing that if the owner hadn't specifically said he was looking for a lost dog, all he would see were those that were already available for adoption.

"Exactly." Jamie nodded. "Although we looked on the security monitors and never saw him come through."

"In Payton's defense," Shane volunteered, "the dog was a mess. I don't think we would have been doing him any favors by making him live here."

"Oh shut up Shane, you thought it was bullshit as much and I or Kim did. Not putting him down of course, his owners should have done that. Just the way Payton handled it, all hush-hush. But there was nothin' we could do about it."

Shane shrugged, remembering. It was not a happy time at the shelter. When the owner first came, Payton denied having the dog there. Then after talking to Dee, she called him back and told him she'd made a mistake. Payton had tried to defend herself by throwing the others under the bus but by then Shane and everyone else were sick of cleaning up after her.

"Kim took it the hardest." Jamie said, "Payton the pussy that she was, made her do it."

"How'd the guy find out?" Laura asked.

Jamie continued, "a volunteer saw me walking him the night before. He knew the guy and told him the dog was here. That's when he finally went to the front counter and asked. Kim showed him the dog and he went through the roof. Screamed at her for like ten minutes for killing his dog."

Shane reached down and petted the alert dog by her feet. Her head was up now and her small ears, sitting high on her head gave her face an upside down pyramid shape. She licked Shane's hand. *Well that's a first!* Shane smiled.

"And he went to the press?" Laura asked.

"His boss's wife worked at the paper," Shane answered looking away from the dog. "It was on the front page the within days. Humane Society kills family pet! The story was completely one-sided and failed to mention the condition of the dog, or that he was given to us or that he was twelve-years-old, but –"

"Then," Jamie interrupted, "none of those dogs came in and we had a run of adoptions that weekend so the paper came and took a picture of empty kennels. Payton was fired the next week. You'd think Dee would have written a letter to the editor or something to explain our side of the story," Jamie said.

"She did. The Board wouldn't let her send it. Said we'd done enough damage, explaining to people why some dogs were still being put down, wouldn't help anyone."

"I didn't know that," Jamie said putting her cigarette out on the bottom of the table.

"So that's why we're going no-kill?" Laura asked.

"Yeah, pretty much." Shane said, "there have always been a few people on the Board that swayed in that direction but once that hit the papers, it was inevitable."

"So no-kill means we don't euthanize any animals ever. What about owner requests? Laura asked.

Owner request euthanasia's were a service the shelter provided to the community. In a rural area like Loma Bonita, many people vaccinated their own animals, so they didn't have a relationship with a Veterinarian. Putting their elderly and sick animals to sleep was a service the shelter had offered for years.

Shane shook her head, but Jamie answered. "You'd think, but you'd be wrong. You can still kill in no-kill."

"I don't understand," Laura looked at Shane.

"It's just not killing for space," Shane tried to clarify. "For overpopulation. Everything else remains the same. We still euthanize unhealthy and untreatable animals but we don't euthanize animals for space; because there's not enough homes. Technically we've been doing it for the last year. At least with dogs."

"Yeah, since you took over." Jamie stood to walk back inside.

"And are you happy about the change?" Laura asked after Jamie had left.

"Happy?" Shane repeated. "No, I wouldn't say I'm happy about it. I guess I just think it's inevitable so why not just accept it."

Amazing, Shane thought, as she was heading back in with Gigit. Jamie didn't mention Hogg at all.

~

"Hey," Shane called out to Kinsey, as she walked up to the front desk an hour later. "We got a chip on that old Shepherd in the back." Shane handed her the slip of paper with the microchip number on it.

"The old one with the grey face? He was an owner surrender," Kinsey responded.

"Yeah, well let's hope it comes back registered to them." Shane headed into her office. Technically they didn't have to scan animals surrendered by their owners but after last year's situation they instituted checks and balances across the board. Scanning all animals, impounds, strays and owned, for a microchip was now required. And they verified all chips, even on animals surrendered to them.

"Hey, Brenda's in medical with those puppies," Kinsey called back.

"What's up?" Shane stopped, turning around in the doorway.

"I don't know. She called this morning saying one was really lethargic. I told her to bring them in."

Shane sighed. It'd been a week since Brenda brought those Hounds and Pomeranian's up from New Mexico. At the time they hadn't looked too bad; scrawny, a bit dehydrated and malnourished, but overall okay. *They had been covered in fleas though, they could be anemic,* Shane thought, quickly walking back to the medical area.

She found Brenda standing at the head of the exam table. Dr. Hunter and Ginny the technician were on either side of it. The doc was talking quietly to Brenda with one hand on an unmoving puppy. *Shit*, Shane thought.

The puppy was supposed to be Pomeranian. Brenda had brought eight up instead of six and they all looked more like miniature Aussie's than Pom's. This one, like most of them, was black and white with small erect ears. Pom's didn't normally get to be more than ten pounds and this dog had already passed that.

"What's up?" Shane asked walking over to the table. It didn't look good.

"Distemper would be my guess," The doc said as he stroked the fading puppy.

Brenda sobbed. "There isn't anything you can do?" She looked devastated. Kneeling, she spoke to the unmoving puppy, "hey there Pumpkin, you hang in there little man."

"Not at this point, I'm afraid." Dr. Hunter patted the pup one more time before turning and walking over to his computer.

Shane made a mental note to find out if the organization didn't give vaccines or didn't have any. It wasn't the first litter they'd transported up to save, only to have them die before it could happen. At least they hadn't been in a foster home. Most families opted out of the foster program when an animal died in their care.

Unlike Parvo, Distemper didn't live in the environment so they could use the home again. But the loss of a pet so young was a big blow to a foster family. It often took a lot of time and coaxing to get them to foster again. Shane wondered how Brenda would take it.

"They told me they had their shots." Brenda said, still face-to-face with the barely alive puppy.

"They may have," Shane put her hand on Brenda's shoulder. "But it coulda' been expired, or they could have done it the day before you took them."

"A recent shot, the stress of moving, poor nutrition and a new environment would be enough to compromise their immune systems and make them susceptible to any number of viruses." Dr. Hunter called out. "And of course there's a good chance that their parents were never vaccinated."

"What about the others?" Brenda asked, just realizing what the rest of them already knew. If it was distemper, all the puppies could succumb to the deadly disease.

Shane looked up at Dr. Hunter. She usually had to give Brenda bad news, telling her they were full when she wanted to transfer in more; Shane figured the doc could be the bearer of the bad news this time.

"We'll have to wait and see," he walked back over to the exam table. "It'll really depend on their immune systems. Chances are those that will go, will do so in the next forty-eight to seventy-two hours."

"Oh my god," Brenda sobbed.

"At that point, whoever is still alive is probably strong enough to survive and we'll take it from there. I'd like you to keep us informed though."

"Is there anything I can do to help them," she wiped her sleeve across her nose, "to make their immune systems stronger, I mean?"

"Not at this point," Dr Hunter continued, "I'm afraid. It's just a waiting game now."

Brenda stood and wiped her eyes. "Okay."

Not a typical volunteer, Brenda wore hair extensions down to her waist, fake nails and eyelashes. Wearing more makeup in one week then Kim, Jamie or Shane did in a year, the aging Barbie still looked good, though much of that was due to the Botox. Shane never thought she'd last at the shelter. The first time she came in wearing heels to walk dogs. After a couple of twisted ankles, she changed to fashionable hiking boots and had been around ever since.

"Okay. I need to get back to the others." Brenda said, wiping at the makeup under her eyes, making it worse instead of better.

"Keep us informed," Shane said walking her out the back door.

"I'm gonna get online. There's got to be something I can do to help them get through this." Brenda walked away, the usual bounce in her step replaced with a hurried one.

Ginny and the doc euthanized the sick puppy while Shane walked Brenda out. Ginny had him bagged and labeled by the time she got back. Before picking him up, Shane walked over to check on Mosi. "How's she doing?"

"Great," both Ginny and Dr. Hunter said at the same time. The doc nodded to Ginny and she continued. "She's picking her up today. The surgery went great. Look for yourself, she's using her litter box and hanging out. She isn't even bothering with it."

Shane visited with the purring cat for a minute. She did seem to be doing really well. "Great. Thanks for taking care of her," Shane said, closing back up her cage and picking up the bag with the puppy in it.

"Of course. She's a love." Ginny said, as she finished washing down the exam table. She sprayed the bleach mixture over the clean table and let it sit to kill the virus.

Dropping the puppy off in the freezer, Shane headed back up to the front. She hoped the puppies didn't suffer while they fought through the crappy disease. *Damn*, she thought, hoping she didn't spread the deadly virus to the other animals at the shelter.

Chapter 14

"So? Shane asked Kinsey, a few minutes later "Were they the owners?" Referring to the microchip check on the old Shepherd she'd scanned earlier.

"Not sure. Microchip was never registered. They're going to call me back and let me know where it was sold to. But they said it may take a day or two." She turned to pick up the ringing phone.

Shane shook her head, *so stupid*. Microchips were foolproof id, practically guaranteeing a pet is returned to its owner after entering a shelter, but only if the owner took the time to complete the form or update their address after moving.

"May I help you?" Shane asked the two kids who had just walked in with a dog on a leash. No matter how big of a sign they put on the door, which asked people to leave their animals in their cars until the paperwork was done, few seemed to abide by it.

"Yeah, we need to turn in this dog we found." The young couple looked like typical college students; scruffy hair, earrings through their eyebrows and lower lips, and clothes made way too small for them. *They weren't covered in tattoos yet,* Shane thought, *that's something.*

She pulled out a found report and attached it to a clip board. "Great, where'd you find him?" Clicking on the lost and found tab on the computer, she scrolled down the listing of animals recently reported lost.

The dog was a gorgeous black and white Australian Shepherd. With the thin, lanky body of a teenager the long-haired dog was a perfect representative of his breed. Aussie's, considered one of the smartest dogs, were popular in town.

"Hmpf," *weird,* she didn't see him. A dog like him has got to be missed by someone.

The guy handed the paperwork to the girl and sat down to play with the dog. Shane watched as he ran the happy dog through a series of tricks. "Sit, good. Round," he twirled his finger in a circle and the dog circled quickly to his left then back to his right. "Good."

It was a really good dog, Shane thought, *there's got to be a report, unless -* "When did you find him?" She asked, realizing why she didn't see a report.

"I dunno, maybe six, seven months ago."

Son-of-a-bitch. Shane pulled out an owner surrender form. "Did you call in a found report?"

"Call here?" The girl looked down at her boyfriend then back at Shane, "Should we have?" She asked, sounding more innocent then her clothes made her look.

"You need to fill these out instead." Shane took back the found form and handed them an owner surrender one. "The dog is considered yours at this point."

Shane looked away, trying to keep her cool. *Breathe. Don't get emotional. Just breathe.* This pissed her off more than anything. They had no idea they did anything wrong. And worse they'll probably do the same thing again. That clinched it for her. "Did you happen to think that his family may have been looking for him?"

They looked at each other.

"That's why you call here when you find a dog. You don't just bring him to your house and ignore the fact that someone is desperately searching for him." Reuniting lost animals with their owners was one of the shelters fundamental services, and something Shane took seriously. Having lost a dog herself, she knew what it felt like to not know, and didn't want anyone else to have to go through that.

"Yeah, of course, but we didn't see any fliers or anything."

"No fliers," Shane shook her head, *so why would you do anything, right? Just because you didn't see any fliers. Unbelievable.* "Was he in bad shape?"

"Yeah," the girl said quickly, then paused and added, "well, he needed a bath."

The boyfriend chimed in, "He wasn't starving or anything."

"We had been talking about getting a dog," the girl said. "Then we saw this one walking down the street. We figured it was meant to be."

"Meant to be, huh? But not anymore?" Shane asked, wondering what changed their minds.

"Oh," she smiled, "schools out and we just found out we're gonna be rafting guides." They looked at each other, smiling, already over the guilt of keeping someone else's dog.

Shane checked to be sure they had filled in where they originally found the dog before taking him from them.

"Sister, that was good." Kinsey said after they left and the dog had been brought back to receiving.

"It took all my might," Shane agreed, "but I didn't say they stole someone else's dog. Which they did."

Kinsey laughed, "I bet they'll still say you were rude."

"Ha." Shane knew she was probably right.

"Hey," Kinsey continued, "I got a call back from the software company. The chip went to a rescue in North Dakota. She dialed a number off the paper in front of her.

"North Dakota, jeezo. That's a little ways."

Shane picked up the second phone and dialed Mary's extension. "Hey Mare, it's Shane. Listen, I need a favor. I need a decent sized picture of a dog that just came in. He was found and kept for six maybe seven months. I want to get him on the website and in the newspaper in case anyone is still looking or wondering." Their marketing guru, Mary Fraser worked wonders with pictures and videos of the animals. She told Shane she'd be down with her camera in a few minutes.

"There's no one there that knows how to search the database." Kinsey said after Shane hung up. "When Joan gets back at four, they'll have her call me." She repeated.

"Too bad we can't search for people that have moved here from North Dakota. Kins, do me a favor and check six to eight month old lost reports for that dog that just came in. Male, Aussie, purebred, probably a year old at the time."

Jamie came through the kennel doors, "I thought that Pit puppy in receiving had an owner. Am I checking him in or what?"

"He does." Shane looked at Kinsey.

Kinsey shook her head slowly, "Not anymore."

"What?" Shane asked, remembering the stinky, tattooed jerk she had brought back to Holding.

"When I told him how much it would be he refused. Said if that's the case it's not his dog."

"Unbelievable. How much was it?"

"I can't remember, like forty-five dollars. Just impound fees and one nights boarding."

"Unbelievable." Shane repeated, rubbing her neck, "though better for the dog."

"He wouldn't even tell us his name or if he was housetrained." Laura added.

"Hi-ho," Brett called, walking Dewey, the leggy Corgi mix in from a walk. Brett Meadows was one of their best volunteers. Completely committed to the animals, he came by every afternoon when he got off work at three-thirty and spent ninety minutes working with and walking anyone who needed it. By then the majority of the dogs had been out with a volunteer, so Brett walked anyone needing extra attention.

"Hey Brett," they all greeted him. A favorite of the entire staff, he had even gotten in Kim's good graces.

"Is it okay if I walk Maggie today?" He asked, letting Dewey check out the front desk area.

"Of course," Shane replied. "She's going back into a kennel today anyway."

"What happened?"

"Happy tail." Shane said, referring to the yellow Lab with the sore on her tail, lying on the bed under the front counter. "But I'd actually like to talk to you about Heidi."

"Yeah," Brett said, "I was wondering. She looks like a pogo stick back there."

Heidi, the brown and white Boxer, had been with them too long. Thinking she was getting worse Shane had fed her that morning to see for herself. As soon as she entered the kennel Heidi jumped straight up, trying to get to her food bowl.

From a standing position, the muscular dog could launch herself five-feet in the air. Though her jumping was impressive, it wasn't a good sign. "Sit." Shane told the bouncing dog. She took a step toward her, to limit the amount of room she had to launch herself. Heidi was doing her best to get to the bowl Shane had in her hand but what she excelled in distance she lacked in accuracy.

Prancing toward Shane then away, Heidi whined and jumped again and again. After three jumps, she kept her back legs on the ground and landed her front paws on Shane's stomach. When she dug in with her nails, Shane bit her lip to avoid yelling out.

Raising her knee, Shane slowly but steadily, inserted it between the two of them. Gently she pushed the dog backwards. Heidi circled once, barked, then circled again. Shane waited until Heidi looked at her. Shane told her to sit again. Heidi's butt almost touched the floor as she assumed the sit position for half a second before bounding up. Again Shane raised her knee. The dog dropped back to the floor and circled. Shane placed the dish down quickly against the side wall.

It wasn't about teaching her manners, at least not during morning feeding. It was about her being polite and not knocking the bowl out of the technician's hands. And today it was about Shane assessing her. *She was going downhill*, Shane thought sadly, hoping there was still something they could do about it.

"I know," Shane said to Brett. "We need to get her an outlet for that energy. And fast. If you have any ideas, or know of any place we can take her to run. A secure place, not like the dog park. A place where she can really run and play but not where she can get loose. I'd love to hear about it."

"Okay," he said nodding his head. "Let me do some checking but I may have a couple of options."

"Great, thank you Brett. Seriously," Shane squeezed his arm and turned back toward her office.

~

"So they sell the chips, but they don't register them." Kinsey said to Shane a little while later. "And they don't track who buys what chip number." Standing in the doorway to Shane's office, Kinsey looked defeated.

"What do you mean they don't track them? Who doesn't track microchips?" The small devices, injected between an animal's shoulder blades, had a unique number embedded in them. By passing a wand-like device over the animal an Animal Shelter could read the number, call the company and find out who the owner was. And since the chips had to be injected, most places registered them for the owners. Identifying what number corresponded to what animal was part of the process. PHS's own Return-to-Owner percentage went up more than twenty-percent when they had started using them. "Unfuckingbelievable."

"Your head must be bothering you," Kinsey said watching Shane, "you only talk like that when you're in pain."

"Hmpf." Shane took a breath. Kinsey was right her head was bothering her again. Shane looked at the clock trying to gage what she should take, one extra-strength Excedrin and four Motrin's should do it. Now if it was only that easy to figure out what to do with another old, sick dog.

Chapter 15

It had been a couple of weeks since Judy first showed up at the shelter. Not missing a day, she followed the staff around with a notepad and pen, scribbling non-stop. Sometimes taking pictures, she seemed to be everywhere that a drama unfolded, and lately there seemed to have more than their share. Anytime Dee or anyone from the Board tried to intervene, Judy made an excuse to disappear, only to re-appear a short while later. She had everyone walking on eggshells. Shane was getting tired of it and tired of her.

Kim seemed more pissed off than usual, ready to yell at anyone who dared talk to her. Yesterday she had Little Laura in tears for not refilling the kitty litter bucket. It was only a matter of time before she went after Judy. Shane wanted to avoid that. So she'd asked Kim to assist with the euthanasia so she could get her alone for a few minutes.

Walking the old Shepherd down the back hall, Shane let him take his time. As they walked, she dropped pieces of hotdogs along his path. The old dog followed, happily scooping them up one-by-one. As they neared the back he poked his head into the only open door in the hallway; the storage room. Sitting just inside the door was a stack of litter boxes, one atop the other. Each held the remains of an animal. Used mainly for extra litter boxes, crates, catch poles and a variety of miscellaneous supplies, this room was also used to store the ashes from the crematory before processing them and getting them back to the animal's owners.

After a body went through the crematory, the large and dense bones often had to be crushed into ashes. Human remains typically went through a large roller to grind the bones to dust. Their second-hand crematory didn't have one so they were forced to crush the bones themselves. Until they could be crushed, the animal's remains were held in kitty litter boxes.
The large boxes were easy to pour ashes into, cheap to replace and had plenty of room to crush ashes inside. Typically there was only one or two waiting to be processed but today there was at least ten.

"What's going on with all those ashes?" Shane asked Kim, closing the door to the euthanasia room. *Shit*, she thought, *that's not how I wanted to start this*. Kim had been at the shelter for years and even though Shane was her supervisor she still intimidated the hell out of her. Shane had wanted to start this off by seeing if she could get Kim to open up to her. *Me and my big mouth*, Shane thought, pissed at herself.

The euthanasia room was located in the rear of the building between Cat Holding and the back hall. Just inside the back door, it was convenient for the public when they needed to have their own pets euthanized. The large room was virtually empty except for the exam table in the middle and the large, walk-in freezer taking up an entire corner. A sink and cupboards were near the only other door in the room which led into the Cat Holding area. Painted blue, the walls and ceiling were offset by big billowy, faded clouds, randomly painted throughout the room. Shane hated it.

"We're behind, I know." Kim said unlocking the cabinet above the sink and pulling out the controlled substance book.

"Behind? Behind is one or two animals not done. You've got like ten in there."

Kim turned and stared at Shane for a second before answering, "I know. I'll get it caught up this week, promise." Kim was responsible for processing any euthanasia's at the shelter.

Providing a crematory service to the public and local Veterinarians was an income stream for the shelter. One that they couldn't afford to lose. *Ten animals behind was a lot.* Shane was surprised she hadn't heard about it before now. *Shit,* she thought, knowing she was going to have to push Kim on the issue.

She pulled the leash off the dog and let him explore the room while she moved the exam table off to the side "You okay if we do this on the floor?"

"Yeah, fine," Kim said without looking up. She noted how much of the controlled substance she was using in the log book. Then, picking up a syringe, she withdrew five cc's of liquid out of the bottle. She removed the used needle and replaced it with a new one, then set it on the counter and drew up the sedative.

After nosing his way around the room, the limping dog found his way to the back of Kim's legs and pushed against her.

"People suck," Kim said, kneeling down. The stately black and grey Shepherd rubbed against her massaging fingers.

Shane pulled a blanket out of the cupboard and laid it on the floor.

Taking a treat out of her pocket, Kim let the dog finish it before walking over and sitting on the blanket. He followed and laid down, half on Kim and half on the blanket. Laying there panting, his forearm draped over Kim's leg, he looked quite content.

Shane glanced at the counter to be sure she had everything she needed; clippers, alcohol, syringes.

"People suck, don't they big guy?" Kim rubbed under the dogs chin. "What's his story, anyway?"

"His name's Shep. He's ten-ish, obese, obviously. He's got arthritis, I'm sure due to his weight, lived outside all his life, and now it looks like he's got Cushing's. Oh yeah, and his microchip was never registered."

"Owner request?"

"According to Kinsey they refused. Said he's a great dog and he'd be a great pet in anyone's home."

"He is a great dog," Kim rubbed either side of the dog's neck. "See, people do suck." The dogs teeth were filed down to small nubs and his gums were almost white. His ears, once erect, laid flat against his head. The grey had taken over his entire face and made him look wise, stately, and tired.

Bringing everything over, Shane knelt down in front of them. "Ready?" she asked checking the syringe containing the sedative.

Kim nodded and turned the dogs face toward hers.

Shane injected the sedative into his rear leg. He didn't seem to feel it but Shane knew in a matter of minutes he'd be sound asleep. Being able to inject the sedative into his leg was great for letting the animal relax before administering the euthanasia drug. Dogs rarely felt the sedative injected into their back leg and were sound asleep when the actual drug was given into their vein.

Kim gave him one more big hug before he swayed and she set his head down. The large dog snored a bit as he completely relaxed. Not moving him, Kim turned his face toward hers and lifted his front leg. Shane shaved a small area half-way up his leg and wiped it down with alcohol.

Kim held his leg at the elbow and circled her thumb over his vein. Rolling it away from his body, she applied pressure, making it clearly visible, "You're a beautiful boy, yes you are, yes you are," Kim repeated over and over to the sleeping dog.

Picking up the syringe, Shane uncapped it and turned the needle until the bevel was facing up. She nodded to Kim who continued whispering in the dog's ear. Inserting the needle slowly, Shane drew back on the plunger. A small splash of red appeared in the syringe and Kim released her hold on the vein. Shane slowly injected the blue fluid.

The dog, already out from the sedative, slumped sideways in Kim's lap. Kim checked the dog's eyes while Shane listened to his chest with a stethoscope. "He's gone."

"Put the blanket in with him." Kim said as Shane began to slide the large, black body bag under the dog.

He must have affected her more than I thought, Shane was glad she did this one. Payton, the old Shelter Director, had always made the rest of the staff do the difficult euthanasia's but Shane couldn't do it. She knew she'd see his face for the next couple of nights as she went to sleep, but it was still better than putting someone else through that.

She moved the bag under the blanket and shimmied both into it while Kim held up the dog's shoulders and head.

"Ready?" They lifted him together and carried him to the freezer. Kim pulled the door open. The smell hit them then dissipated. Pushing past the hanging flaps, they entered the cold chamber. The room was lined with bodies. Still backed up from when the crematory went down, they were running it 24/7 now to catch up. The public's animals got done before the shelters so most of the animals inside were theirs or one's that had arrived D.O.A. Shane was happy everyone was bagged.

They placed the body on the second tallest pile. While Kim stayed and straightened him out, Shane headed back out, eager for fresh air. She had wanted to talk to Kim but it didn't seem like the right time, so she put it off, again.

~

"I told you it was true." Jamie said as Shane closed the door of the prep room, a few minutes later. Jamie had Amadeus, the huge Mastiff puppy in with her and was trying to get him to sit. *She knew better than to have an owned animal in here.*

"What are you doing? Get him back to Iso. He shouldn't even be in here."

"Oh he called," Jamie said, referring to the dog's owner. She had a treat hovering over his massive nose. "Said he'll be in in the morning. He's just finishing the fence."

"Good, another night of boarding fee's and we'll have that room back tomorrow." Shane opened the dryer and pulled out the towels to fold them.

"Sit. Sit Amadeus. Sit." Jamie held a treat above the large dog's nose.

The oversized puppy leaned back as she moved her hand farther above his head. But as soon as he felt his weight shift he dropped his head and resumed his stance. Woof! His bark rattled the drying food dishes.

A second later, Amadeus shook his head. The drool that had been forming and gathering in his floppy lips flew from his mouth. The sticky, shiny substance covered Jamie, Shane and the towels she'd been folding.

"Nice." Shane said looking down at the long line of slobber that now connected her with the newly folded towels.

Training the dogs had become standard practice six months ago, once Shane was able to get everyone through training. But it still took constant reminders to work all the dogs and not just the staff's favorites. The kennel staff and many of the volunteers wore bait bags around their waists, and everyone carried cut-up pieces of hot dogs, cheese and dog treats to reward any dog doing something right.

Teaching all the dogs to sit, lie down, and shake hands had been relatively easy, but the public's reaction was overwhelming. So Shane decided to add an additional trick. Now besides the three basic tricks they taught all the dogs; every dog now also learned to either put their heads down between their paws, salute, or circle, depending on which they were more inclined to do. It went over great anytime the dogs were at offsite adoption locations and gave the staff something tangible to do when working with them.

Jamie handed Shane a paper towel then wiped herself down. "Big changes are coming."

"What are you talking about?" Shane asked, pulling the sticky saliva off the towels in one long strand. She tossed the towels back into the dirty clothes basket. *No dogs in the prep room, why was that so hard to remember?*

"It's true. I heard Big Bird telling Dee in the back hall."

"Big bird, huh? I can see it." Shane smiled, *leave it to Jamie.* Judy's height combined with her disheveled hair made her look a bit like a character but it was her love of yellow that made the staff constantly comment. Judy wore yellow every day. Shane didn't know how Judy did it, she couldn't stay clean for five minutes but somehow Judy never seemed to get a spot on her many shades of yellow.

"So that's why we've been enjoying the Sesame Street song?" Shane asked. "Did she say anything in particular?"

"I didn't hear it all. But it sounded like Big Bird was telling Dee to back off."

"Really?" Now Shane definitely doubted it. Gossip spread faster than kennel cough around there. And anyone telling Dee to back off was impossible to believe.

"I couldn't hear what Dee said, but Big Bird was telling her to get onboard with somethin'."

Shane finished folding the last of the towels and loaded the contents of the washer into the dryer. Pulling out a dryer sheet she set the timer and turned to leave.

"It could mean all our jobs." Jamie said, wiping the drool off Amadeus's face and chin.

"I doubt it." Shane said, holding the door open. And if it's gonna happen, it's gonna happen. Get that dog back to his kennel." She let the door close behind her then smelled poop and pushed it back open, "I need you to scoop, now." She said before turning to go find Dee.

~

Shane caught up with Dee, in her office an hour later.

"Do you mind if I finish?" Dee asked, referring to her lunch. She was scooping up hummus with a stick of celery. "I have a meeting at two."

"No, of course not." Shane moved Dee's purse off the chair and pulled it away from the desk a little so she wasn't right on top of her. Picking up a pen, Shane twisted it between her fingers.

"What's on your mind Shane?" Dee asked after wiping her mouth with a napkin.

"I was just wondering what you thought of this no-kill stuff." She weaved the pen over her ring finger, under her middle finger and back over her forefinger before switching hands.

"This no-kill stuff," Dee repeated. "What do you mean?"

"Well, I mean, what do you think about it? Are you okay with switching?"

"What makes you ask?" Dee grabbed a handful of crackers and sat back in her chair.

"Well, Jamie was talking about it earlier. And I said that it's no different than what we've been doing for the last year or so. You know, implementing different alternatives and getting the community to help. That's true, isn't it?"

"Yes and no." Dee brushed off her hands and leaned forward. "You know better than anyone the delicate system we are forced to balance every day. That system only works because we have flexibility. Every no-kill shelter in existence is some form of limited admission. We don't live in a limited admission society. Until we have the number of animals being born, matching the number of available homes, nationwide - we cannot afford to be limited admission. And in this area, where we're bordered by so much homelessness and suffering, it's going to be years."

"Yeah but we're able to euthanize unhealthy and untreatable animals and still be no-kill, so why do we have to become limited admission?"

"Good question. I can't answer that because I would never be a part of one. We're the Animal Shelter. We can't say no, ever – it's our responsibility to take care of animals in need. Part of the no-kill doctrine is to turn animal control back to the local government. That means that we still have an organization, actually worse, a government organization that's caring for the stray and impounded animals, usually those surrendered by their owners too. So we're not helping any of the public's animals, for the most part they'll be completely on their own. We're just helping the one's we invite in."

"Sooo, if we went no-kill but not limited admission, would you be in favor of it?" Shane asked struggling to understand.

Dee took a swallow of water and put the lid on it before standing. "I don't know Shane, maybe I'm wrong. No one else seems very concerned about it. And like Judy's always saying, no-kill is everywhere."

"But you're not convinced." Shane stood and walked to the door.

"No, I'm not convinced." Dee said, picking up a pen and pad of paper and walking out with her.

Chapter 16

Later that same day Shane was on the phone trying to get a long-term courtesy hold moved out of the shelter. "Reverend Wright," Shane took a deep breath and reminded herself to breathe. She'd been on the phone with him for fifteen minutes and didn't feel any closer to getting him to understand than when she started.

"I appreciate your concern for Gayle, and I would love to continue holding onto her dog, but I don't have room. I know we had room, but we don't anymore. Please, isn't there someone in your congregation that can foster the dog?"

Tilly, an English Setter, had been with them for almost four months. Every time they tried to move her the minister came up with another reason or excuse, and amazingly they had had the room. But not any longer. Her owner, Gayle had moved into a battered-woman's shelter with her two sons; no dogs allowed. Now she talked to them through her minister, who didn't seem to understand or care about their dilemma.

"No one that I know of."

This is crazy, Shane thought, *enough.* "Let me be blunt, because this is not our dog I cannot foster her out. She is taking up an entire run that I could have two adults or an entire litter of puppies in. We are not a boarding kennel. It is not in the dog's best interest to stay here long-term. Please, speak to your congregation and see if there is someone willing to foster her. If not, I will be forced to take custody of her and adopt her out to another home."

"No please, please. Gayle's doing better, she's finally getting her life together. And she loves that dog."

Gayle had been doing better every month for the last three, and Shane was happy for her. But she couldn't watch her dog any longer. "Wonderful. Then I need you to make it a priority to find her dog a place to stay. We can no longer keep her here. We are reaching capacity and I will not," her pace had quickened so she paused, trying to get it back under control. "I will not euthanize a homeless dog because this one has been here three months longer than she should have been. I won't do it. Reach out to your congregation, you have until Wednesday, after that she becomes ours."

"Can you even do that?" He asked.

"I could have done it a long time ago, but we had room, so I didn't. We don't have room anymore."

"I understand." He said, sounding defeated, "I'll see what I can do."

"By Wednesday. Please." Shane hung up the phone.

"How much longer does he want us to hold her?" Kim asked. They'd been trying to do her annual review for weeks and were constantly interrupted with something that couldn't wait.

"Just a couple more weeks," Shane shook her head. The woman's shelter called them a couple of times a year to watch someone's dog. They were always willing, provided space was available. But this one was getting out of hand. The program stipulated that the woman had to stay in touch with them and that they would only hold the dog for thirty days. Both stipulations had been ignored. *There is no way I'm going to euthanize a dog because this woman can't get her shit together,* Shane thought.

"She's a good dog. We could find a home for her in a minute." Kim said.

"Where's that dog in the back?" Judy called from the front desk, loud enough for both Kim and Shane to look up.

Shane's stomach tightened as soon as she heard the question. She knew exactly who Judy would be asking about.

"Which dog?" Kinsey asked.

Shane smiled, "I need to remember never to play poker with that girl."

"Hmpf," Kim said, standing and heading out to the front desk. It was obvious they weren't going to finish.

"Oh you know who I'm talking about. That old Shepherd mix that was in the Holding area."

"Shit. Shit. Shit. Shit." Shane said to June, the large grey cat who shared the office with her. June walked past Shane's face and let her fluffy tail linger against her nose.

Shane pushed it away, "Shit." She knew Judy was going to say something about euthanizing that dog. She'd say something about any dog that was euthanized at this point but that old guy was a perfect example for her cause.

Walking to the door, Shane stopped and leaned against it. *Might as well get it over with,* she thought. "Who you looking for?"

Judy was standing on the other side of the front desk while Kim and Kinsey were trying to look busy behind it.

"That old dog in Holding. C'mon, you know who I'm talking about, Shep, I think. The Shepherd mix I walked yesterday."

"You walked him yesterday?" Shane asked, jumping on the breech of protocol. "You walked a dog in Holding?" This was not the first time Judy had broken procedure and Shane was getting tired of it.

"Yes. And what's the problem now? He's a sweetheart."

"You just have no respect for us, do you?" Shane heard Kinsey suck in her breath but went on anyway. "You're not qualified to walk the dogs in Holding. As I've said to you more than once, you have to follow the rules. Being on the Board doesn't mean you get to do anything you want."

"Qualified? As if. I'm certainly as qualified as any of you." She waved her arm to include everyone standing behind the desk.

Kim slammed down the phone book and turned toward Judy.

"Judy," Shane said quickly, taking a couple of steps forward hoping to intervene if she needed to. "Dogs in Holding don't get walked by anyone but staff and you're not staff."

"Yeah, they could bite." Kim glared at her.

Shane put a hand on Kim's arm then continued, "They could bite, or escape or any number of things, we just don't know those dogs yet. But the point is a trained individual only – whether you agree with our credentials or not – handles those dogs."

Judy crossed her arms, "you still haven't answered my question."

Shane had to give her credit, she was holding her ground, considering it was three against one. "I put Shep down earlier today."

"What? You What? Why?" Judy looked horrified.

"Because he was surrendered to an Animal Shelter at ten years old, obese and with serious health issues."

"You don't know that. He just came in."

"I do know that." Shane could feel her hands sweating. "If they couldn't keep that dog, they should have put him down themselves. We have six senior dogs, all in better shape than Shep. A dog like that," Shane nodded toward the kennel, "One in a thousand homes may possibly be interested in an overweight, elderly dog. Add to that, he's never lived in a house, so he's not housetrained, ignoring the fact that we would never adopt a senior dog to live outside and you've just lowered his odds down to like one in ten-thousand homes."

"A lot less than that," Kinsey added.

"So you killed him." Judy snapped.

"Are you fucking kidding me?" Kim spoke through clenched teeth, "who do you think you are?" Her hands were balled into fists at her sides.

Kinsey stepped in front of Kim, trying to turn her towards Shane's office.

After two weeks Shane was as fed up as Kim. All her efforts, all her hard work over the last year just to have this woman walk in and trash it. She was sick and tired of being on guard all the time. They weren't doing anything wrong. If anything it was the opposite. For the first time since Shane started there, everyone was doing their job, and doing it well.

Technically the Board had never been on Shane's back. And if she thought about it, she really liked her job; liked feeling like she was doing something bigger than herself. And she was doing good, she knew that. But she was confused about the no-kill stuff. Sure they put down some animals, it was part of their job. What else would they do with the dogs that went kennel crazy? Or those that were too old or sick to be adopted out?

The Board understood that, at least she thought they did. Many of them had said told her how happy they were with her. She would have loved to go to them about Judy but how could she? Dee was her boss and was well aware of what was going on. Plus it was the Board who put Judy in charge in the first place. They had to be aware of what she was doing. They certainly had her support with the Hogg issue.

Shane reminded herself that they didn't stand up for the organization or staff last year. *They wouldn't even let us tell our side of the story.* Most of them disappeared for months after the article came out. She wondered if they ever really knew what had happened.

Screw this, Shane decided, *Kim was right.* "Well I suppose we could have checked him in, injected him with a bunch of vaccines, then put him on the adoption floor," she stared directly at Judy. "Made him live in a three-foot by six-foot concrete run, only able to see a couple feet on either side of him. He'd spend his days watching kids run right past him and adults barely slow down. The question would be, which will come first the diagnosis of Cushing's disease or him disconnecting from us and the rest of the world."

"Of course," Shane continued, "by the time that happens we'll all be in love with him and heartbroken when we have to put him down. Oh and let's not forget, he'll have spent his last three months in a kennel instead of just his last night." Shane tried to swallow the knot forming in her throat, she wanted to finish. "Same outcome, less pain and suffering, for everyone including Shep." *Why can't I control my emotions around this woman?*

Shane turned to see Dee sitting on the corner of her desk. She never heard her come in. *Fuck it,* she thought, storming into the office. "She accuses us of killing animals at the front desk!" Shane slammed the door behind her. "You tell me I have to make these decisions and then she stands there and accuses me of killing animals. Are you fucking kidding me? I don't understand what," her voice cracked. *Damn*, she thought taking a breath. "I need some air." She walked out without Dee saying a word.

~

By seven o'clock that night Shane had completed the grant for the mobile spay/neuter vehicle she'd been working on. Relieved to have it done, she sat back in her chair petting June. She'd pushed the cat off her lap three times since they closed but June's persistence won out. Shane smiled at the large cat who now made biscuits in her lap. Kneading Shane's stomach like it was a lump of dough, the huge cat circled three times before settling in.

June had been up for adoption for months before Shane agreed to take her. The burly cat had spent her time curled up under whatever bedding they gave her, earning her the nickname; June bug. Although friendly to the staff, June spent every day hiding from the public, refusing to interact or show any interest at all. After three months Lily, the foster coordinator recommended she become an office cat. Shane agreed and now welcomed the company.

Weighing a whopping twenty-two pounds, the large cat quickly took over the office and made every surface her own. Able to stand up to the toughest dogs, she was a great cat to use to seeing if a dog got along with cats. If they got fresh, June stood up on her hind legs and smacked them with her muscular arms and large feet. When she slept she curled her front feet under her and looked more like a bloated June bug than a domestic cat.

"Hey there," Dee walked in and squeezed Shane's shoulder. "End of another long day, huh?" She put her bags down on the chair and leaned up against the small desk Jamie used.

"Hey," Shane said sitting up and pushing June to the floor. "I didn't know you were still here." Everyone else had already left. She had thought she was alone.

"How'd the euth go earlier?" Dee asked referring to Judy's concern over Shep's euthanasia.

"Fine. Nothing unusual."

Nodding, she stared at Shane then continued. "You sure? You seemed a little, sensitive."

Shane picked up a pen and threaded it between her fingers. "Not about the procedure," Lacing the pen through the fingers of her right hand, she balanced it for a minute on her knuckles then flipped it to her left. "Maybe about being questioned on it."

Dee waited until Shane looked up at her. "Owner surrender, huh?" If the dog had been a stray they would have had to wait the mandatory three or five days before he officially became theirs. Owner surrenders became theirs immediately. Though PHS always held these animals for at least 24 hours in case the owners changed their minds.

Shane nodded and flipped the pen to her other hand.

"No owner request?"

Another policy instituted after the incident a year before, was requiring owner request euthanasia forms for any senior dogs surrendered to the shelter. To avoid older dogs suffering in the kennel and to encourage responsibility on the part of the owner they now asked any individual surrendering a senior animal to also sign an owner request euthanasia form. This way the animal could be put down immediately and not have to spend their last days stressed out in a kennel.

Shane shook her head.

"I wonder," Dee began, then paused.

Shane looked up at her, "What's that?" She spun the pen back through her fingers quicker this time. She was getting good it.

"What options are there in a situation like that?"

"You mean besides keeping the dog?"

"Well sure, ideally, but sometimes kids, job, life comes first. You've never had to give up a dog?"

Shifting in her seat Shane dropped the pen on the floor. June pounced on it. "Yeah, back in college I had a dog that I couldn't keep. They could have brought him to their vet." Shane countered.

"To be euthanized?"

"Yeah, sure."

"Well since we offer that same service, they could have brought him here and done it."

"Uh-huh."

"So their only options were to keep him or euthanize him."

"No, they could have tried to place him with someone else."

"We both know how that would have worked out." Dee said referring to the dogs that were handed between family members and co-workers. With no one actually accepting ownership of the animals these were the ones that were often forgotten, ignored or left behind.

"It doesn't change the fact that it sucks." The pen flipped out of Shane's reach. This time she let June have it and crossed her arms.

"You're right it does suck, but that doesn't make it anyone's fault."

"Maybe, but he wouldn't have had to spend his last night in a kennel with strangers."

"Who knows, maybe that was one of the best nights of his life. Just because he was over fed, doesn't mean he was happy, warm or loved."

Shane hadn't considered that. "I wouldn't have had to euthanize him."

"Maybe, but then I'd argue that's part of your job."

"Okay, so I wouldn't have had to euthanize him without his family present."

"That happens all the time when family members don't want to be present. It's being questioned on it that's got you upset."

June walked over to Dee and rubbed her round face up against Dee's leg. She leaned down to pet the large cat.

"Do *you* think I rushed it?" Shane asked, biting her bottom lip.

Dee straightened up, picked up her bags and put her hand on Shane's shoulder. "No Yahzi, I think you did the right thing. And I think maybe the people that owned the dog did
the right thing too, by bringing him here." Squeezing her shoulder, Dee wished Shane a good night and turned to head out. "I wonder," she looked back at Shane. "You seem to grieve the most when there's no one else to. Have you noticed that?" Turning, Dee left through the Kennels.

Chapter 17

The next day Shane was in a much better mood. She didn't have a headache for the first time in days and she was working with Little Laura, who always made her smile. Maggie, the Lab with Happy Tail had healed enough to be back in one of the wider runs and Shane had Gigit up front with her.

The small dog didn't seem to mind being attached to Shane's waist with a short, four-foot leash. She wouldn't have gone farther than that without it. Nervous whenever the dogs barked, Gigit cowered every time she walked through the kennel. Shane was working to desensitize her to the noise, and she was getting better; she hadn't submissively pee'd in the last couple of days. But the scared little dog still froze and cowered between Shane's legs anytime the dogs erupted.

In the office, Gigit stayed curled up under Shane's desk for hours or until she was made to come out. *The little girl certainly found comfort in a den,* Shane thought, making a mental note to be sure whoever adopted her wasn't opposed to crates; otherwise she'd take over their closets. Of course that was if they could get her adopted at all. At this point it still wasn't worth behavior assessing her – she'd fail for sure.

"Gigit, huh?" Laura asked, watching the dog slink behind Shane.

Shane laughed. "I know, it's horrible. It's not gonna last. But I need to see more of her personality to name her so I figured it would work temporarily."

"She seems more like a Merlin or a Casper. She wants to be invisible."

"You're right. When we finally get around to behavior assessing her, I'll let you name her."

"Really?" Laura asked excited.

Naming animals was something everyone loved when they first started working at the shelter. Typically done at check-in, those handling the animals and those with the most seniority usually got to pick the names. But it surprised Shane that Laura hadn't named any yet.

The phone rang and Shane picked it up, "Pinewoods Humane Society, can I help you?"

"Yes dear, I'm calling about that little dog that was on the news last night."

I should have let Laura answer the phone. Damn it. "Yes ma'am." Picking up the clipboard, Shane made another slash. Anytime a dog made the news, people came out in droves to adopt him or her. The Hero Phenomenon drove Shane nuts. Even if the dog did nothing but put himself in a bad situation, people wanted him – and only him. With a kennel full of animals needing homes it was frustrating to receive one call after another for only one particular animal. Tallying up the calls was Shane's way to diffuse her frustration.

The dog they were calling about was just being curious yesterday when he was hit by a car. A woman with a litter of Fox Hound puppies, sat outside the Vic's grocery store. Sitting under an umbrella, armed with a cooler full of two dollar tamale's and five puppies, she drew a constant crowd. Both went quickly and within a couple of hours she was down to her last puppy. The runt of the litter, he was only eight-pounds and had much longer hair than any Fox Hound 'ought to have.

Then an argument ensued. A customer swore he gave the woman twenty dollars for his three tamale's but the woman didn't have a twenty in her stack of bills so she gave him change for a ten and told him to be on his way. The customer refused and reached for her money sack. While this was going on the puppy tipped over the box he was in.

Seeing the whole world in front of him, he took a step off the curb and then another. Two more and he would have been under the first parked car. But he wasn't fast enough. A woman, searching for a parking spot never saw him. She ran him over with her front tire. The tamale selling woman, now realizing the puppy was missing, turned just in time to see him struggling.

Screaming, she ran toward the car, stopping the driver before the back tires got to the puppy. Not really wanting the small animal, and not able or willing to pay for his care, the tamale/puppy selling woman brought him to the shelter.

"Well I was wondering how he is. I mean is he okay?" The caller asked.

"Yes ma'am, he's fine." Shane waited, not offering any further information. The story only hit the paper's website the night before and came out in print that morning but they had already received thirty-three calls. No matter if the dog looked exactly like ten others in the building, no one wanted anyone but that dog. Shane had heard stories of other shelters adopting out the hero kitten fifty times or more, *maybe that's what we should do*, she thought, not for the first time. The woman either wanted to adopt the dog or donate money for his care. So far it was ninety-four-percent in favor of adoption.

"Well I was wondering, if I wanted to adopt that little guy, what would I need to do?"

"Ma'am, I'm sorry but he's not available for adoption at this time." Shane began the spiel. "He's going to be spending some time in a foster home until he's feeling better and then we'll put him up for adoption. I should tell you though, we already have quite a few applications filled out for him." Shane continued quickly knowing she was about to lose her. "You know we have a lot of other dogs available for adoption, great dogs, many just like the little guy in the story."

"Oh no, no it's got to be him. I've been thinking about him all night, ever since I first heard about it. I just have to have him. When did you say he would be up for adoption?"

Shane sighed, "in a couple of weeks." *Why do I bother?* "Ma'am keep an eye on our website and we'll post it there." She hung up before the woman could say anymore.

"Jesus, what am I doing?" Jamie said loudly from Shane's office. Picking up the blue kennel card she'd been working on, she crumpled it up and threw it in the trash before walking out to the front desk.

It was three in the afternoon. Shane was hovering between the front desk, her office and the kennels. Kinsey didn't work on Sunday's and she wanted Laura to do as much as possible. Knowing that her patience was running thin for people calling for the hit-by-car dog, Shane figured she should let Little Laura handle the phone.

It was surprisingly quiet for a Sunday. Judy hadn't been in all morning and the Mastiff's had finally gone home. The Reverend had promised to bring a family by that afternoon so Shane spent the morning writing up notes about Tilly, the Setter still on courtesy hold, including some specific area's that needed to be addressed. Fifteen minutes ago the minister called and cancelled.

Shane could hear Betty, one of the regular dog walkers, at the front desk talking to a couple of women.

"Oh I rescued mine too," the woman with the blue hat said.

Obviously a tourist, Shane thought. *Who else would buy a straw cowboy hat dyed blue?* They had just come from the kennel area.

"You rescued your dog?" Jamie asked.

"Yes, I did," the woman turned to her smiling.

"Did you run into a burning building?" Shane knew Jamie could look deceptively innocent at times, and now was one of them. "You said you rescued her," Jamie added when the woman just looked at her, confused. "I was just wondering what situation you rescued her from."

"I, uh, I, I got her from a shelter."

"Oh," Jamie said, smiling. "I wondered." Turning her back on the three women, she rolled her eyes.

Shane followed her back to the office. "Nice. Taking a page from Kim's book?"

"I'm sorry Shane," Jamie turned back toward her. "I'm just so frustrated. I love my job, usually. But lately, I don't know. I'm like hyper-sensitive. I mean, you know me. I don't slam people like that. I don't know what it is, I just feel like no matter what we do - ," she trailed off. "That just drives me crazy that people say they rescued the animals from us. Newsflash," she raised her voice, "we already rescued the animals from the bad situation. You adopted them."

"I know," Shane said, "me too. I'm not being a very good role model for Little Laura today. I hate the fact that there's so many people out there willing to take a dog - but only a popular one that has a story behind it. I don't get it. It drives me crazy. What's up with this?" Shane asked pointing to the stack of blue and pink kennel cards sitting on the desk.

Since she knew all the animals and had excellent penmanship, Jamie was in charge of writing up the detailed cards which hung on the door of each animal's kennel. Providing a brief description of every pet, their circumstances and their preferences, the cards were an invaluable tool.

"Nothing." Jamie said, drinking half of a bottle of Mountain Dew in one gulp.

Typically when she was stuck like this it was because she couldn't think of anything to write. Being creative was difficult when you do the same thing day after day. Shane looked in the garbage and saw a stack of crumpled cards. "What's up?" She asked again.

"I just wrote kennel cards for three different animals and they're exactly the same as Leroy's, Bowser's and Sassy's."

"Exactly the same?" Shane thought about the dogs Jamie was doing cards for, *Shepherd mix, Shepherd mix, and damn, another Shepherd mix*. Keeping a variety of dogs on the floor was something never mentioned in her job interview. The need to have different types, colors, and sizes may be possible for a pet store, but when you had no say over who was available, it was a different matter entirely. And one that weighed on Shane more often than she'd like.

Studies had shown that in order to keep the public coming in they had to have a variety of dogs. And in order for the public to keep coming back, the dogs they had available had to change. But knowing that and making that happen were two different things.

"Shit, you're right." Shane agreed with Jamie, "c'mon, and bring a piece of paper." They went into the kennels and counted the number of Shepherd's, Rottie's and Pit's they had. Tallying them up a few minutes later, the picture was bleaker than she originally thought.

Of the forty adult dogs, almost half were Shepherd mixes, with four more in Holding, waiting to come up on the floor. Their Rottie and Pit numbers were okay but the Shepherds were off the charts.

"We need some small dogs in here." Shane said once the kennel door closed behind them.

"Small, adult dogs."

"You're right. Let me see what Durango has, maybe we can swap a couple of Shepherd mixes for some Cattle dogs or Aussie's." Shane made a note on her to-do list.

"See if they have a Dane over there. I miss Jade."

"Yeah, top of my list." Shane said, rolling her eyes. Jade was a black and white Great Dane who'd been with them for three months before she was adopted. She was so bonded with Jamie that the day she left she jumped out the car window and ran back to the shelter.

"Oh good, I'm glad you're both here." Judy said, coming into the office.

Jamie looked at Shane surprised. Judy barely acknowledged her existence.

"I want to know why you put the reason an animal is surrendered on these." Judy held up two dog kennel cards.

The half-page blue and pink cards were the same one's sitting on Jamie's desk and in the wastebasket. They held the basic information about each animal; name, age, breed, when they came in, if they were housebroken, if they were good with children and cats, if they were already altered and how they came to be at the shelter. A third of the page was left open for specific notes about the animals. Jamie often used this area to list what tricks they knew or any special needs or quirks they had. The cat cage cards were half the size and contained a similar summary of each animal.

Shane looked over at Jamie, these were her babies.

"What do you mean?" Jamie asked Judy.

"It says here that Aldo was surrendered for pee'ing in the house. That's a horrible thing to put down. People won't even look at him with this on there."

"Would you rather we lied?" Jamie asked, turning toward her.

"No, you don't have to lie, but you don't have to put it down, either." Shane watched as they talked. Judy had involved herself into so many areas of the shelter it was hard to imagine a time when she wasn't around. She knew Jamie, Laura, even Kim probably didn't feel her impacts as much as she and Dee had, but it was impossible to ignore her completely. And the toll it was taking on the staff was obvious.

Shane couldn't stand being around her. Not able to keep her emotions in check was part of it but she was also more defensive than usual and she hated that. Talking about her with her sister last night, Sheila told her this was just the newest obstacle in her path. She thought that Shane should be the bigger person. "Maybe offering an olive branch might make the situation less tense," she had said. "You said her dog was killed when she was away, that sucks for anybody. Tap into that the next time you talk to her."

"You don't think that's important to know?" Jamie fired back. "That a dog or cat isn't house or litter box trained? Seems like it's something I'd want to know if I was interested in one."

"All I'm saying is that you don't put it on the kennel cards. I've seen the way you take in dogs. All you do is have people fill out a form. That's it. How do you know the person is telling the truth?"

"We give them the benefit of the doubt. So, what if the dog has separation anxiety, climbs fences or attacked the cat?"

"What about it?" Judy asked. "All I'm saying is to not put the worst features of the animal on the kennel cards. Those things may be due to a bad owner instead of a bad animal."

"Let's remember," Shane said, deciding this was her olive-branch opportunity. "Kennel cards are a means to answer questions without involving the staff. If someone wanted to meet a dog then finds out the dog doesn't get along with cats or kids they could get pissed that they wasted their time. Plus it takes time for the staff to answer simple questions. So most of the things on the kennel cards are there to let people know if the animals will work in their families or not, before considering them."

"All I'm saying is," Judy held up the kennel cards again. "Not to put it on the cards. Have the people get to know the animals a little first. See if they really like them. And anyway some of the reasons are probably not true and others may be due to the owners not putting the time in with them."

It wasn't the first time Shane had heard this argument from someone. Just a few weeks ago, she had a discussion about it with Brett the volunteer. Ever since, Shane thought it may be worth trying out. "You know, when we first meet someone we aren't given a list of all their problem areas. We see all the things we like and once we're in bed with them, so to speak, then we learn their issues."

Judy stared at Shane for a minute before responding, "Exactly. That's exactly what I'm saying. We don't have to withhold anything from them. Just let them get to know and meet the dogs first then tell them why they were surrendered."

"But I will say this," Shane continued. "When we transfer animals, the surrender form is looked at with as much weight as behavior assessments. And not because the assessment isn't valuable, it's because the owner's experience is equally as important." *Am I really telling a Board member that she should trust the public?*

"I don't know," Jamie said, looking at Shane. "It sounds dishonest; here, fall in love with this dog. Do you love him, isn't he great? Now you should know he's not housetrained and his owners said that he barks all the time. I think I'd be pretty pissed if a shelter did that to me."

"But maybe he isn't housetrained because the owners never bothered to housetrain him." Judy responded.

"That could always be the case." Jamie said. "And wouldn't you want to know that going in? Not everyone tolerates project dogs, you know. A lot of people just want a plug-and-play dog. One's that don't need much in the way of training or even time to adapt to the new environment. We get dogs and cats back after a day because they didn't bond quick enough. Do you really think people are going to be patient if the dog pee's in the house and we knew about it ahead of the time?"

"You're not hearing me." Judy said, louder this time. "I'm not saying to withhold it, I'm saying to not list it front and center on their kennel cards, that's all."

"Shane, Brenda's on line two," Laura called from the front desk.

"Alright, I need to take this. " She turned towards Jamie, "I think it's worth a shot. Don't change anything we already have on the floor, but on the new ones, don't list the reason for surrender and we'll tell them before they spend time with the animal. But I still want to see if we're recommending them with kids, cats, fence height, all that. Got it?"

"Do you want me to make up completely new cards? I have tons of these left." She gestured to the stacks of pink and blue cards on the bookshelf.

"For now," Shane said picking up the phone, "just use the back. You have great handwriting, so do everything you'd normally do but leave off the section "Reason for Surrender" and we'll see if it's worthwhile."

"Fine, whatever." Jamie said, without looking at Judy who stood smiling, satisfied in the doorway.

Chapter 18

An hour later Shane listened as Little Laura worked on an owner surrender. The dog, a young, Lab mix seemed like a great little guy. He stood near his owner, gnawing away on his leash. In another few minutes he'd be all the way through it.

"Ma'am," Laura repeated, "What seems to be the problem?"

"He's just too much. I'm mean look at him." She pulled the leash out of his mouth and dragged him towards her. Squirming backwards, he didn't look like he was used to being on a leash.

"He's a puppy." Laura said smiling. "He just needs to work off that energy, just like kids. Have you brought him to a training class or a puppy socialization class?"

"No. I don't have time for that." The heavyset young woman looked like she didn't have time for much. Her hair was still matted from where she had slept on it the night before and there was ketchup on the corner of her mouth. Her sweatpants had seen better days. Shane wondered what it took to wear holes through thick sweatpants, as she reached for the puppy's leash.

"What about the training classes?" Laura offered. "We have them here. They're really great. I can sign you up for one now. A little training would help a lot. But really he probably just needs some exercise."

"No. I don't have the money. And he's such a spaz. I'm not dealing with him anymore. Plus someone hit him, he flinches all the time. Do you want him or not?"

"Of course," Laura sounded dejected. "Is he neutered?"

"No."

"Has he had his vaccines?"

"Yeah, before I got him."

Laura finished the rest of the owner surrender process without saying a word. The woman signed her name with big circular letters. "I'd like my leash and collar back," the woman demanded, her arm outstretched.

Shane had walked the dog around the counter using a slip lead. Laura reached down and removed the Lab's leather collar. She handed it back to the woman without a word.

By watching the scene through Laura's perspective, Shane was having an easier time tolerating it. When she first started it surprised her how many people turned in their animals then took back the only thing the pets owned; their collars. But today, having seen it hundreds of times, she was able to keep her mouth shut.

Shane had left Gigit in the office, sleeping under her desk. But as she called the puppies vet to have the his records transferred over, Gigit poked her nose out the door.

Laura was sitting on the floor, the new puppy twisting around in her lap. He was thin and gangly, and small for a year old Lab. Laura rubbed him down while he covered her with kisses. He was all black except for two white toes on one of his back feet. "Has someone hit you, Pumpkin?" Laura asked the active dog.

"If I had a dime for every time I heard that," Shane said watching Gigit. The still-nervous dog watched as Laura played with the puppy. Taking a few steps forward, Shane thought she was going to come all the way out of the office, then Laura laughed out loud. The puppy had tangled himself up and was now sprawled spread-eagle on the slippery floor. The sound scared Gigit and she froze, watching.

"You don't think he's been hit?"

"If every dog out there that flinched had been hit in the past, we should be worried about the country going to hell. Dogs are just smart, they flinch because they don't want to be hit now, not because they've been hit in the past.

"Shane," Laura said looking up, "she wouldn't even listen to me. This is a great dog. If she'd just brought him to some classes and maybe got him some exercise, she wouldn't have had to give him up."

Finishing her call, Shane nodded. "Dee told me a story a while ago, one that kinda put it in perspective for me."

Hummer, the Lab puppy suddenly realized another dog was around. Spotting Gigit in the doorway, he headed towards her. Shane and Laura both watched as Gigit stood her ground, stiff and unsure.

Hummer stopped in front of Gigit, the two of them nose-to-nose. After a few seconds the puppy walked around Gigit to smell her butt. Gigit didn't move but she didn't growl either.

Shane watched, holding her breath. This was huge progress. Now if she would just relax enough to play.

Hummer apparently had a similar thought and circled Gigit completely before play bowing in front of her. Gigit didn't respond so Hummer barked, a high-pitched, puppy bark.

Shane watched, wondering if Gigit would run back under the desk or towards her.

Hummer bowed, barked, and circled in front of the frozen dog.

After a second, Gigit shook from head to toe and laid down where she was.

"That's huge," Shane said smiling and turning back to Laura. "Okay, you've flown, right?"

"Sure, of course."

"Have you ever taken them up on the free ticket when they've oversold the flight?"

"Right when we're boarding? Like when they offer to fly you anywhere if you'll fly standby? No. I've thought about it, but I've never done it."

"How come?"

"I don't know. I guess 'cause I have plans. I need to be somewhere at a certain time."

"Exactly. Dee says trying to help owners who are here to surrender their pet is like trying to get people to take a standby ticket. We don't like change much. We're planners and we like to know what's coming. When people bring their pets here, they've already said good-bye. They've already made up their minds and put away their bed and food bowls. They don't want ideas, they want it over, just like they planned when they got into the car."

"That's depressing." Laura said, reaching over to pick up the ringing phone.

"What's depressing," Shane said, "is that she'll get another dog in six months."

By four o'clock they had ninety-six calls for the previous day's hit-by-car puppy. None of the callers wanted any of the other dogs, just that one. Now comfortably sleeping in the medical bay, the little guy was going home to stay with Dr. Hunter for the next couple of weeks. His tail had to be amputated and he'd have pins in his back leg forever but Shane knew he'd be adopted in a heartbeat.

"Hey check it out," Shane said holding up a check they'd just received. She was going through the mail and had opened a card addressed to all of them. It was from Mr. and Mrs. Markovitz, the older couple who had adopted Mattie, the lonely-heart Shepherd with Pancreatitis.

"Thank you all for giving us this soul we didn't realize was missing from our lives. We love her dearly," Shane read out loud. They included a picture of the two of them sitting on matching recliners. Angled toward each other they faced a large T.V. with an oversized dog bed between them. On it was Mattie, staring up at the camera, her mouth open, her eyes bright. Shane handed the card and picture to Laura but held onto the check.

"How much is it for?" Laura asked scanning the card and smiling at the picture.

"Ten-thousand."

"Dollars? No way." Laura looked at the check. "I've never seen a check for so much."

"Amazing," Shane said, feeling great. She hung the card and picture up on the alumni wall. So much of their work went unnoticed or at least it seemed that way. Fighting with the city for adequate boarding fee's, dealing with the press every time a horrible story came to light, stuff like that just came with the job.

What were the chances I would have met Mr. and Mrs. Markovitz? Shane thought, she rarely handled adoptions any more. *And to adopt such a worthwhile dog. Mattie was great and deserved to live out her life in a wonderful home. It was perfect. And the icing on the cake, a ten-thousand dollar check,* sometimes Shane really loved her job.

"I got an idea," Jamie said, walking in with a tennis ball in her hands.

Hummer, who had given up on Gigit for a minute, was back at it by bowing repeatedly to the unmoving dog. Play bowing, a method used by dogs to entice others to play, involved placing their front legs flat on the floor while keeping their butts in the air. It was usually accompanied with a happy face and wagging tail. The posture, known by all in the canine world, was a terrific sign of a friendly dog and a dog that wanted to play with another.

Hummer continued his bow, bark, circle routine as Gigit watched. After another minute she tried to copy Hummer's play bow, but ended up falling over sideways. Standing back up, she shook off just as the puppy launched himself on her back.

Jamie bounced the tennis ball to grab Hummer's attention. It worked. He jumped off Gigit and headed over to investigate. Jamie tossed the ball and the small dog galloped after it, his oversized feet making him look silly. Gigit followed behind him.

Still sitting on the ground, Laura took the opportunity to reach out to the still fearful dog. Already closer to her than she'd ever been before, Laura held out her hand. Gigit looked away from the puppy, took a couple steps forward and smelled Laura's fingers. After a second, she licked them.

Laura looked up, smiling from ear-to-ear.

Shane was smiling too, this was the best they'd seen of her yet.

"I got an idea," Jamie repeated. "Why don't we leave the faucets on tonight?"

"What?" Laura looked up at her shocked.

"Think about it. The building will flood, everybody will live but they'll all make the news. They'll all be survivors, heroes. We could get everyone adopted in one clean sweep."

Shane couldn't help but smile.

Chapter 19

The next afternoon Laura stood waiting in the office. "Ready?" Shane asked her. She'd called Little Laura to help her do behavior assessments but had gotten caught-up on the phone. "Kins, tell anyone else who calls, I'll get back to them in a couple of hours." Shane motioned Laura to follow her, grabbed the paperwork and quickly headed out before the phone rang again.

Jamie and Kim usually did the assessments but Shane wanted to train Laura herself. Training people was a great way for her to keep up-to-date on the different jobs she was responsible for. And Little Laura reminded Shane of a sweet little sister. She enjoyed spending time with her. Today there was a good variety of dogs to do, it would be a great day for her watch.

"Does Los Mochis want to send up more animals?" Laura asked, referring to the call Shane had just hung up from.

"Yeah, them, Flagstaff, Phoenix. I've gotten calls from all of them this week."

"Why?"

"To see how far my rubber-band can be stretched before it snaps." Shane smiled briefly before explaining. "It's typical. They're dealing with puppy and kitten season just like us. I just wish they had more options."

Shane held the door for Laura, "don't get me wrong. I love to help, and we do constantly. But phone calls every morning reminding me of how bad it still is, gets a little old."

They used the front exam room to conduct the behavior tests. With doors to both the front desk and into the kennel it was a convenient alternative to walking the dogs up to the boardroom - where they used to do the tests. Before the surgery suite was added on they used this room for intake exams and to care for any medical situations. Now it was used as an overflow room and for behavior assessments.

The walls, lined with old kennels, traps, and cat adoption boxes were painted the same drab green as the rest of the building. A bank of old, and mostly broken, kennels stood against one wall. Every cage held large cardboard boxes filled with old paperwork, mostly adoption records. Shane moved a box of blank adoption contracts onto one of the kennels. With only a few feet of counter space, she needed all of it.

Pushing aside an empty soda can and candy bar wrappers, Shane spread the dog's paperwork out in front of her. Each dog had a PetDirect form stapled to their intake paperwork. PetDirect was the software the shelter used to track the animals. The form wasn't ideal but it had all the basic's and was easy to read, once they had gotten used to it.

Stray and impounded animals also had Animal Control forms. The half-page forms held the basic information regarding how and why they came to be at the shelter. The codes on each form indicated why the dog was with them. D.A.L., short for Dog-at-Large was the most common.

"What about some of the other shelters?" Laura asked, walking around the room and peering into the kennels.

"Who? Everyone south of us is in the same situation. Durango and Boulder help whenever they can but they're getting calls as often as I am."

"That sucks." Laura said walking over to the sink to wash her hands. Shane had just finished and handed her the towel.

"Okay, who's first?" Shane asked, thumbing through the paperwork of the different animals. She put them in order of importance, then looked back through the stack. She wanted to start with a good dog that would have a perfect score so she pulled out Hummer's paperwork.

"Let's do Hummer first." Shane said, grabbing a two-page assessment form and handing another to Laura.

"Yeah! I love Hummer."

Most employees adopted an animal in their first eight weeks. Laura was quickly approaching that mark. Shane wondered if Hummer would be the lucky one. The cute Lab mix was Laura's first solo intake, one that she'd tried hard to get the owner to keep, he probably had a special place in her heart.

"Okay, we're going to start in the kennel. The first thing we want to see is how he reacts to us standing in front of his run." Shane grabbed a handful of treats and put them in her pocket. "After that, we'll bring him in here and do the rest. Questions?"

"Tons, but maybe I should wait until we get started."

They walked back to the holding area, where Hummer was staying. The small, cute dog was doing great and would make anyone an ideal pet. His face looked like a Labs, but his long, black tail was thin and whip like. He also had a small build; Shane figured he'd top out at forty-five-pounds.

Hummer ran to the front of the kennel. His tail wagging so hard it looked like his entire body was involved in the task. After a second of them not responding, he performed a perfect play bow, his tail still madly wagging above his body.

Shane saw again how cute he was, she hoped Laura would adopt him. His ears, still a little too big for his face made him look young. He circled once then looked at them as if to say, "hey I'm here, what are you waiting for?" After bowing again, he ran to the back of his kennel, grabbed the stuffed dog he'd been destroying and brought it to the gate.

"Can I talk to him?" Laura asked, looking like she was going to burst.

Shane shook her head and pulled a treat out of her pocket. "Not yet." Dropping to one knee, Shane brought the treat up to the fence and the dog quickly gobbled it down.

"Okay," She handed Laura the leash and unsnapped the collar from his kennel door. All dogs were able to keep their collars, if they weren't too trashed. But to avoid injury they never wore them in the kennels. Laura had found a good, used one for Hummer and attached it to his kennel once he was set up yesterday.

"When we go back in with him," Shane said, snapping the collar on the leash and handing it to Laura to secure around his neck. She leaned in closer so Laura could hear her over the barking dogs. "Just drop the leash, don't call him or entice him to play. It's fine if he does come to you but don't encourage it."

"Okay." Laura nodded and walked him back to the exam room. The barking followed them as they walked the puppy back through the kennel area and into the front exam room.

"No, let him drag it around." Shane said when Laura bent to unfasten the leash. They weren't going to have a problem with Hummer but a dangling leash was a great safety measure if the door opened or if they needed more control.

Hummer headed toward the kennels to investigate, his nose to the ground, his tail still wagging.

"What are we looking for now?" Laura asked, as Shane put the dog's name at the top of the assessment form.

"Can you make sure the sign is on the door?" Shane asked Laura while she opened the opposite door and hung the "Assessments in Progress Do Not Disturb" sign on it. "This part is called affiliation. We're looking to see if he comes back to us on his own. Is he bonded to humans or is he independent or aloof?"

Just as Shane finished, Hummer ran, or more precisely, wagged himself back to Laura, looking for affection.

"Next time he goes off, I'm going to call him to me." Shane set down the pen and watched as the dog tried to get Laura to play with him. When that didn't work he went back over to the kennels, investigating.

"Hummer," Shane called, not bending down. He turned around, glanced quickly at Laura then came directly to Shane.

"That's good, right?" Laura asked, smiling.

"Yeah, that's great," Shane said, marking the appropriate box on his form. "See how he's still wiggling and his mouth is open?"

"He smiles," Laura said looking at the dog, now in her lap. "You do, don't you cutie."

Shane grabbed the food bowl out of the sink and opened a can of dog food. This immediately got his attention and he headed straight back to her. Shane smiled, *he was a perfect dog to start with.*

"Okay," Shane said after she got the food together. "Why don't you stand up, so he's not distracted. I'm going to test him with food." She tapped the spoon on the edge of the bowl and grabbed the Assess-a-Hand.

"What's that?" Laura asked.

"This is our finger-keeping device." Shane said, pushing against the duck-tape that held the rubber hand to the mop handle they had attached it to. She set the food bowl down onto the floor and let Hummer have a few seconds to enjoy it. Then she reached in with the fake rubber hand. After a few seconds she tried to pull the bowl away from the dog. Hummer followed the bowl at first until Shane pushed his nose away with the hand. He looked up at her, his tail wagging. After a second he reached for the food again. But when the rubber hand got in the way he whined and sat down.

Laura laughed "What a good boy."

Shane smiled, *he was great.* She picked up the food and pulled out a tennis ball and a squeaky toy. After squeaking it she tossed it to the other side of the room. Hummer ran after it and brought it straight back to Laura, who looked up at Shane, begging with her eyes.

"Don't pet him yet," Shane said. "Toss it again."

He ran to get it and brought it back to Laura. This time lying down in front of her with the toy between his legs.

"Ohmigod, I love this dog." Laura said, hardly able to hold herself back from petting him.

"Alright, let's do body handling." Shane said getting down on one knee. She reached out for the leash and pulled Hummer toward her. The puppy came happily. Shane ran her hands from the top of his head down to the tip of his tail, than repeated it.

"Once we do another dog a lot of this will make sense to you." Never one to explain what she did, Shane's training method was to lead by example. It worked great for behavior assessments which were always easier to show than tell.

Shane picked up the puppy's feet and wiped each down with the towel, then looked in his ears and tried to look at his teeth. The quick puppy squirmed away backwards. "Settle," Shane said, pulling him back to her. She lifted his lips and looked at his gums and teeth a number of times before he got fidgety again.

"Okay, that's it for in here. The last thing we need to do is see how he is with other dogs. Go get Snickers and bring him out to the play yard, will you?"

"Sure." Laura said, standing.

Shane walked Hummer out to the play yard. It was a beautiful day. She hadn't realized how nice it had gotten after the rain shower earlier. As she waited for Laura in the fifty foot square, chain-linked enclosure, Shane tilted her face to the sun. The heat slowly penetrated. After a minute she felt her jaw loosen and she moved her neck around to break up the building stress. *What the hell?* She thought, *I've had a decent day.*

Laura walked out with Snickers, the fifty-pound Golden mix who'd been brought to the shelter three times and adopted twice. A perfect helper dog, they used Snickers as a test with other dogs and cats to see how they would get along.

Snickers was a beautiful red dog with a white chin, belly, and legs. With folded ears and a white stripe up the center of his nose he looked more like a puppy than an adult. But the noticeable limp in his right rear leg gave away his age.

Reservation leg or Res leg was a term used for common leg issues seen on street dogs in the area. Either hit by a car, shot or caught in a trap, limping dogs seemed to far outnumber those that didn't limp. Snickers was no exception. An x-ray revealed an old break that had healed improperly long ago. Since he wasn't in pain, they didn't feel there was a good reason to put him through the long ordeal of trying to fix it.

Given to the shelter because of severe separation anxiety, Snickers had issues. When he was young he clawed his way out of every crate and room his owner locked him in. But it wasn't until after he broke two teeth and a couple of nails trying to follow his owner to work that she realized she had a serious problem. She put him on an anti-anxiety medicine and thought the problem had cleared up when she left for work one day. As she drove out of her driveway

Snickers jumped through the front window. The owner was devastated to give up her pet and wouldn't have done it except her landlord made her.

Shane had worked with him for months using both drugs and behavior training and thought he was doing better when she finally adopted him to a family of four. A stay-at-home mom sounded like the perfect scenario for Snickers. He made it for six weeks before he freaked out. This time it was due to a thunderstorm.

Each summer Loma Bonita experienced four to six weeks of afternoon thunderstorms. A welcome relief to the heat, the storms often brought the temperature down as much as twenty-degrees. But the electric storms also upset many dogs in the area, including Snickers. The day that got him brought back to the shelter, he dug at the bathroom door until he got it open. Only wanting to hide next to the toilet, he probably didn't understand what his owners were so upset about. They didn't seem to mind the ruined door or doorframe, it was his bloody paws that scared them. Nervous for a dog so obsessed that he'd hurt himself, they brought him back to the shelter, heartbroken.

The third home he went to belonged to one of the volunteers. She was sure he'd come around with the homeopathic remedies they'd used successfully with their previous neurotic dog. Not wanting the dog, they agreed to foster him and try the therapy out. It didn't work. In the three weeks he was there, he ripped down four shower curtains and couldn't be coaxed out of the tub for hours after a storm passed.

Feeling the dog was truly terrified, the volunteer brought him back, declared defeat and recommended the shelter euthanize him for his own good. That was nine months ago. Now, after a couple of simple modifications he was the perfect shelter ambassador, and their go-to dog any time they needed to bring an animal to an event, business or school.

At first Shane was nervous about having a dog stay at the shelter long-term. Though Snickers didn't seem to mind. Because of the motion sensors, he spent his nights locked in Lily's office, upstairs. During the day he walked between the upstairs offices and the front desk but spent most of his time lying on the balcony with his head through the bars, watching over the front area. Shane loved having him around and could tell he had a positive influence on the place.

Animals cycled through the shelter continuously. The nature of the business was to keep animals moving quickly so they didn't have to spend too much time in the stressful environment. And unfortunately, most of the long-term residents had issues. But Snickers and June provided a presence, one that went beyond the people and politics. They made the shelter their home and the staff seemed more comfortable with them there.

"So this is just a typical dog meet," Shane said as Laura walked Snickers into the enclosure. All dogs adopted to homes that already had dogs in residence had to go through a dog meet to finalize the adoption. Laura had done it many times before.

"Hold onto the leash for now," Shane instructed, unnecessarily.

Snickers, an old pro, walked in and stood. Hummer ran over and smelled his backend. Snickers followed suit. After a few seconds Shane told Laura to drop the leash and she let go of Hummers. After more smelling, Hummer play bowed to Snickers and then barked, a high-pitched puppy bark.

Shane let them play for a few minutes before calling it. "Perfect." She picked up the leash. "Okay let's put these guys back and we'll get to the next one."

The second dog they tested was Cheech, one of the hounds Brenda brought up from Los Mochis. He also tested well. He was less than stellar on his affiliation test; preferring to smell the room and investigate each spot on the floor rather than play with them, but since he was a Hound, that wasn't unusual. Shane gave him a little extra time and after a few minutes he came back to them.

After finishing Cheech's test they went and did the same for his brother, Chong.

"Shane," Kinsey called out as they walked Chong to the testing room. "Second Chance has called twice. Something about seventy dogs possibly coming in."

What the hell do they want me to do? Shane thought. *I'm not turning out my adoptable animals for transfers. I've already got unadoptable transfers I can't move.* "We're working as fast as we can," she said to Kinsey. "We've gotta get these done. As soon as I'm done I'll call them back," she turned to go back, "though I don't know what we can do."

"Seventy dogs? Phew, that's a lot. What will they do with them all?" Laura asked.

"Depends. If it's a hoarder or a busted rescue they'll probably need to be put down, most do. If it's a court-hold, they'll have to board them until the trial."

"Busted rescue?"

"Yeah, you know, best of intentions and all that. People open rescues because their hearts are in animals. But to have any chance of success they have to have some basic business and people sense as well. And a lot of them don't."

"And all the animals need to be put down?" Laura asked, looking both shocked and sad at the same time.

"When you have a bunch of animals you can't give them the individual attention they need. Sores, issues, problem behaviors all go unchecked. Plus these places usually have the animals in chain-link enclosures which causes them to have fence and boundary issues, stuff that takes a long time to fix."

"I don't understand, do they keep the animals or adopt them out?"

"Depends on the rescue. Most will keep them their whole lives if no one adopts them. The poor things are stuck living in cages forever with little to no human contact. The one near the state line has had litters of puppies born there that are so unsocialized by the time they're six months old they're completely unadoptable."

"That's crazy. It's got to drive the people crazy. Especially since they love animals so much."

"I don't know if they even see it, but maybe. When Animal Control does bust them they're burned out. Most, I think, are relieved when we take the animals off their hands."

"It's probably the first time in a while they have time for their own animals."

Shane smiled, Laura was probably right. "Okay," she said, refocusing. "So tell me, what did you see Chong do differently in the kennel than either Hummer or Cheech?"

"He wasn't as friendly. Like he wasn't trying to entice us to open the gate."

"Uh-huh, what else?" Shane asked, jotting down some notes.

"He was happy, or at least his mouth was open, but he, I don't know, he seemed more wary of us, I guess. He wouldn't stop barking and he pulled at my shirt when I put the leash on him."

"Yeah, I'd agree. The things I noticed were that he held his tail very high over his back. Did you notice the other two? Hummer wagged his entire body and Cheech wagged her tail but it was low, below her spine. Do you see how he's standing now?" Shane gestured to the dog. "His weight is forward on his front legs."

"Does that all mean he's dominant?"

"It could, they're certainly signs of a more confident dog. But that's why we have the test to check different areas. Has he come by to see you since you released his leash?" Shane asked, watching the brown speckled dog with the oversized ears and wrinkly skin.

"No, not once."

"Chong." Shane called. Not knowing if he knew his name she clapped her hands and employed her best happy-dog voice. "Come here baby, come here."

Nothing. He didn't even look towards her. She tried again.

Finally, after two long minutes he walked over, circled around Shane and slammed his nose into her calf.

"That was a muzzle punch, wasn't it?" Laura asked, excited. "I just read about them the other day but I haven't seen one."

"Well now you have. That was a textbook muzzle punch."

"The book said that they're a closed mouth bite. Is that true?"

"It is. He's trying to tell me he's boss and he doesn't have to come if he doesn't want to."

"That's not good," Laura said as she watched the independent puppy. "He's so young."

"Any animal that chooses to fight or be aggressive isn't a good sign. But this is a young dog, less than a year old." Shane watched him; he had no desire to get affection from them. "So he's not giving me a direct stare," she said. "He looks like he assumes he rules the roost."

A little concerned after what she'd just saw, Shane decided to continue, carefully. "Let's try food. This should be fun." Shane set the bowl of food down on the floor and slid it to the middle of the room. Chong immediately came for it. After a couple seconds of eating, Shane put the Access-a-Hand on the edge of the bowl.

The strong-willed dog started eating faster.

"Can I have it baby?" Shane asked in a steady voice. She pulled the bowl towards her, slowly.

Chong froze, his nose holding the bowl under him. A low, steady growl came from deep in his throat and Shane pulled back the hand.

"Was that a growl?" Laura asked, "he's so young."

"That was a growl. If I would have pushed him farther he would have bit the hand. Shit." She thought he would need work, but this might take more than she figured. "Alright. Let's put him back and I'll have Kim retest him in a day or two." Shane wrote a note on a sticky pad and stuck it to the front of his paperwork.

"Your brother is much nicer than you are," Laura said, reeling in the extra slack in his leash. She seemed more cautious with him than when they first walked in. "He's panting."

"See the stress wrinkles?" Shane pointed to the lines that circled the sides of his open mouth. Stress wrinkles were formed when a dog pulled their lips away from their teeth. Like Shane's neck and jaw getting tighter, they were a sure sign of a dog that was feeling stressed. "Have you seen this one bullying the other?"

"I haven't, but they just came in from foster yesterday."

"When you feed tomorrow, make sure Chong's not taking it all. We may need to separate them." After they were done, Laura walked the small, dominant dog back to his brother.

What am I gonna do with that puppy? Shane wondered.

Chapter 20

Shane was still trying to think of what she could do with Chong when the door opened and Judy walked in.

"There you are. I need to talk to you." The pushy woman held two kennel cards up in front of her.

"Judy, we are in the middle of behavior assessments. Did you not see the sign on the door?"

Judy looked around, "It doesn't look like you're doing anything to me. Just look at these. You have to see what that girl did."

She was still flapping the blue kennel cards so Shane yanked them out of her hand. *Of course I'm not doing anything. Why would she respect a sign on the door? Obviously I'm a small step above the gum on the bottom of her shoe. Bitch.*

"What?" Shane asked shrugging, she didn't see anything.

"What? Just look at them. It's ridiculous. It's her game. Her way of winning. I swear, working here is no different that working in kindergarten class, you're all a bunch of children."

Staring at her, Shane wondered if Judy realized she had just insulted her as well. "What?" She asked again, her patience now completely gone.

The other door opened and Laura walked back in. "Oh, I'm sorry."

"You're fine, come in." Shane said, welcoming an ally. "Apparently Judy has an issue that can't wait until after behavior assessments. Because you know," Shane turned back to Judy, "fixing these is much more important than getting dogs onto the adoption floor." *Stow it Shane*, she cautioned herself. *Not in front of Laura.*

"Now," she refocused on Judy. "Judy would you be so kind as to tell me what, exactly is the issue you're having with these?"

"Just lo –"

Shane raised her hand to stop her. "And don't tell me to look for it," she stared directly at Judy, daring her to say it again.

"Look at the Reason for Surrender," Judy spit out the words as she folded her arms. Her pursed lips were formed into a deeper frown than usual.

Reason for Surrender – See front desk

Shane had to bite her check to keep from smiling, *God damn it Jamie.*

"This is blatantly disregarding a direct order. Now I want to know what you're going to do about it."

"She didn't do it on purpose," Shane said, knowing Jamie wouldn't have realized the issue.

"Didn't do it on purpose? Jesus you're as blind as they are. Of course she did, she ignored you. I heard you tell her not to put that line on there. She ignored you and she ignored me and by doing so, she didn't do her job. And I want to know what you're going to do about it."

Instead of using the back of the kennel cards as Shane had suggested, Dana used the front. Shane couldn't blame her, they'd had them printed a couple months ago and they looked great. Dana knew how much they spent on them and probably didn't want it to go to waste.

Shane rubbed the crease forming between her eyes. "I'll take care of it." She said, not knowing yet what she was going to do other than tell Jamie what she and apparently Judy already knew; by putting See the Front Desk on the cards it was actually worse than saying the dog pee'd in the house. It was human nature to assume the worst and putting something cryptic like that on the card would guarantee people would assume the dog was surrendered for something bad, very bad.

"She should be fired."

Shane heard Laura gasp. "This is hardly a firing offense. And Jamie is one of our best employees," she couldn't keep the smirk from her voice, "she's not going to get fired over a power struggle."

Judy leveled Shane with a stare, turned abruptly and walked back through the door she'd come in.

"Unfuckingbelievable," Shane said shaking her head and feeling her pulse soar. She was trying to curse less, especially in front of Laura, Lily and Dee but that woman made it difficult. Rubbing her temples, Shane willed her headache to stay at bay.

"Would she really fire Jamie?" Laura asked.

Shane shook her head. "One would hope she doesn't have the power." *If Jamie gets fired over this,* Shane thought, *if they let her go after all she's done.* She threw her pen down, sick of the bullshit.

She shook her head to try and clear it. *No time to think about it now.* "Pedal's is next."

"Oh, she's so sweet." Laura said referring to the stray Border Collie the college kids kept for six months before bringing to the shelter.

Shane nodded, unable to think about anything but that damn woman. She couldn't figure out what she had done to deserve this. *If she gets Jamie fired*, Shane thought, continuing to work herself up.

Together they walked back to Holding and down to the kennel with the surrendered Border Collie.

They had only found one lost report for a missing Border Collie over the last eight months. They called the people who filed it but they had already found their dog. And so far they hadn't received any responses to the ad in the paper. She looked like a purebred. Her long black and white coat was shiny and thick. Her face and ears were black except the half inch stripe of white that circled her muzzle and ran up between her eyes, stopping just before her ears. It split her face in two making her look like she had a mask on.

A happy and relaxed dog, she acted more like a five-year-old than an adolescence. Pedal's had taken to kennel life immediately. As they stood in front of her she watched them from the bed. Lying with one paw dangling over the edge, her mouth was slightly open and her eyes were animated. Less than a minute went by before she jumped off the bed and came to the gate. Sitting sideways, she leaned against it looking for some loving.

"Hey girl," Shane said, handing her a treat through the chain-link. Gently, she took it out of Shane's hand, swallowed it and looked for more. Shane nodded for Laura to open the gate.

Looking around, Shane expected to see Judy lurking in one of the corners taking notes. It felt like she'd become Shane's nemesis; coming to the shelter to make her life miserable, or force her to quit. Sometimes it felt like all Shane could think about was a woman best described as Big Bird with a grudge.

It amazed her how things could change so quickly. Just six weeks ago the Board told her how great she was doing and how she was really making the place better for the animals and the community. Now, she was second-guessing everything she'd done and wondering if she'd have a job in a couple of weeks.

They walked back to the exam room. "Shane?" Laura began tentatively, "remember earlier with Chong, you said one thing you saw was his tail wagging, above his back?"

Shane nodded, "Uh-huh." She was looking through Pedal's paperwork.

"Well her tail was wagging above her back." Laura said, referring to the happy dog in the room with them. "It still is. What's the difference?"

"The wag," Shane said, shaking her head to clear away any remaining thoughts of Judy. "When Chong was holding his tail up, it was stiff, especially close to his body. His tail wasn't so much wagging as it was vibrating with tension. With this girl, her tail is up, she's comfortable. Her wag is nice, slow and easy, there's nothing frantic or stressed about it."

Laura nodded, watching the dog systematically check one kennel after the other. Pedal's passed her evaluation with flying colors and they moved on to Gigit.

"I don't think we're going to be able to test her yet," Shane said, picking up her paperwork, "but let's go look."

She opened the door to the kennel just as the dogs erupted. The barking was intense. Shane looked around trying to find the source of the commotion. *Please don't let it be her*, she thought trying not to see Judy's face every time she closed her eyes. Shane headed around the center aisle and was almost run over by two young boys.

"Whoa," she hollered grabbing one by the shirt. "No Running!" There's no way they could have heard her over the ruckus but they got the message. It took the dogs another couple of minutes to calm back down and one or two continued with a random bark while Shane and Laura walked back to Holding.

"I'm going to have you stand in front of her kennel alone. If she approaches the gate, we'll try the test. If not, there's no point." Shane waited off to the side as Laura stood in front of Gigit's gate. She could tell it was hard for Laura not to engage with the small dog. After a couple of minutes she shook her head and walked back down the aisle toward Shane.

"Another day," Shane said, wondering how much longer she'd be able to avoid running the dog through the mandatory test.

"So," Laura began, "what happens when they fail? I mean, why exactly do we do these tests?"

"Two reasons. One, so we know what they need training on and ideally we work on it while they're here and two because we want to match them up to the right family. If a dog has a problem we confirm it using the test, like with Chong. It's the only way we can develop a treatment plan. So for Chong we'll start with free feeding.

By providing him with a constantly full bowl of food, he may relax his guard. It works great for hungry Res dogs. If that doesn't work, which I don't think it will for Chong, we'll pull his food and put it in a bucket on the front of his kennel."

"Oh," Laura said, "like when we ask visitors to feed them."

"Exactly. Dogs that don't affiliate well with people do not get adopted. So to get them to start liking and wanting to be close to people, we have people, anyone and everyone, feed them. It's a great way to motivate dogs that hide in the back of their kennels or those that are nervous. For Chong we'll get him into some training as well."

"So to answer your question we use the information we get during the tests to treat the animals, adopt them to the right homes and to transfer them. The shelters we transfer with all use the same assessment so we know the scoring scale which helps a lot when we're transferring."

~

At six-thirty Shane was finishing up her paperwork and shutting down her computer when Dee came in. Setting two beers down on Shane's desk, Dee reached into the top drawer for the opener.

Taking a swallow of the beer, Shane sighed, "That's good." She looked at the label; El Diente Stout. *One thing about Coloradoans,* Shane thought, *they were good at beer.* Every town seemed to have its own micro-breweries and all were pretty good. This one, named after one of the 14,000 foot peaks in the area, was heavy, malty and delicious.

"You know," Shane said after they had spent some time discussing a bit of everything. "Laura said something today."

"Yeah, what was that?" Dee asked, petting June.

"We were talking about rescues gone bad and I was saying that the people seem almost relieved when we take the animals."

"Uh-huh," Dee took another drink of her beer.

"She said, in that innocent way of hers, it's probably the first time in a long time they've gotten a chance to spend any time with their own animals."

Dee laughed. "That's a different point of view, isn't it?"

"I had never thought about it before. But it's true. I bet they just wanted to help and took one then another and another and soon their own animals probably became a pain in the butt, when they had to take care of so many others."

Dee, who was still smiling, agreed. "I don't know about you, but as much as I like to foster, I also like having time for just me and my pack. I have a finite amount of time, I can split it between four animals or forty. The time's the same, it's what I can give each of them that changes."

"I had always thought about them in terms of what they did to us. You know, like when we did that house over in Montrose? That was right after I started."

"That was certainly a tough one," Dee agreed, referring to the hoarding house Animal Control busted not far away. Never able to do an accurate count of the animals, the shelter was understaffed and overwhelmed. Trapping and euthanizing over a hundred feral cats and thirty dogs, it was a long, horrible experience. The twenty-two dogs they brought back with the shelter were undersocialized and difficult to adopt. One by one they succumbed to illness or turned on other dogs. The shelter was forced to euthanize many of them. Only two cats and four dogs had been successfully adopted out.

"We lost four employees over that. And the freakin' nightmares. I couldn't get that barn out of my head for weeks. Oh, and the smell," Shane shivered remembering the smell and wiping her nose. "Anyway, I never thought about how it was for them."

Dee nodded.

"You know it made me think," Shane picked at the label on her beer bottle. "You know The Nation, Flagstaff, and Los Mochis are calling a lot lately looking for help."

Dee didn't look like she was aware but nodded for Shane to continue.

"Well you know they tell me I'm their only hope. If I can't take them, they have to put 'em down."

"How often does that happen?" Dee asked, trying to look unconcerned.

"Lately? Three or four times a week."

"And they're calling you here?"

"No, on my cell. I usually get the calls at home or on my way in."

"I'm sorry, go ahead," Dee said, prompting her to continue.

"Well, I don't know exactly. I was just wondering if I could look at it a different way, like Laura did with the rescue's." Shane paused, trying to figure out what she was trying to say. "Like right now I'm pissed. Every morning I feel like I've condemned dogs to death just because I can't take them. So no matter how good we're doing, I'm still responsible for the deaths of dogs because we don't have room to take in more transfers."

"That's a pretty self-destructive attitude to take," Dee said, finishing her beer.

"Well I never thought about it. Like, I never thought I had a choice on how to think about it. Does that make sense?"

"And now?"

"Well I don't know. I was just sitting here wondering if instead of thinking about it being a burden and focusing on all those I can't take, maybe there's a different way to think about it. I mean, I take in any we have room for but still, maybe there's a way for me to think about it that doesn't make me want to slit my wrists by nine every morning.

"Not funny," Dee said seriously.

Not serious about the threat Shane forgot who she was talking too. Dee's brother committed suicide a few years before. On The Nation suicide was a more common occurrence than in other areas of the country. Shane immediately felt horrible for saying it.

"I'm sorry, Dee. You know what I meant."

Dee nodded. "Well you could focus on the fact that they're reaching out. They're trying to move their animals. That's a big step all by itself."

"Yeah. That's true." Shane agreed without much enthusiasm.

"Seriously, think about it. Moving animals between shelters like this was unheard of five, ten years ago. And now it's the norm. It's great everyone's onboard – even out here in this part of the country.

"I guess." Shane was hopping Dee would come up with something more that she could grab onto.

"I'm going to head out." Dee said standing and grabbing their empty beer bottles.

"I can take care of those."

"Better we get the evidence out of the building." She said slipping them into her oversized bag. "Sleep on it Yahzi. Maybe tomorrow something will occur to you."

Chapter 21

Kim and Shane sat down to do Kim's evaluation again. Already two months overdue, Shane couldn't put it off any longer. Dee was supposed to do this one with her, since it was Kim, but she wasn't available. Shane would have waited, except Kim was pushing for it.

The yearly reviews were the only opportunity the kennel staff had of getting a raise. Ranging between ten and fifty cents, it was a pitifully small amount to give. But they still looked forward to it. Shane was surprised Kim was pushing for hers though. Most of the staff put it off for as long as possible so that when they got their retro-pay they received a decent-sized check.

"Okay," Shane said, pulling out the review form and pushing June out of the way. June preferred to lie in the middle of Shane's desk, and often got miffed when she was handled. This time she just stood, flicked her tail back and forth and headed for her food bowl.

Shane was a little nervous. She knew how she wanted this to go, but she had assumed Dee would have been there for it or they would have at least had a chance to talk. "Hey, before we get started." Shane said, stalling for time. "I want to warn you about Judy. She's taking notes on everything and she seems to have an agenda."

"You think?" Kim said holding up June's favorite toy; a black wand with purple and white feathers on the end.

"I'm just saying watch her."

"Fuck her," Kim said, still flicking the feathers back and forth. June sat back on her hind legs batting at the feathers.

Just then the door opened and Judy's head appeared. "Oh, there you are." She came into the office and waited while the door closed behind her. "I wanted to tell you that I found a rescue for Hogg, I mean Harley." Glowing, Judy looked like she had just won the lottery.

"Oh yeah?" Shane said, not able to muster much enthusiasm.

"And it's great," Judy gushed. "You should see their website. They're only a couple hours from here and they foster the animals in people's homes until they're adopted."

"Who is it?" Shane asked hoping it wasn't someone they were already transferring with. She knew once they saw and met the dog, they'd never take another from them. Transferring animals was touchy business. The receiving shelters demanded, just like PHS, that animals transferred-in be adoption ready. Shelters got enough hard-to-place-dogs from their own communities, transfers had to be healthy and adoptable, otherwise the sending shelter quickly got a bad reputation.

"Pet Orphans of Central Colorado. Do you know them?"

"I've heard of them but never worked with them. Are you going there to check them out?

"They said they'd meet me."

Shane shook her head, *she apparently didn't have any problem trusting them.* "Do they temperament test?"

"What? Oh, behavior tests like that?" Judy gestured as if to dismiss it. "No, I don't think so."

Shane shared another look with Kim. It was probably a good thing. No shelter that checked incoming dogs to see if they were adoptable, would agree to take him. "So when's he leaving?"

"A couple of days," they need to check with their foster homes to see who's available.

"Judy, do not let him go to a home with kids." Shane warned.

"Oh I'm sure these guys know what they're doing, they're very professional."

"Got all that from their website, huh?" Kim asked.

"I talked to them too. And they were great." Judy turned to leave, then turned back. "Neither of you can obviously let go of your own hang ups and be happy for this dog, so just make sure he's ready."

After she left Shane put her head down on her desk, "Oh my god, that woman."

"She busts in here like she owns the freakin' place, Shane. These guys know what they're doing, they're very professional," Kim repeated Judy's words in her Big Bird voice. "Just goes to show what a good website can get ya."

~

"There's just four more after this, I promise." Andy Hasting said as he stood in the lobby with Shane, surveying the rows of boxes.

It was just after one in the afternoon and the shelter was unusually quiet. *Thank god*, Shane thought since Andy had shown up with the rest of the cats he had been trying to trap.

"Jesus Andy, what am I supposed to do with all these cats?" Shane ran her hands through her hair. They'd been bringing cats in for the last few minutes and now stood looking at them all lined up. *Shit,* she thought rubbing her neck. Eighteen boxes lined the three benches and the floor in front of them.

"What's here?" she asked, knowing there had been more than one cat in most of the boxes she carried.

"Kittens, mostly and a couple of adults."

"How many?" Her head was throbbing again. She had downed three Excedrin's after lunch knowing it was coming on. She could still function but damn if that vice didn't feel like it was trying to carve a hole in the side of her head.

"Twenty-six kittens and seven adults."

Shane looked up at him, sighing. "You could have called." *What the hell am I supposed to do with all these cats?* "Andy, you're going to take the four that are ready today, right?"

"Oh sure, but I've got to go to the store first, I'll be back in a couple of hours," Andy said smiling. He'd been trying to get the cat population under control at his place for years. But it wasn't until late last year when the woman next door, who had been feeding them, passed away, that he'd had any real success.

Now he was a regular, bringing in ten or more a week. The first time he came in he had a big smile on his face, "I brought you presents!" When none of the staff got excited he repeated it and showed them a litter of eight-week-old kittens. Genuinely hoping to make their day, he looked hurt when Kim snapped a rude comment his way.

Since then, Shane had been trying to make it up to him. First she explained that they really were grateful he brought in the kittens, after all she'd make sure they were spayed and neutered before going to new homes. But then she showed him their reality of far more cats than homes. Not completely catching on, he had at least begun thanking them on occasion.

Last time he came in, Andy had told her he wanted four of the cats back. "We have more mice this year than ever before. I knew there'd be some, but the first barn we already cleaned out, it's like they're trying to make up for lost time. It was overrun by cats was now it's overrun by mice. But I got more for you, and I'll be bringing them as soon as I catch them." Shane didn't realize he meant all at once.

After Andy left, Shane stood looking over the mound of cats. "Sure, whatever," she said to no one in particular. "We'll take care of them."

"Holy Shit!" Jamie exclaimed with a long whistle.

Shaking her head Shane said, "I know, can you help me move them to the back?"

"Why are they up here, anyway?" Jamie asked taking a picture of all the cat boxes. They used the back door for drop-off's of this size. The front lobby, where the dogs walked through, was no place to have so many cat carriers lined up.

"He had them unloaded at the front curb before we even knew he was here," Shane said, motioning for Jamie to put another carrier under her arm.

"Do you want me to call Lily?" Kinsey asked, picking up the phone to call the foster-home coordinator.

"Not yet," Shane said. The boxes seemed a lot heavier than they should be for kittens. Maybe due to the towels, food or any of the unnecessary toys Andy put in there for them. At least that would be the best case scenario. But Shane knew chances were that the cats were adolescence instead of kittens, which would be bad.

During kitten season, May through October, PHS was inundated with kittens, sometimes having as many as seventy percent of their cat population under three-months of age. When this happened it was virtually impossible to move anyone older. Even though adolescent kittens, four to six months old still exhibited all of the typical kitten charm, they moved off the adoption floor a lot slower. If these were outdoor adolescence they would be even more difficult to place.

"I'm hoping some of the kittens are small enough to go out to foster with the mom's." Shane said to Jamie as they walked back up front.

The look on Jamie's face told her not to expect it.

The first couple dozen cats Andy had brought in had been pretty sweet. Some needed socialization and all needed a little extra time, but they all moved, eventually. Of course that had been late in the season last year, when kittens weren't always available. Lately, everyone he brought in was feral. Hopefully that wasn't the case here.

"Where did he get all these boxes from?" Jamie asked as she grabbed the last few.

It was a good question. All the cats were in identical cat adoption boxes; the temporary enclosures used to bring cats home from a shelter. The handles were soft and badly frayed and there were oil stains on some of them, but overall they were in pretty good shape.

The shelter sold similar boxes for seven dollars each. The newer ones they carried now had a coating of thin plastic over the cardboard, making them impervious to liquids and body fluids.

"Jesus, that's a lot of cats," Jamie said surveying the now over-full cat receiving room. The room, one of the smallest in the shelter, was so narrow only one bank of cat cages could fit. They started putting the boxes at either end of the unit but quickly ran out of room and were forced to set some on top each other. The floor was completely covered except a small path that ran through the middle.

What the hell are we going to do with all these cat? Shane wondered again. They didn't have an open kennel in the building. Maybe Lily could get some in foster but Shane doubted it. They had already lined up their last foster homes for the three cats in back and the mom and litter coming in tomorrow. Shane's head hurt.

Jamie reached down and opened one of the identical plain boxes. Unfolding the flaps, she closed her eyes, "I'm guessing two adolescence," she peeked in. "Hey, check me out. Two brown tabbies, maybe five months old." She held onto both top flaps as she peered in but without the side flaps in place one of the cats saw the opening and took it.

Jumping up through the top corner of the box, his head and shoulders were out before Jamie could slam shut the sides. By then it was too late. He pulled his thin back end easily through the small opening. Ran up the front of Jamie, across her shoulder, and then leaped to the top of the kennels.

"God damn, son of a bitch," Jamie cried out, as Shane closed the box tightly. Jamie lifted her scrub shirt. Red welts had already begun forming where the cats' claws had impacted. At least half were open punctures with spots of blood beginning to form, others had closed as fast as they had opened.

"Son-of-a-bitch." Shane said. Cat scratches were some of the more painful things to endure. Often filthy, a cats nails typically caused small infections everywhere they punctured. Shane knew Cat Scratch Fever was no laughing matter.

The room wasn't easy to pin a cat down in when it was empty. With so many carriers piled up it became virtually impossible. The bank of kennels ran the entire wall, leaving only a couple feet of open space on each end. The bank itself was large, three kennels tall and four wide. Made completely out of steel, it was bulky and even on wheels, hard to move. The missing kitten had quickly explored the top of it then climbed down the back, making it necessary for Shane and Jamie to move the entire unit.

After carrying half of the carriers into the connecting euthanasia room, they pulled the kennels out away from the wall. A three-inch gap existed between each of the mounted kennels, enough room for a slim, five month old kitten to hide.

It took forty-five minutes to catch the hissing, spitting little cat. By the time they did, both of them were sweating, the room was trashed, and Shane had a long gash down her forearm, but they had him.

Jamie held the brown tabby with the thick cat gloves. Shane never used them, they were so bulky. She'd typically use a towel in a situation like this, but also ended up with scratched and torn up arms.

Jamie started singing her most recent favorite song, "If you're going through hell, keep on going, don't slow down. If you're scared, don't show it, you might get out. Before the devil even knows you're there."

Shane held the panels of the box while Jamie lowered the growling cat towards it. He had already tried to bite her, but she held him by the scruff of his neck with one hand and his back legs with the other. Now he just growled, continuously.

Jamie shook the cat to try and distract him, then went back to singing "Well I been deep down in that darkness I been down to my last match. Felt a hundred different demons, breathing fire down my back. And I knew that if I stumbled I'd fall right into the trap that they were laying. Yeah, if you're going through hell, keep on going, don't slow down. If you're scared don't show it, you might get out, before the devil even knows you're there."

Shane smiled, knowing Jamie was trying to distract the cat as much as herself. She held down the flaps until the cat was inside, then secured the sides. Immediately a fight broke out between the two cats. Shane shook the box to break it up. A second later it was quiet.

The two of them sat down heavily on the floor. Shane leaned against the door, breathing heavily. She was trying to figure out how they could see the cats without having to play hide and seek every five minutes. They could open the boxes in a kennel, but they only had one empty kennel, and they needed that for cleaning. Plus they'd have to clean between each box and there was no guarantee the cats would come out quickly.

Jamie opened the door to the euthanasia room. There wasn't a window in this room and it felt like a hundred degrees. After a few minutes, she got up and put peroxide on her welts while Shane lined up the boxes according to the number of cats they guessed were in each. Most of them felt similar to the one they had already opened. If they were all as old as the one that got out, they wouldn't be able to go with their mom's. Shane made a path through the room, clearing out the area in front of the kennels.

When she was done, Shane opened a kennel with a large orange tabby inside. He'd been watching them since they'd come in the room. He had huge cheeks, long whiskers and was solid as a rock. *He must weigh twenty-pounds*, Shane thought. With scars on his face and ears, he looked like a big old outdoor Tom, her favorite. She rubbed his face and scratched his ears as he leaned in, purring.

The door from dog Holding opened, "Shane, there you are," it was Little Laura. "Wow that's a lot of cats."

"More than one in most." Jamie called out from the euthanasia room.

"Wow. Um, we've been looking for you. There's a Ms. Clay here to see you, from the Marketing something or other."

Shane looked down at her watch, three o'clock. *Jesus where did the time go?* "That's that PR woman who wants to create a brand for us." She gave the huge cat one last pat before closing the kennel and turning to go. "I'll take care of this later," Shane told Jamie gesturing to the cats. She rubbed her scrub shirt across her face and tried to smooth down her frizzy hair before walking out for the meeting.

~

By the time Shane got back to Cat Holding it was after six. The shelter was closed and finally quieting down. The phones were still ringing and a couple of the dogs were up and around, mostly the puppies, but half the lights were off and the radio was switched to the nighttime channel. Jamie was checking in a couple cats while Kim and Shane headed to the back.

"Holy shit, we're gonna be busier than a cat coverin' shit." Kim said walking through the path and directly to the far door leading to the euthanasia room.

"I haven't been able to look at any of them yet, so we'll have to evaluate as we go along." Shane would rather have had Laura or Jamie help her but if she had to euthanize a lot of them, Kim would be best.

"What's to evaluate?" Kim propped the door to the euth room open with a block. "Where ya gonna put 'em? Bet none are nice. Did you see Jamie's neck? She's gonna be feeling that for a while."

The scratches on the back of Jamie's neck were the worst. Apparently digging in to launch himself, the young cat had left deep, inch long gashes behind. Shane had cleaned them up as much as possible, but knew Kim was right. Jamie was going to be feeling them for a while.

Shane rubbed her temples and stretched out her jaw. She knew Kim was probably right about the cats too. She hated these. Euthanizing a bunch of animals at the same time was one of the hardest things to endure. Especially young animals. There was nothing they could do with feral cats. With all the domestic ones they had available there was no place for them to go.

"Do you want to just do it in there?" Kim asked as Shane brought in the first of the carriers.

She looked back into the room at the bank of kennels filled with onlookers. The cats, perched on towels and in litter boxes, surveyed the activity. Usually completely shut-off from the rest of the shelter, the room had become a busy place, and all the cats in residence were watching. Shane saw the orange and white Tom looking her way. "No, let's do it in here." With so little in the euthanasia room, losing a cat wasn't a possibility and she didn't want the other cats to watch.

Shane lined five boxes up in the room while Kim pulled out the controlled substance log and began writing down Andy Hasting's name over and over again under the heading that read Owner. The cats couldn't be too bad considering he had gotten them into the carriers, but Shane wasn't taking any chances. She had the cat gloves and a couple of towels sitting ready.

~

By quarter after seven they were done.

Shane closed the freezer and told Kim to take off while she restocked the syringes and put away the sharps container. The freezer was getting backed-up and Shane toyed with the idea of putting the cats directly into the cremator but didn't have the strength. Closing off her emotions was the only way she could endure taking lives but it took a toll on her. Even the knowledge that she could use the cremator for feral cats did little to change her mood.

In the past the animal's bodies were sent to the dump, per city ordinance. It was one of the first things Shane had changed when she took over. Across the country, city and municipal protocol required deceased animals be sent to the local dump, to be disposed of like household garbage. Shane knew she couldn't expect her staff to treat the animals with respect if they were made to throw them in the garbage after they were gone.

Feeling dirty and utterly heartless for what she had just done, Shane turned off the lights in the euthanasia room and went out through the Holding areas. Stopping again at the big orange cat's kennel, she opened the door and rubbed his face, chin and around his ears. The large cat purred in response. His long whiskers tickled the cut on Shane's arm.

Three large dog crates now lined the far wall. *They must be the cats back from foster,* Shane thought they weren't coming in until the next day. Each crate contained a litter box, bed, food and water. As Shane scratched the face of the muscular Tom, she wondered where they would put them. He rubbed his head against her hand again and again. His left ear had been tipped, indicated he'd been altered in a TNR program, but his right ear was also a mess and Shane made a mental note to have Dr. Hunter look at it in the morning.

She watched, as the kittens in the far kennel played. They had one of the toys Madge's mom made, full of catnip. Rolling on top of each other, they smacked into the litter box, food bowls and the water dish.

The big orange pushed his head against Shane's hand hoping for more petting.

She looked at him, "I don't think you'd be doing that if you knew what I just did." She scratched him once more, wiped the tears from her eyes and closed his cage. Cleaning the kittens up as best as she could, she gave them more food then headed up front, finally able to go home.

Chapter 22

"I can't put my finger on it," Shane continued. Dee and her were sitting down to their weekly meeting in Shane's office. Their agenda each week including the animals they were responsible for, dispositions of each, any euthanasia's, any concerns and of course the staff. They never had time to cover everything but Dee always made sure they covered each, at least once a month. Today staffing issues were dominating the conversation, mainly Kim.

"She's different. It's weird. I don't know." Shane struggled with the vibe she was getting from Kim. Shane was the one that brought it up so Dee waited while she formed her thoughts. "It's like she's the same with the animals as she's always been. Disconnected from the majority, but she treats the dead one's like they're gold. I mean she's done that for years now, but it seems more than before. Like, the other day she was in the freezer for ten minutes with Shep making sure he was laid out perfectly. If I didn't harass her she probably would have stayed in there longer. And her attitude with Judy. I don't know, it seems like she wants to get fired."

"Maybe she does." Dee replied calmly.

"Maybe, and who'd blame her? I don't know, I think sometimes it would be the best thing that could happen. I mean working with her is stressful. Kinsey comments on it, she had Little Laura in tears the other day, and I notice it. I'm definitely on guard when she's around."

"Why?"

"Well for starters she's a bitch. I mean she's just such an unhappy person and for some reason she blames us for that. Or at least takes it out on us. And she's got no filter when it comes to the public. God help whoever comes in when she's behind the front desk."

"How was she last night?" Dee asked, referring to Kim helping Shane put down Andy's cats.

"Weird. Well weird for Kim. For some reason she's behind on ashes. I mean really behind, like there's ten litter boxes back there, full. I asked her about it the other day when we were putting Shep down and she apologized and promised to get it done this week."

"Wow," Dee said.

Kim never apologized. And promising something wasn't her way. You took her at her word and that was that. "I know, weird." Shane continued, "then last night, I didn't bring it up at all. I figured I'd go back there later this week and help her catch up. But she brought it up, a couple times. Mentioned the coffee grinder, and breathing in pieces of animals. It wasn't Kim, at least not the Kim I know."

"Sounds like she needs to be pulled off euthanasia and the crematory for a while." Dee said, looking concerned.

"Jesus what else can she do? I can't have her talking to the public, she rips them apart. She's okay with the animals, but the one's that really need behavior modification need someone with patience, and she doesn't have it."

Sighing Dee said, "We've got to find something. Kim has been through a lot here. A lot more than anyone else that's still around. Have you checked to see if she's still going to her weekly appointments?"

"She's goes, but I haven't checked to see if she actually goes to the place. What are you thinking?"

"She sounds like she's depressed. Depressed people often don't do the very things that make them better, like talking to someone. Does she talk to you about her home or family?"

"Never. And to tell you the truth her husband sounds like such a looser I tune her out when she mentions him," Shane admitted, feeling guilty.

"She's euthanized more animals than anyone else currently working here. She grew up here, this is all she knows. She spends the majority of her days in the back with the bodies and ashes. Is it any wonder that she's struggling? And like you've said, her husband's a jerk and her people skills are severely lacking so chances are she doesn't have anyone close."

Shane watched Dee, wondering if she stuck up for her like that. Of course she would, Shane knew. Dee looked out for all of them, empowered them, held them to a higher standard and encouraged them daily until they achieved it. Though it seemed like Shane was seeing less and less of her lately.

"We work with animals because we aren't people-people, we're animal-people." Shane said, repeating a saying she'd latched onto early in her career.

"I would add that there is a broad spectrum of both," Dee said. "Some animal-people can still function fully in the people world, while others can't."

"Kim's the later."

"It would seem so," Dee said. "Don't be too hard on her Shane. It may just be her way of crying out for help. Let me see what I can do." She grabbed her notebook, standing to leave.

~

An hour later Shane left for lunch. It was another beautiful day so she decided to bring Gigit out to the yard with her. Finally secure at Shane's side, the little dog had finally stopped cowering between her legs. She was still uncomfortable in the kennel, but she was progressing, slowly.

Jamie made a bed for her under her desk and Gigit ran straight to it every morning. At first Shane couldn't believe she'd taken to it so quickly, then she realized Jamie was leaving treats on it. Every morning Gigit was treated to a smorgasbord of dried liver and small salmon bites. Luckily June was a picky cat and would have nothing to do with dog treats.

Shane walked Gigit over to the large pine tree and spread out a towel to sit on. Sitting down first, Gigit took up the entire towel. "Oh you think so, huh?" Shane asked her while she switched the short leash for a retractable one. She showed Gigit the tennis ball she had brought out and threw it a short distance. Gigit ran after it and Shane quickly took over the towel.

Gigit loved the ball. She'd dive on it, toss it over her head and bring it back — but never drop it within Shane's reach. Now, seeing that Shane wasn't going to go for it, Gigit laid down and gnawed at the felt covering. Shane pulled out a soda and her sandwich; a chicken wrap with pesto and horseradish.

As she watched Shane eat, drool bubbles the size of large marbles formed on either side of the small dog's mouth.

"Pretty," Shane said.

Then Gigit shook her head.

Shane shielding herself but most of the drool landed overtop of the dogs nose. "Really pretty."

Shane threw the ball again hoping Gigit would follow it. But she didn't move. Sitting a foot in front of Shane, she stared at the food, drooling. "You keep coming out of your shell and I'm going to have to teach you some manners." Shane tossed her a piece of tortilla shell and took a drink of soda.

"Does she need a home?"

The young voice came from behind Shane. Choking on her soda Shane turned to see a boy Jeremy's age standing nearby. She hadn't heard him come up and by the looks of it, neither did Gigit. The terrified dog bolted to the end of the twenty-foot leash and was now pulling against it trying to get further away.

"It's okay baby," Shane said quickly. "You're okay." She clapped her hands together.

Gigit didn't look convinced but had become used to Shane's clapping being a good thing, so she made her way back, slowly.

"Hi," Shane said turning to the boy. "You scared us."

"Oh," he said, sitting down next to Shane. He reached for an ant hill and started poking at it with a pine needle.

"Does she need a home?" He asked again, pointing the pine needle toward Gigit.

Gigit had come the majority of the way back but kept herself as far from the boy as possible.

"Not yet, but hopefully soon. Right now she's still a little scared." Scared was an understatement. The kid had startled Gigit and she didn't look happy. So intent on Shane's lunch, she had hadn't heard him. Now she stood on the far side of Shane, her tail securely between her legs, quivering.

"Can I pet her?"

"I don't know, maybe. Why don't you sit down over here and we'll see if she'll let you feed her." Shane motioned for him to move off to the side a little more. She hoped Gigit would use her as an anchor to investigate the young boy. Though Shane didn't expect Gigit to let him pet her. The scared dog had gotten better and was starting to come out of her shell, but kids were so unpredictable, just what Gigit hated.

The boy looked a lot like her nephew so she asked if he knew Jeremy.

"No, but we just moved here."

Shane gave him a couple pieces of the hotdogs she had brought out. "She loves hotdogs. Hold out your hand."

He reached his hand toward the dog and waved it back and forth, "What's her name?"

"She doesn't have one yet."

"She needs a name." He said, matter-of-factly.

He was right she did need a name, a better one that Gigit. Shane had been putting off thinking of one since she still couldn't get her to pass a behavior assessment, but the dog had been there for weeks now, she needed a decent name. And Shane needed to make a decision with her. She'd been putting off letting Laura name her just in case they needed to put her down, but she couldn't imagine that happening at this point.

"What do you think a good name is?" Shane asked the boy. He had gotten bored holding out the treat and had gone back to digging away at the ant hill near her soda. She picked up the can, took a swallow and set it on her other side.

"My dog's name is Boomer. But my cousin's dog is Bella."

"Boomer or Bella," Shane repeated the names.

"But she doesn't look like either of them. Why is she out here with you?"

"Just wanted to give her some sunshine and time in the grass, or pine needles." Shane smiled, then remembered that she needed to check Jeremy's baseball schedule, *I think he has a game this weekend.*

"She's not afraid of you."

Gigit still didn't trust the boy, but anytime he sat still or seemed distracted she reached for the hotdogs he had left in the dirt. So far she still hadn't gotten close enough to nab them.

"No, not anymore but she was." Shane handed the boy another treat. "Here, toss this one to her, gently."

He did and she ate it immediately. Smiling he turned back to Shane, "She just needs a chance to not be so scared."

That was exactly what she needed, Shane thought. Wondering for the first time where the kid's parents were.

"Hey, that's what you should call her. Chance." He looked at Shane with the wide-eyed excitement she loved seeing in her nephew.

"Chance. Eh? I like it." Nodding, she looked over at the drooling dog, "What do you think of Chance?"

A woman's voice called out. "Oh I gotta go. Bye." He said, standing up and running toward the parking lot. Turning back after a few steps he called out, "Bye, Chance."

As soon as he was away, Gigit pounced on the treats and devoured them. Shane gave her the rest of her sandwich. "Chance, eh? Seems pretty appropriate I suppose. Let's see what Laura thinks."

~

"I want that god damn dog locked up!" The woman yelled.

She had been yelling for more than a half an hour and Shane's nerves were shot. Bringing Gigit in from lunch she found Kim, Jamie and Laura trying to deal with the irate woman. The dog she wanted locked up was Jake, the German Shepherd that spent as many nights at the shelter as he did in his own home. Also known as the neighborhood prowler, he had impregnating most of the unaltered females in the neighborhood.

Of all dogs, it had to be Jake, Shane shook her head. The German Shepherd had gotten into the woman's backyard, and then into her Poodle, Sophie. The woman heard a ruckus and found Jake and Sophie stuck together.

"I tried to separate them," she gestured with her hands. The movement making her already too tight shirt nearly pop a button.

"And now my Sophie is ruined." She sobbed "How can she ever be taken seriously again after that beast raped her? How?"

Raped her, unbelievable. Shane shook her head. The dramatics were actually pretty entertaining. She'd never gone to an opera but thought this must be what it felt like. *The poor woman, her only claim to fame in this world, her dog Sophie – has been soiled. Her champion lines marred forever by the neighborhood wanderer. Life would be over as she knew it.*

"Ma'am, as I said, I'm very sorry for your," Shane paused not sure what she was sorry for, "for your dog. Animal Control has your statement. There's really nothing more that can be done. Why don't you go home to Sophie now?"

Jamie had gone back to the kennel but Shane couldn't get Kim to let her take over. Now, after thirty minutes they were both getting a little punchy. Kim had been good, so far and Shane hoped they could get through this without any additional drama.

"You know," Shane began, thinking of an alternative. "They have that day-after drug for us. Call your vet, maybe they have something similar for dogs," she paused, wondering if she should continue, "or of course, you could have her spayed."

"Spayed!?" Are you kidding me? Spayed?! This dog has had seven, count them, seven AKC champions. And two have gone on to be Grand Champions! Do you know how rare that is? Well do you?"

Shane shook her head slowly, "No I really don't." She said realizing she had just gotten dragged into the opera.

"Spayed, as if. You talk like she's your run-of-the-mill mutt." The woman gestured toward the kennel. "Hardly."

"Hardly," Shane mimicked, after turning her back on the woman. Always fond of mixed breeds, Shane never understood the fascination with purebreds. A good dog was a good dog. And she'd met enough purebred dogs to know they could be good or bad. But most, just like mixed breeds, were unique and people who stereotype them usually paid the price.

"Here they are," Kim scrolled down the webpage in front of her. "Shepadoodles, I knew they had to exist."

Shane smacked her on the shoulder. *What the hell was she doing?*

Ignoring Shane, Kim spoke directly to the woman. "See," she turned the monitor and pointed to the picture of the puppy. "Shepherd, Poodle mixes. Right there, see that, you're expanding your line, that's all."

The owner of the Poodle, took more interest in the monitor than Shane would have expected. So she leaned down so only Kim could hear her, "You're not helping."

"Sure I am," Kim said sarcastically. "I'm helping *her* out."

Just then the front door swung open and Jake's owner Cody came striding in. "I can't believe you picked up my fucking dog again. This is harassment you know, you can't keep doing this to me." He hadn't even reached the counter when he started in on them.

"Awesome," Kim said leaning back in her chair. "I've been waiting for this."

"Your dog?" The woman turned toward him. "You're responsible for that beast of a dog?"

Cody looked briefly at her before turning back to the front desk. "Where the hell's my dog?"

"Is he the one?" the Poodle owner asked Kim.

"Sure is," Kim confirmed.

The woman turned on him, "You're dog raped my Sophie."

"Huh?" Cody finally turned toward the woman.

"You heard me. Your dog raped my little girl. He's ruined her, forever."

"Wait a minute," a look of recognition crossing his face. "You're that crazy bitch from the end of the road with all them Poodles? Those fucking mutts never shut up." Laughing, he turned back to the counter. "Priceless."

"How dare you? My Dool's are wonderful pets, don't you dare call them mutts. They've sired champions, you know."

"Well here's her chance to do it again," he smiled, "with a real dog."

"I want to know what's going to happen to him. He's got to be charged for this." She spoke directly to Kim, who was enjoying the show.

"No charges, just congratulations" Kim responded. "Jake and Sophie will be the proud new parents of Shepadoodles. You can probably sell them for hundreds of dollars apiece."

Both Cody and the woman looked at Kim, confused.

"Nothing like taking a strong solid name like Shepherd and dumbing it down. Shepadoodles, so stupid," Kim repeating, "Shepadoodles."

So called designer mixes could be distinguished from purebred dogs by their names. These dogs, gaining in popularity only recently, were named by blending the names of the parent's breeds into some sort of hybrid name. Some like the Labradoodles and Bassadors had become commonly accepted. Others like the Morky's, Alusky's, and Wheatables were just plain silly to Shane.

She hated the fact that first generation mixed breed dogs could garner hundreds or thousands of dollars because they were labeled "designer" while identical dogs and second generation mixed breeds lingered in the shelter for months. But that didn't excuse Kim's tactics.

"What?" Cody asked, annoyed again. "What the fuck are you talking about?"

"I'm talking about Jake making puppies." Kim stood and pointed at him. "I'm talking about your dog making us kill other dogs because you're too lazy to keep him locked up. I'm talking about the same thing we've been talking about for months."

She paused, Shane jumped in hoping to stop her before she said something worse. "Okay," she began, not quickly enough.

"And I'm talking about penis envy." Kim blurted, her face reddening as soon as she said it.

"What?" Cody asked, as everyone looked at her wondering the same thing.

"You've got penis envy." Kim repeated her face now bright red.

"I've got what? What the fuck are you talking about, bitch?"

"If you didn't you wouldn't care that he got neutered. If you weren't trying to live through him and his exploits, he'd be neutered already. You've got penis envy."

Oh for god sakes! Shane couldn't believe she had just said that. "Okay, enough, Kim, to my office."

Cody looked as surprised as Shane felt. She turned toward Kim, hoping to prod her when she saw both Dee and Judy sitting in her office, listening. *God damn it,* she thought, *now I'm screwed.*

"You bitch, who the hell do you think you are?" Cody's shocked expression had turned angry.

"I'm the person that takes care of your dog, as much as you do. And now I'm the person that has to clean up his mess," she gestured to the woman. Her voice had risen to match Cody's.

Did every opera have to have a tragedy? Shane wondered as she prodded Laura to get the woman out of there and pushed Kim into her office.

The woman had backed down once Kim took up the fight. "I wonder if I could sell them?" She said, picking up the items that had been in her purse before she emptied it on the counter "I'd have to do it under a different name," she continued, more to herself than anyone.

Shane put her hand on Kim's arm. Speaking in her ear, she let her know they had an audience.

Shane wondered if she should have sided with Kim and brought up the fact that none of the puppies would be altered. But it wasn't the time or the place. She was pissed, so pissed she didn't think she'd be able to speak clearly. She handed Cody the Return-to-Owner form and followed Kim into the office.

Chapter 23

"Shane, is something wrong with the cremator, again?" Kinsey asked closing the door to the cupboard and heading back to the phone.

"Not that I'm aware of." Shane answered from her office. It'd been almost a week since her conversation with Dee about the backed-up ashes. Kim had gotten caught up the next day so Shane assumed they were good. Ever since her talk with Dee, she had tried to stop thinking about Kim as a pain in the ass and had tried to cut her some slack, but she wasn't making it easy.

Kinsey picked up the phone, "I'm very sorry ma'am but they're not done yet. Can I get a number for you and I'll give you a call right back, just as soon as I know when they'll be ready."

Hanging up, she turned to Shane, "I've had to do that for the last two days. What's going on?"

"I don't know," Shane said, closing the press release she'd been struggling with. Kim was off so she figured it was as good a chance as any to see what was going on back there. She also needed a break from the computer. The piece she was working on was to implore the community to come and adopt an animal. They were busting at the seams and Shane needed a really good hook to get the piece picked up and run in the paper.

Shane told Kinsey she'd let her know when the ashes would be ready and headed out back. Walking through the kennels she smelled poop. It took her a minute to find the culprit; it was Bowser. *Weird,* she thought, *he didn't usually go in his kennel.* Not seeing anyone in the prep room, Shane grabbed a scooper and cleaned it up.

Bowser, the large black and tan dog was beautiful. Weighing close to 100 pounds, his thick, shiny coat made Shane think of him more like a bear than a dog. His size and muscles were intimidating, but he had a good personality; friendly not happy like a puppy but nice enough. But he was a dog that needed a job. Shane knew he'd go stir crazy lying around all day in a house but he was there because he chased livestock, so it was taking forever to place the large animal.

Oddly enough, the storage room was worse than when she saw it last. A four-foot tall stack of litter boxes stood just inside the doorway. *What the hell was Kim doing?* Shane looked inside each. The ashes indicated that the animals had run their course in the cremator, but who was who? She looked up at the white board, where they listed the animals needing to be cremated.

"God damn it Kim," Shane said under her breath. She lifted the top box. In the box below it was the slip of paper typically attached to the outside of the body bags, "Daisy Goldsmith" it read. Well at least that was something. Looking at the board on the wall, there were fifteen animals listed. *That many, again already?* Shane thought. *What the hell was going on? Had she only run the cremator? What about the ashes? This had to be everyone, but - ?* To figure out what was going on she needed to start at the beginning. Dusting off her hands, she headed across the hall into the euthanasia room and opened the freezer.

Three stacks of bodies lined the back wall and another two stacks sat closer to the door. The animals against the back wall were theirs; the others had come in already deceased. Each stack sat on a number of pallets to keep them from freezing to the floor. DOA's short for Dead-on-Arrival, were typically held for two months to give their owners a chance to find them. But there were still more than Shane expected.

Each of the bodies in the freezer was in a separate bag. Each bag had a label on it indicating what animal it was. Animals that arrived at the shelter already deceased had a complete description so they could be identified without opening the bag. Shane looked at the tags attached to the farthest row:

DLH, M, HBC, Main/10th 6/11/11. A Domestic Long Hair Cat, Male, Hit-by-car on Main and 10th on June 11th.

The second read DLH, M/N, Blk/Wh, DOA, 6/7/2011. Another long-haired cat, this one was a black and white, neutered male who was brought in already deceased

The third was a Border Collie, F, HBC, 5/25/11 Female, also hit-by-car.

The last read Mutt, DOA, 5/29/11. *Mutt? What the hell is that?* Shane turned the card to see if she could recognize the writing. Mutt wasn't descriptive at all, any kind of dog could be in there. Animal Control would never have written that down, and they're the ones that brought these animals in, usually. Shane couldn't tell who wrote it.

Identifying the Dead-On-Arrival's with at least one breed of animal, their sex, markings and color allowed the staff to determine if they had to open the bag or not. The last thing they wanted to do when an owner came in looking for their lost dog, was open up body bags.

The undescribed dog was on the bottom of the first pile. After moving the others, Shane pulled at the bag but it didn't give. Pulling again without any luck she realized it was frozen to the pallet under it. "Shit." Rubbing her hands together, she tried to warm them back up with her breath. Her fingertips were numb but she should still have been able to move the dog, she thought, wrestling with the frozen bag.

Shane knew what had to have happened. The dog must have been newly deceased when he was put in the freezer. When that happened, the body fluids pooled at the bottom of the bag. Shane glanced through the opening in the pallet immediately under the body. Sure enough, the bag, filled with fluids had sunk through the openings in the pallet. Then froze, "damn."

Shane walked out of the freezer, rubbing her arms.

"There you are," Laura said from the doorway. "Brenda's on the phone for you. Didn't you hear the page?"

"I was in the freezer. Tell her I'll have to call her back." Shane had a thought. "Hey, are you busy?" She realized she was going to need help getting caught up.

"No, just doing laundry," Laura paused. "What's up?"

"I need some help back here."

Laura glanced at the freezer, "okay. Sure of course. Just let me get back to Brenda."

By the time Laura got back Shane had managed to break up and turn enough of the frozen fluids under the mystery dog to unlock him from the pallet.

She carried the body out and placed it on the exam table. Closing the door behind her, Shane stood for a moment enjoying the fresh air and rubbing down the goose-bumps on her arms.

"What's up?" Laura asked, looking at the bag on the table.

"I need you to process ashes, but first I need to find out who's in here." With her hands still numb Shane knew she wouldn't be able to peel the tape off the gathered plastic. So she walked over to the sink, turned on the water and waited while it heated up.

"It says mutt?" Laura asked, looking down at the stained tag.

"Have you filled those out before?" Shane nodded to the card Laura was still holding.

"Not yet, but Jamie's showed me how. I thought we had to have at least one breed on here." She flipped the card over but the back was blank.

"You do. Which is the problem we have right now. We have no idea who's in that bag. You also should have," Shane stopped herself, remembering to let Laura answer. "What else should be on there?"

"Um, I guess um, the color or any specific markings." Laura looked up at her.

"Uh-huh." Shane's hands had warmed up under the running water. She dried them and headed back to the body. "Think about lost reports, what kind of information do you take down or what stuff is important to identify an animal?"

"Is it male or female."

"Yep, what else?"

"Oh uh, where they found it."

"Exactly." Shane peeled away the thick tape and glanced up at Laura before opening the bag. She turned her head away but not quick enough to avoid the smell. The freezer preserved the bodies until they could be cremated but the distinct smell of decay still permeated. Shane took shallow breaths through her mouth, trying to avoid the odor as much as possible.

Laura pulled her scrub shirt over her nose. Making a face, she squinted and looked away.

Let's get this done quickly, Shane thought, pulling back the plastic. The dog was a cute little black and tan spaniel mix. *Didn't someone come in looking for a spaniel?* She tried to remember, "I think this dog's owner came in. I checked the board, do me a favor," Shane looked up at Laura. "Go check the board and see if this dog is listed."

Laura looked grateful to get away from the smell and quickly turned back to the door.

All animals coming into the shelter deceased were listed on the dry erase board next to the freezer. It provided a listing of animals that people may be looking for. When the animal was cremated they were erased from the board. Shane knew she would have looked at the board when she walked the woman around. She always did. And she was sure she'd remember if the word "mutt" was listed.

Trying to pull the bag away from her or him, without breaking any of her frozen appendages was difficult. But working slowly Shane was able to uncover the dog almost completely. He'd been hit by a car, luckily the crushed side was facing down and Shane wasn't forced to see the damage. At least there weren't any maggots, she thought, flinching again at the smell.

The dog looked to be male, but without moving and possibly breaking something Shane didn't think it was worth checking. He was wearing a collar, though. *Unfreakenbelievable,* Shane thought. Knowing the collar would have given her everything she needed. She tried to unlatch it but it was the kind that needed to be slid over the dog's head, which Shane wasn't going to do.

Laura came back in, "Nothing."

Shane nodded. Not able to stand the smell any longer, she did a quick inventory of everything she could see without disturbing the poor guy. "Long coat and tail. Black on top but belly and legs all brown. Brown around his eyes and under his chin." Shane cut the dog's collar off, took a picture then motioned to Laura to help her with the bag.

The smell didn't go away after they got the bag back around the dog, so Shane avoided taking the deep breath she wanted. Laura taped the bag closed while Shane wrote down what she saw before she forgot. Picking the small dog up, Laura put her back in the freezer and came out for the tag Shane was finishing.

After they were done, they headed out the back door, eager for fresh air. Standing together, they let the sun warm them and melt off some of the death they had just dealt with.

"Damn, that woman's been looking for that dog for weeks now." *Son-of-a-bitch*, Shane thought, shaking her head. *Why do I bother writing up procedures if no one's going to follow them?* "God damn it, I've gotta call her back. This is gonna be a fun conversation."

Shane shook her head trying to clear it. "Have you crushed bones yet?"

"Excuse me?" Laura asked, her eyes growing wide.

"Today's your lucky day. We've got boatloads to do." Heading back in, Shane showed her the pile of litter boxes in the supply room. "See these litter boxes," she gestured to the two stacks. "Each is an animal that has been cremated. They need to be crushed, bagged and labeled.

Laura poked at the partial skull that sat in the top box.

"I know," Shane said seeing her reluctance. "I had no idea they didn't come out as ashes the first time I had to do it either. Then Dee told me they do the same for us."

Laura looked up at her shocked.

"For us they use huge rollers to crush the bones. Some shelters use a coffee grinder or these bulky bone grinders but the sound is horrible, like disturbingly horrible. So we just use the sledge hammer method."

Pulling her hand back, Laura wiped her fingers on her jeans.

With only a couple feet between the items stored on either side of the space, there wasn't enough room to do it in there so Shane grabbed the oversized hammer and walked back into the euth room. "Grab that box on top, would you?"

Laura brought the box into the exam room and set it down on the table in the middle.

Shane handed her the safety glasses. "Some you can do on the table, but some are tough and you'll need to do them on the floor." Picking up the oversized hammer, Shane held it so the handle was straight up and down. The skull, pelvis and one two-inch bone were the only things recognizable but they quickly turned into powder with the hammer.

Shane pulverized what was left and set down the heavy tool. After fanning the air she brushed off her hands and grabbed a bag from one of the drawers. Pouring the contents of the litter box into the bag she got most of it out. Using a small broom, she swept up what was caught in the scratches at the bottom of the box.

Closing up the plastic bag, Shane set the small package into an urn. "That's all. Now they should all have a name or some kind of id. This one, let's just put a note that it was in the top box. We might be able to tell who it is if they're in order." She looked up at Laura, "you good to try?"

"Um, sure." Laura looked up at her. "Is there a mask or something I could wear on my face?"

"Oh yeah, sorry. Jamie wears them." Shane opened the drawers until she found one.

"I want to go call this woman about her dog." Shane gestured to the one in the freezer. "Have at it; call if you have any questions." She knew Laura would never call.

By the time Shane tracked down the dog's owner she wasn't thinking about how pissed the woman would be, just that she'd have closure. Unfortunately, she was pissed. Really pissed. And she had no qualms with saying so. Shane didn't blame her. She knew as well as anyone how important closure was and felt horrible the woman had had to wait so long to find out her dog was there the whole time.

God damn it, who did that? And how did no one notice? That dogs been in the freezer for weeks and no one knew. No one thought this woman was looking for her? No one cared? Shane made a note to call Animal Control and talk to them about the tag to make sure it wasn't one of their officers, but she knew it wasn't. The only one who would have done it, the only one who would have caught it had someone else done it, was Kim. *What the hell?* Shane thought, *all those ashes again. Dee's right, I've got to pull her off cremations. Damn. What am I going to do with her?*

Kinsey appeared in the doorway so Shane covered the mouthpiece and nodded to her, "Shane, I'm sorry there's an owner request here. Jamie's at lunch. Can you do it?"

PHS performed owner requested euthanasia's five or more times a week. Most people called ahead of time so the shelter could have the room ready and the right staff on hand to take care of it. The woman on the phone was wrapping up so Shane waited while she repeated how much they disappointed her and how she would find it hard to trust them again.

Shane apologized for what seemed like the hundredth time and hung up. *If they'd done their jobs the woman would have been upset over her dog but she wouldn't have had any reason to be mad at them. When she was ready for another dog they might have been able to get her to look at one in the shelter. Ripples,* Shane thought, annoyed.

Walking out to the front she remembered she needed to talk to Kinsey. Leaning down to avoid being overheard she said, "Kins, Kim's off euth's for a while. Make sure there's none schedule when only she's here." Shane turned to go in the back, then turned back around, "and give me like five minutes, Laura's using the room right now for ashes."

"How long for ashes?" Kinsey called back.

"A day or two." She headed back to the euth room and found Little Laura wearing an oversized baseball cap, safety goggles, and a mask. She had pulled her sleeves down and looked more like she was fumigating a house rather than crushing bones.

"How you doing?" Shane asked looking around. Three closed and tagged urn's sat on the counter by the sink. She walked over and picked them up. Opening the door to cat Holding, she set them down just inside the small room.

Laura finished the one she was doing and brushed off her entire body. Shane brought her a bag and urn.

"Have you done an owner request yet?" Shane asked, knowing the answer but wanting to see the young girl's reaction. Assisting with owner requests was the second step in training. The first was to assist with euthanizing their own animals. Laura had assisted her with two reservation dogs that came in last week. Both older and in horrible shape, the female had had multiple litters, her nipples hung down to the ground and she'd lost her coat years ago. The male's ears had been completely eaten away by frostbite and he was anemic. Neither dog had any teeth left and Shane made the decision to put them down. The euthanasia's had gone smoothly. Laura seemed to take it in stride but those were a lot different than owner requests.

"No," she took off the glasses and mask and fanned the cloudy air in front of her. "Do you need me?"

"If you wouldn't mind. We've got a walk-in and Kim and Jamie are both out." Labeling the last urn Shane set it out with the others.

Chapter 24

Laura wiped down the table while Shane unlocked the cabinet and withdrew the sedative and barbiturate. Just as she logged the date in the controlled substance book she heard the car pull up. Shane took a deep breath and headed out to the back door. Not sure how big the dog was, she left the wheeled cart behind and held the door open for Laura.

The dog's owners, a couple Shane's age, were reaching into the backseat of the car. The man stepped backwards before turning with a large, chocolate Lab in his arms. Tears were running down his face.

Shane turned around and opened the door back up. Laura followed her lead and guided the man into the euthanasia room. The woman, also crying, passed Shane carrying a large, green and blue plaid dog bed in her arms.

Laura had spread a blanket on the table but Shane asked if they'd rather have the dog bed under him. Neither said anything but a second later the blanket was on the floor and the dog bed was on the table with the large dog on top of it. His breathing was labored and he hadn't moved when he was picked up or set back down.

He looked ancient. His entire face was grey, his eyes cloudy and unfocused and he smelled like urine. *He probably didn't have control of his bladder any more*, Shane thought trying not to show that she had noticed the smell. Closing the door, she approached the table.

The husband was on one knee talking to the dog. "You've been a great dog Charlie. Really you have. I couldn't have gotten through all this without you." He stared into the dogs face as he stroked his ears and head.

Charlie's head was slumped on the table between his paws. *A couple more hours, and he'd go on his own*, Shane thought. Estimating his weight to be around sixty pounds, she smiled sympathetically to the woman and went to pull the sedative and barbiturate up. Taking another deep breath, she grabbed a box of tissues and headed back to the table.

The woman was now talking quietly to the dog. "Thank you Charlie. Thank you so much. Thank you for teaching me and for being patient with me and for making me see all the beauty in the world. I'm going to miss you so much." She sobbed loudly.

Shane set the tissues on the table in front of her and looked up at Laura.

Barely keeping it together, Laura was standing behind the couple blinking madly. Her nose was red and her bottom lip quivered. *Damn it*, Shane thought. *Hold it together.*

The guy had moved around to the dogs back and continued stroking him. "Whenever you're ready," Shane said quietly. She never wanted to rush people at a time like this, but she didn't know if Laura was going to be able to keep it together.

Owner request euthanasia's were always the most difficult for Shane. With the owners present and crying over their babies it made it easy for her to feel for them. She'd shed more than her share of tears with grieving people before and understood Laura doing the same. But she didn't know how bad the girl would be, some people completely lost their ability to function once they began crying.

"You've been the best dog ever Charlie." The woman rubbed the dog's head as she spoke. "Thank you for giving us so much. For bringing us together and for making us so happy." She buried her head in the dog's coat. "Who's going to lick away my tears Charlie?" Sobbing, she brushed her sleeve across her mouth. "I love you so much you big lug."

The woman nodded to Shane. She looked towards the man. Tears were running down his face as he dug his hands into the fur on the dogs back. Shane looked away quickly.

Damn, she thought fighting to stay in control. She quizzed herself, *how much sedative? Four cc's. How much blue? Seven cc's. Breathe*! She took a quiet breath and felt in control enough to look up at him again.

He nodded, sobbing loudly.

"Okay," Shane spoke quietly. "What we're going to do is give him a sedative, just like he'd be given before surgery. After he goes to sleep, we'll administer the drug. He won't wake up after I give him the sedative. Laura," she nodded to the young girl whose nose and cheeks were bright red, "will be assisting me."

I'm going to inject the sedative into his back leg. Shane pulled the cap off the needle, checked the syringe and then placed it into the dog's rear leg. He didn't move while she did it.

"I love you Charlie. We love you so much." The woman repeated slowly as the dogs eyes gradually closed. As he began snoring, his mom repeated over and over, "we love you Charlie. Thank you baby, thank you for everything. We'll never forget you."

"Whenever you're ready," Shane said quietly, her voice scratchy.

The man nodded.

Not wanting to disturb the dog, they let him lay where he was. Laura knelt at the head of the table so she had access to his leg. She picked up his right arm and held it at the elbow. Shane shaved a small patch half-way up the dog's leg, directly over his vein. Laura placed her thumb over the top of his leg and rolled his vein outward, applying pressure as she did. Shane knew older dogs could be difficult because of their low blood pressure and took a breath to steel her nerves. Placing her thumb against the side of the dog's vein, Shane wiped it down with alcohol and turned the needle. Once the bevel was facing up, she inserted it slowly. Bright red blood filled the hub. Shane nodded to Laura to release her hold then slowly injected the drug.

The syringe was half empty when the dog let out a deep, long breath. "Oh, Charlie." The woman buried her head in the dog's back, his loose skin completely covering her face.

Shane was having a hard time holding back tears. She looked down at Laura to see how the young girl was doing. Tears streamed silently down her face. Shane could tell the dog was gone before Laura stood up. But she brought over the stethoscope and listened to his chest to be sure. "He's gone," she confirmed quietly to the couple. Walking back over to the sink, she noted the drug used, put everything in the cupboard and locked it before turning back to them. "We'll give you a couple of minutes."

Laura and Shane headed out the back door both eager for fresh air. Just as they were closing the door to the euthanasia room Shane heard the woman humming Amazing Grace. *Jeezo,* Shane thought feeling tears burn her eyes. *Just when I thought I had it together.*

They both stood, not saying a word, letting the sun and slight wind wash over them.

"Jesus that was hard. How do you hold it together?" Laura asked.

"I think owner requests are the worst." Shane answered after a minute. "I don't know if it's because it's easy to relate to or because we feel their pain, but damn if they don't get me every time."

"Guys crying," Laura said after a minute, "gets me every time."

Shane nodded, "yeah, me too."

After a few minutes the back door opened and the couple walked out. "What now?" The woman asked, after blowing her nose.

"Are you having his ashes returned?" Shane tried to ask as delicately as possible.

"Uh-hum," The woman nodded.

"We'll call you when they're ready. It'll be a couple days."

"Thank you." She said pulling her shirt tightly around her.

"Can I ask a question?" Laura began after they had bagged the chocolate Lab with his bed.

"Hum?" Shane was looking at the mess in the control substance book. The pages were out of order and the math didn't add up.

"Why do you bother to swab with alcohol? I mean isn't it used so the animal doesn't get sick? It's not like he has to worry about that."

"Just good practice," Shane said smiling, *the girl thought of everything.* "If you don't use it before you insert a needle you might think there's times when it's okay not use it, it's just a good thing to practice. Plus it makes seeing the vein easier."

"Thanks Shane. You really held it together."

"Think about the process."

"Huh?"

"Emotions are dangerous. The best way to not experience them is to think about the process. If you find yourself getting upset concentrate on what we have to do next, the health problems with the animal, the amount of fluids we need, something, anything that isn't emotional. Do a math problem, make yourself think."

"That works?"

Shane nodded, "It takes practice, but, yeah, it works."

Chapter 25

The next afternoon Kinsey stood in the office doorway, "Shane?"

"What's up?" Shane asked, pushing back her keyboard and looking up. *It felt good to look away from that screen*, she thought rubbing her eyes.

"I just thought you should know, we've had seven impounds, and eight owner surrenders so far today." She paused, "and no adoptions."

Shane looked up at the clock, four-thirty. "Eight owner surrenders?" she asked. They were in no position to handle that right now.

The dog population had been steadily rising over the last five weeks. They had exceeded capacity ten days ago, both in the shelter and in foster. Just yesterday, Shane asked a woman to hold onto a litter of Aussie mixes for another week to give them a chance to move some.

Kinsey continued. "Two came in due to the death of the owner, one because the daughter is allergic, another was moving apparently to a state that doesn't accept pets, two were this crazy woman's -"

Shane didn't know what she was going to do with all these dogs. Their foster homes were full, they were transferring animals out as often as possible and they were actually adopting out a lot. But more kept coming in. *What am I supposed to do with them all? They never stop. Every time I get a litter into a foster home another comes through the door. And the dogs, she knew the spay/neuter clinic was working but they just couldn't keep up.*

"Oh," Kinsey waved her hand, continuing as if Shane had asked her about the crazy woman comment. "I don't know some long story about they were her sister's before she gave them to a woman she works with who couldn't keep them and they ended up with this other woman, but now they're ruining the laundry room door. Long story."

Shane nodded not really caring to hear it, "and the impounds?"

"Two are definitely owned, purebred Airedale's, the other had tags. ACO tried to bring him back to the house but there wasn't a fence, just a dog run, so he left them a message."

Well that was something at least, Shane thought. Those ones should be out of there by the end of the day.

"Can I help you?" Kinsey asked the man who had just come in.

The Reverend, who Shane had been talking to about the English Setter, Tilly on Courtesy Hold was supposed to come by. When Shane heard him ask for her she took a quick look around the office to see if there was anything that needed to be put up. Not seeing anything she headed for the front. Up till now, her pleading had gone on deaf ears and she was hoping he might understand better if he saw their reality.

"Reverend Wright?" Shane asked, extending her hand.

"Very pleased to meet you, Ms. –"

"Hillard, But please call me Shane."

He smiled, a pleasant looking man she could see why the church appealed to him. He seemed a lot like Mr. Rogers with his gentle handshake, cardigan/loafer look and soft voice.

Wonder how he's going to deal with the kennel, she thought before criticizing herself for thinking something negative about a minister.

Not having ever belonged to a church herself, Shane never knew what the correct way to address ministers was or what she was supposed to say for that matter. She assumed people said some pretty crazy stuff in confession so they had to be used to it, but she didn't think Rev Wright was catholic, so maybe he didn't get to hear the dirt.

"Mr., I mean Reverend Wright, I asked you here today because it's time for me to make a decision concerning Gayle's dog, Tilly."

He nodded, waiting.

"But before we talk about her, I'd like you to meet her." Shane led him through the kennel doors but instead of heading directly back to Holding, she walked along the first row of kennels to the far end.

On either end of the long room were the puppy pens. Four per side, the five-foot square, concrete kennels were surrounded by three-foot-tall walls. Mounds of shredded paper were in each, as well as blankets, toys, food and water bowls.

Every pen was in use, some having as many as six puppies in them. Shane hated the pens. Since they were wide-open people constantly picked up the puppies or went in with them, it was a nightmare. If she had a choice she wouldn't use them but she didn't have a choice right now.

The minister slowed and smiled at the puppies. In one pen two brown Dachshund mixes wrestled with each other while their siblings slept on the fluffy bed in the corner. One woke while they looked on. She stretched, yawned, then stood slowly. A second later she shook herself, lost her balance and tumbled back into bed.

Shane turned to continue on. She walked down the middle run slowly. The barking made it impossible to talk but she wanted the minister to see how full they were. Tilly was in Holding, not on the adoption floor but he wouldn't know the difference.

Every run had the maximum allowed; two dogs in each, and all seemed to be barking at the same time. Many of them barked because volunteers were walking dogs in and out, others were barking at Shane and the minister and still others barked just to join in. At the other end were four more puppy pens, all filled. The minister followed at Shane's pace, not rushing to avoid the noise.

Opening the far door, they walked into the Holding area. The dogs erupted in chaos anytime visitors came through and they were in full swing today. Shane braced herself to try and block the piercing barks from her ears.

She stopped in front of Tilly's kennel. The dog had been at the shelter for four months and it looked like it was taking its toll on her. When she first arrived she was a happy, upbeat dog always at the front of the run and excited to be talked to. Now, she watched them from her bed. Not moving or even picking up her head, the dog just rolled her eyes in their direction.

Shit, Shane thought. She hadn't realized she'd gotten this bad. As an owned animal Tilly couldn't be taken out by volunteers like the others. She was walked by the staff every day but it wasn't the same. And since she wasn't up for adoption she had to be held in this stress-filled room. *No, this wasn't good at all.*

Tilly was a beautiful, English Setter. Her drooping eyes and long nose and ears gave her a pathetic but aristocratic look. Her long hair, mainly white and brown had grey spots scattered throughout and was as soft as an angora sweater.

Shane knelt on one knee to try and entice the dog to the front of the run. She looked completely uninterested but after two long minutes, finally stood, stretched, shook and made her way to the gate.

"Hey baby, how are you?" Shane asked the speckled dog. "You hanging in there?" She sat next to the fence and let Shane pet her through the chain-link.

Shane hadn't planned on taking the dog out, but after what she saw she figured she should. Pulling a slip lead out of her pocket, Shane opened the gate and quickly looped it over the dog's head. Tilly burst out of the kennel, chocking herself. She would have pulled Shane off her feet but knowing what was coming, Shane held onto the metal gate. The leash pinched her hand but there was no way to pull the dog back.

After taking the long way back there, she didn't want to get back up front too quickly, so they walked down the last run of dogs. As they passed, many of the dogs charged the fence to bark at Tilly. At first the tall, stately dog pulled away from the dogs and closer to the wall. But as they neared the end of the row she began lunging back at them, barking. Her hackles raised, she trotted comfortably down the last half of the aisle.

Shane opened the door to her office and ushered the minister inside. As soon as it closed behind them the sound of barking dogs was cut off, giving them a welcome break.

The minister shook his head, rubbed his ears and stretched his jaw in an extended yawn. "I don't know how you do it."

Turning, Shane looked at him. She didn't know which 'it' he meant.

"The barking." He clarified.

"Ah, you get used to it," she shrugged.

"So this is her dog?" He asked, not making a move to engage with the dog.

"It is." Shane got down on one knee and called Tilly to her. The dog didn't seem very comfortable but came when she was called. Shane stroked her back, noting how stiff she was. "When I asked you to come in today, I was going to offer you an option. Either take her or we adopt her out. But I can't do that anymore."

The minister watched, waiting.

"Did you notice when we stood in front of Tilly's kennel that she didn't come to us? That I had to call her and she still took her time?"

He nodded.

"That's a sign of her disconnecting. She has lived 24/7 in that noise you just experienced. You experienced it for three minutes, she's lived in it for the last four months. Consider if your hearing were ten times better than it is, if your nose could smell the minutia in the air and on the floor. She hears nothing but that, smells nothing but that. Since she's not one of our dogs, volunteers can't legally handle her. So she's only getting two short walks a day, the rest of the time she's locked in that run in that room."

God he had good eye contact. It made Shane wonder if the church made people patient or if patient people were just drawn to the church. "Also, I'm sure you noticed her barking and lunging at the dogs before we came in here?"

Again he nodded.

"I'm afraid at this point I can't put her up for adoption. I would not be doing her any favors. She needs to be in a home, immediately or we're going to lose her completely."

Tilly walked the perimeter of the room. Taking her time, she investigated every corner, dust bunny and spot she noticed.

"Lose her?" He asked.

"She will continue to disconnect with us until there won't be anything we can do."

"How long does that take?"

"It's different for all dogs, but looking at her today, I can tell you it's already happening. If we don't move fast we're not going to have a chance to save her."

"Do you need me to sign her over to you? Is there a place you can send her to?"

"What I need from you, what I've needed from you for months now, is for you to take her."

"Oh no, I can't take her. I don't have animals."

"Reverend," Shane took a deep breath trying to figure out how to get through to him. "You have a congregation that has what, a hundred families or so in it?"

He nodded, "more or less."

"Can't you reach out to them? I'll bet you'll find someone willing to do it."

"Oh no, I'm not comfortable doing that."

"You're not comfortable asking your congregation to take in a dog for one of your own, but you'll ask me to do it?" *Stay cool* she reminded herself, realizing she had started talking fast again. "You saw how full we are. You won't even consider helping, even for one of your own?"

"It's not that, I'm happy to help. It's just the congregation comes to church to get something out of it. Not to be asked to do more or carry a greater weight."

Shane shook her head. She hadn't expected this to be so difficult. "So you don't have pets?" She asked, thinking of a different tactic.

He shook his head, "I care for my mom's cat from time to time. But no, I don't have any myself."

"Does your mom get enjoyment from her cat?"

"Enjoyment? Oh she loves that cat." He laughed briefly.

Shane nodded. "Couldn't there be someone in your congregation that could benefit by loving something that much? I mean, there could be someone thinking about getting a dog or the opposite; someone thinking how bad or how lonely life is. Then you make an announcement that a member of your congregation needs help."

"You explain about this wonderful dog that needs a place to stay. Don't you think that the process will make one of your people's lives richer? Can't you see them thanking you in a couple of months for giving them something to live for? This is a good dog. She could be a great dog again if we can get her back into a home environment. But she cannot stay here any longer. I can't do right by her here."

Ten minutes later, with assurances that he would have her out of the shelter in the next two days, Shane said goodbye to the Reverend and headed upstairs to Lily's office with Tilly in tow.

Chapter 26

The office shared by the Volunteer and Foster Home Coordinators was on the second floor. Almost an exact opposite of Dee's office, this one was busy, cluttered and a non-stop parade of people in and out. Posters from the shelters past events lined the room while pictures of already adopted animals filled in any open spaces. Two desks sat face-to-face against the far wall and a three-tiered, free-standing cat kennel was on the other. Today there was a litter of six-week-old brown tabby kittens inside.

A long rectangular table sat covered with foster-home supply bags, filled with food, toys, information guides and litter boxes. Behind it was a large white board. Upcoming trainings and important phone numbers were listed on it and a row of paw prints were drawn across the bottom.

In the far corner, boxes of cat and dog toys were piled on top of each other. Madge's mom was in one of the local nursing home. Having a ton of energy, she'd begun a program at the home that made cat and dog treats for the animals at the shelter. The cat treats were a simple sock stuffed with crumpled paper and catnip and tied at one end. The dog treats were made from toilet paper rolls. Each was stuffed with dry dog food then the ends were folded in on each other.

Shane checked on the litter of kittens in the kennel while she waited for Lily, the Foster Home Coordinator to get off the phone.

"Shane, how wonderful to see you." Lily said. She reminded Shane of the grandmother she always wished she had. A put together older-lady, Lily was classy, smart and very good at reading people and situations.

"Any openings?" Shane asked.

"For what?" Snickers, the shelter dog, had been lying under Madge's desk. Hearing Shane's voice he came out and. After a minute of Tilly and Snickers reacquainting themselves, Lily took Tilly's lead and Snickers sat down next to Shane.

Wearing his storm shirt, Snickers rubbed his back and butt against Shane for scratching. Storm Shirts, tight fitting "shirts" that surround a dog's torso, helped to alleviate stress in neurotic dogs. PHS owned ten of the crucial behavior modification shirts though Snickers claimed three of them for himself.

Shane loosened the Velcro straps and rubbed the dogs coat underneath them. Most dogs only had to wear the shirts before and during thunderstorms, though they also worked great for any dogs that were freaked out or who couldn't relax. But Snickers wore his shirt all the time. Shane was afraid it had become a new neurosis for the crazy dog but at least it seemed to alleviate all the other ones.

"Dogs, adults. We're busting at the seams." Shane refastened the shirt and fished a treat out of her pocket.

"Puppies maybe," Lily said watching, "but I can tell you without looking we don't have any openings for adults. Most people want puppies."

"We need more." *Oh god,* Shane thought, *did I just sound like Judy?*

"I could put out another press release," Lily said.

"I'll add it to the volunteer newsletter, if you'd like." Madge offered.

"That'd be great, but there has to be more we can do," Shane had a thought. "How about this, let's announce that we haven't euthanized a dog for space in a year. Explain that we want to continue, but we need their help. We need homes that can foster dogs when we get backed-up. And we need them ASAP. We'll need them on short notice and we'll need them at different times throughout the year."

Damn, who would sign up for that? She wondered. "Hell, let's give them something. Free vaccines for a year if they sign up and foster a dog for say, twenty days. I don't know, think of something."

"I like that," Lily said, jotting down some notes. "Free vaccines for a year," she repeated.

"For one animal," Shane added.

"How much would that cost us?"

"Depends what we want to include. Rabies and the yearly are obvious. They would cost us, maybe ten dollars, combined."

"So could we throw in another vaccine?"

"What, like Bordatella? Feline Leukemia or FIV? Those are a little more. But your right, if we just gave them a choice of one additional, we'd keep it around twenty bucks."

"So we could offer everyone that fosters for at least twenty days, free vaccines for one pet a year?" Lily repeated, her excitement growing.

"If you think about it," Shane said, "it could save us money. It costs us twenty-three dollars every night they're here. I'm happy to give them the free vaccines, plus they'll probably get their other animals done at the same time so we'll make a little money to boot. The vets won't be happy but I'm sick of catering to them, they're going to have to learn to advertise for themselves and build their own clientele."

"It certainly is a great way to show our appreciation to the foster homes," Lily added.

"You're right," Shane smiled, "good, and we could really get some overflow space and not be so stretched in here." She felt a bit of the weight lifting off her shoulders.

Thanking them both she headed back to her office to get an email out to Dee and get her approval. As she got to the foot of the stairs, she found Brenda, the volunteer that loved to transfer dogs, waiting for her in the lobby.

"Shane, I was wondering if I could talk to you?" Brenda, began tentatively. She wasn't a small woman but she had a mousy personality – except when it came to animals. Her passion couldn't be questioned. She had a desire to save as many as possible. Remembering that gave Shane the patience to deal with her.

"What's up?"

She followed Shane into her office. "Shane, I'm sorry to bother you, it's just. It's Los Mochis"

"Oh Brenda," Shane interrupted. "Please don't ask me to bring in more, you can see how full we are."

"I know, I was just wondering if there was somewhere else they could go. I mean do you know any other shelters that have space and could take them? There are so many fantastic animals down there and they're euthanizing constantly. There's just so many."

"I know," Shane signed. "Unfortunately everyone seems to be in the same boat, at least around here."

"Okay but that girl up front is telling people there isn't any more overpopulation. That there are empty shelters back east, if that's true there's got to be a way to get the animals to them."

As the meeting approached the Board had been advertising it more and more. As they did, the number of calls and people with questions about the meeting increased. To handle the questions, and Shane figured to circumvent the staff, Judy brought in a number of woman who stood at the front door, greeted visitors and explained what the change meant to anyone who asked.

"I've heard that too. But we've only transferred within Colorado. It's got to be a logistics nightmare to move the dogs far. It's a couple days drive and to make any kind of impact you'd have to have a lot of dogs which would mean you'd have to have a special truck."

"I heard in Massachusetts they're taking in dogs from Puerto Rico, if they can take dogs from there, you'd think they'd take them from here. Is it just a matter of finding transportation? Do you know anyone I could call? Or are there any foster homes we could maybe put some of them in?"

"Jesus Brenda we're busting at the seams. Listen," Shane said, taking a breath. "I know it's hard. I don't know how you go to those places still so out of balance. I get calls constantly to transport-in more so I know what it's like. But right now I have to look out for what we have here. Some of the ones I'm juggling are transfers-in that haven't moved." Seeing her face Shane offered the only glimmer she could think of. "Dee mentioned Larimer or Longmont may be able to take some and maybe try the shelters in Denver but I think
most of those are full too. Your best bet is to call shelters back east. They're the ones that are supposedly empty. I'm sorry I'm just having a hard enough time trying to figure out what to do with all we have here, I can't help Los Mochis right now. I'm sorry."

~

By the end of the day, through Lily's desperate pleas, they only had three dogs more than they had space for. If the next day was similar they were going to be in trouble, but Shane knew three dogs was workable.

"We could triple a couple up." Jamie volunteered, standing at the front desk with Kim and Shane. It was after six o'clock and everyone else had gone home.

"There's only a couple we could do that with. And it would only open up one kennel," Shane responded.

"We could set up crates for a couple." Jamie tried again.

"For who?" Shane asked. "We'd need someone small enough to spend the night in any that we have."

"We should put down Bowser and Aldo, and you're not gonna like this, but we should do Chance too." Kim looked directly at Shane. "C'mon Shane you know as well as me, that dog's not going to get any better. There's a reason we don't adopt out dogs that act like that, they come back to us. And there's your third kennel."

Jamie looked at Shane, her eyes wide. "We've got time with Bowser and Aldo's fine. Shane you know that."

Shane held up her hand, "Don't worry. I'm not putting anyone down tonight." She hadn't actually considered putting anyone down at all and was as surprised as Jamie at the thought.

"I'll take Bowser home with me tonight," Jamie said, not looking at Kim.

Good idea, Shane thought looking over at her. "I'll take Chance home." She looked back at Kim, "I agree with you, but I'm invested at this point. That just leaves one spot. I'm concerned about putting three in a run. Two is the max to keep everyone healthy and we haven't done it before. No one's gonna be here and god forbid anyone gets sick when we have so many."

An outbreak had been on Shane's mind more and more as the number of animals increased. Up until a week ago both the dogs and cats had been moving pretty fast through the shelter, but adoptions had slowed. Having too many animals and for too long was a recipe for an outbreak. The dogs could break with kennel cough or Parvo and the cats with Upper Respiratory Infections. An outbreak of any kind could be deadly and any would stop adoptions completely.

"Speaking of that," Jamie said, "Cheech is coughing. I heard him this morning. I thought he had just eaten too fast. But he's been doing it on and off all day."

"Great." Shane said, her heart dropping. Coughing was the first sign of kennel cough. As common as a cold in an elementary school, kennel cough was just as contagious. The dogs were inoculated against the annoying virus when they arrived, but some still broke with it - mainly due to stress. Cheech, the Hound from Los Mochis was a perfect candidate.

"Who's he paired up with?" Shane tried to remember. His strong-willed brother, Chong had been fostered out to the local agility club. One of their trainers was a pro with dominant dogs and promised to do what she could with him.

"Duncan."

Shane nodded. "Well that's something." Duncan was a strong, three-year-old Rottie mix who had gotten vaccinated weeks ago. *It could have been worse. But it did mean they needed two spaces now.*

"Okay. Who's in exam?" Shane asked, referring to the room used for behavior assessments.

"Just those two litters of kittens that came in earlier."

"Bring up a large kennel from the back, one of the big wire one's. Cheech is small enough to stay in there for the night. Give him a place to go to the bathroom, as well as a blanket and water."

"Do you want me to give him some Amoxi?" Jamie asked.

Doxycycoline was the drug they used for kennel cough. As an antibiotic it was great, not just for clearing up the cough, but also for alleviating the secondary infection in the lungs they used to be plagued with. Unfortunately it wasn't good for puppies. Amoxicillin was the best they could do.

"Yeah, go ahead."

"We're still one short," Kim reminded Shane.

She nodded. Getting an idea, she pulled the phone book from the drawer. *They may already be closed but, maybe not.* She picked up the phone and dialed the number she'd found.

"Good Afternoon, Paula's Pets."

"Paula, its Shane at Pinewoods." Shane had never called in a favor like this before. The boarding kennel and grooming parlor was only a couple miles away but she didn't know if they had any space. Always needing last minute kennel cough shots for her borders, they had traded favors often, but never this.

"Shane! So great to hear from you. I hear you're doing good things over there."

"Thanks, that's nice of you to say. Paula I'm sorry to bother you so late but I'm wondering if I can call in a favor. We're a little crowded here and I'm wondering if you could spare a kennel for the night?"

"Of course. Do you only need one?"

"Yeah, oh Paula, that's great. Thank you so much." Sighing, Shane felt the tightness in her shoulders ease a bit. "Kim will leave with him now. And I'll be by in the morning to pick him up."

"Thanks for volunteering me." Kim said after Shane hung up the phone.

"Jamie and I are both bringing home dogs." It's just a couple miles down the road. "Track your mileage. Now go, don't make them wait."

"Who am I taking?"

Shane thought quickly, "take Tilly. She's supposed to be out of here tomorrow anyway."

By the time Shane cleaned Tilly's kennel and got the stray Lab set up it was close to eight o'clock. *Another night with less than twelve hours before I have to be back, Damn my kids are gonna be pissed,* Shane thought feeling bad that she couldn't give them the attention they needed. Thank god they loved her nephew Jeremy and he loved them.

Checking on Cheech before she left, Shane put a blanket over the wire kennel, leaving just the front area open. He did sound like he had the familiar deep chested, hacking cough, Shane hoped they caught it in time. She said goodnight to the cute long-eared puppy, grabbed some food for Chance, and went back to get her. Shane wondered how she'd ride in the car...and what her sister was going to say.

Chapter 27

The next few days were a non-stop parade of the same. Each day they ended up with more dogs than they had room for but every night they managed, somehow. Shuffling dogs through the shelter and out to foster had become Shane's primary concern each day. She called in favors, gave away free medical procedures, and signed off on hours of unworked community service all to entice people to foster a dog.

Chance came home with Shane every night and stayed in her office each day. Not having room in the back for her, there wasn't much else she could do. Shane's own dogs were upset. Juice and Henry, the Shepherd/Hound mixes she'd adopted her first year, put up with the way she smelled every day. They tolerated the long days and her occasional need to go straight to bed because of a headache. But they were having a hard time tolerating a dog that got all of her attention.

Since Chance got to go to work with Shane the temporary boarder was on a different playing field than the others, who weren't allowed to go. Luckily the small dog loved Juice and Henry as much as Shane and she'd won both of them over. Her sister also seemed to be tolerating the disruption but Shane knew it was only a matter of time before she'd say something.

"How you doing, Shane?" Dee asked from the doorway.

Shane glanced up from her computer, surprised to see Dee. "Good. Just finishing up the stats from last month." It was ten o'clock on Wednesday morning and she was trying to get all her paperwork done for the upcoming meeting.

Chance wagged her tail from under Jamie's desk. A happy dog, she wagged her tail anytime someone came in the room. Or anytime someone petted her, talked to her or just looked at her. Every time Shane moved, Chance's tail thumped. Sometimes Shane felt like she had her own cheering section. Thump, thump. Thump, thump. Thump, thump.

Dee bent over to pet her, "does she stay up here all the time now with you?"

Uh-oh, Shane thought, *here it goes.* "There's no room in the back. I've been bringing her home at night but she really needs socialization."

"No, no. I think it's great." Dee smiled. "In fact I'd like to commend you on all you've accomplished. I know this has been a difficult time."

"You could say that." Shane said, thinking what an understatement it was. Things had gotten a little better with Judy gone, but Dee had also been M.I.A. a lot of the time. Shane felt like her and her staff had been left to bail out the boat. "Judy hasn't been around, that's helped."

After weeks of Judy micromanaging everything from what kind of toilet paper they were ordering to what cats were being put to sleep, she suddenly announced she had everything she needed and would see them at the meeting. Her abrupt departure didn't change much at the shelter. Leaving behind the six women that worked the door, Judy stayed apprised of everything going on.

Keeping to themselves, the women took shifts standing at the shelter's entrance. They greeted visitors, asked them if they were aware of the upcoming vote and offered literature on the benefits no-kill. Though polite, they rarely interacted with the staff. Judy had taken over the upstairs kitchen before she left and now they used it as their staging area.

Shane desperately wanted to ask Dee what was going on, but she had made it clear she didn't want to talk about it. For weeks Dee had been pulling away. At first Shane thought it was something she'd done, but then she heard Dee's words in her head, *"I'll never work for an organization that calls itself no-kill." If Dee was thinking about leaving, it made sense that she'd pull away and try to protect herself from the pain.*

"Kinsey tells me," Dee said, still petting the happy dog under the desk, "we've got dogs fostered at almost all the area kennels and at two of the day cares. Congratulations Shane, I don't think that's ever been done before."

"And we have one at Cherry Creek." Shane said proudly. Of all the vets in town Cherry Creek was the one that would come back to them the fastest, but it had still taken a lot to get them to agree.

"Wow," Dee exclaimed, "how did you manage that?"

"I went to lunch with Dr Martinez," Shane said referring to the lunch she had with Cherry Creek's head veterinarian. Shane hoped it marked the beginning-of-the-end to the cold shoulder they'd been receiving from the veterinary community. Since the shelter had opened up the low-cost medical clinic the local Veterinarians had formed a coalition, threatened to pull their cremation business, and bad-mouthed the shelter at every opportunity.

"It seems to me that if a Veterinarian came into the area and opened up a low-cost clinic you'd be upset," Shane said to Dr. Martinez after their food arrived, "but after a couple of years you'd chill and treat them like everybody else. Why can't you do that with us?"

"Shane you have to understand our point of view," Dr. Martinez said. "You're opening a government funded clinic in our area. Why shouldn't we be upset about that? It's not a level playing field any longer."

"Why would you think the clinic is government funded?" Shane asked, surprised.

"You're non-profit and you've got contracts with both the city and county, of course it's government funded."

"Dr. Martinez, you're wrong. The clinic is completely funded with grants, donations and the profits it makes. We do have contracts with the city and county but that only covers the cost to hold stray and impounded animals their first three or five days. And technically they don't even fund the whole cost of that. They certainly don't pay for the clinic."

"Don't you think the people who donate to you want their money going to homeless animals and not to pay the medical bills for people who can't afford their own pets' care?"

"I think they entrust their money to us because they want us to look out for the best interest of the animal – no matter what the owners like or their resources. You tell people that if they can't afford your $2,000 procedure they should euthanize their pet. Right?"

"We are a business Shane," Dr. Martinez responded. "I employee sixteen people, I need to make money to pay their salaries."

"It's just kinda funny if you think about it." Shane said, deciding to share a thought she'd had, "if a person comes to you and can't afford your $2,000 procedure you recommend euthanasia, or surrendering the dog. We on the other hand put the value of that animal's life above money. Our goal is to keep that relationship, that bond intact, so we look for or provide an affordable alternative. But yet we're the ones always being blamed for high euthanasia rates. Weird, huh?" Shane shook her head.

"You could have stayed with the voucher program. That was working." Dr. Martinez said referring to the grant-funded voucher system the Animal Shelter used before opening the clinic.

"You're the reason we had the stop the vouchers," Shane said. "Our grant funding was not going up as fast as your rates and all of a sudden we were only doing half the number of animals for the same amount of money. We were going to lose the grants. We needed a low-cost option and you refused to provide it. So we opened the clinic. Do you know that we do double the number of surgeries in that clinic in a year than we ever did through the voucher systems? And it only took eighteen months for us to start seeing a difference in intakes numbers. We never saw a drop through the voucher program."

"Let's face it," Shane continued, "by only offering minimal services we can perform spay and neuter surgeries faster and cheaper. Especially since we have a vested interest in having them done. And when people come to us to tell us they need to surrender their seven year old dog because they can't afford to get the porcupine quills removed from his face, would you really have us take their dog from them? If you weren't a Veterinarian would you really want us to take someone's dog because they can't afford a simple procedure?"

"Shane you know as well as I do that pet ownership costs money. If people don't have the money to care for their animal, they shouldn't have one. We aren't asking more than fair market price. These calls are typically in the evenings or on the weekends, shouldn't we get compensated for being on call and having to come out during our off time?"

"Of course. But fair market price to you is a mortgage payment to the pet owner. What kind of Animal Shelter would we be if we separated someone from their pet instead of pulling porcupine quills? I'm proud that we have a shelter that puts peoples relationship with their pets above all else. It's important. Animals are not disposable or interchangeable. What's so wrong with that? Do you really think we'll take that many of your clientele?"

"That's not what I'm worried about. Giving away things free and lowering the prices like you have devalues the entire profession."

"Do you really believe that?" Shane asked. "Does having a flu clinic in Wal-Mart lower a Doctor's value? You're a Veterinarian, you're so much more than vaccines and spay and neuter surgeries. You diagnose, treat, understand drug interactions and breed idiosyncrasies, you deal successfully with the public and you run a business. How could we, the Animal Shelter, possibly undervalue all that you do? We're not trying to replace you, by any means. But I need animals altered and people aren't going to do that when you're charging them $300 or more for the procedure."

The dispute between the Veterinarians and the Shelter weighed heavily on Shane. No matter how good the shelter was doing, they could never get full community support with the vets bad-mouthing them. The shelter had never set out to have a clinic and many on the Board had actively fought against it - which was the reason they still only offered limited services. But Loma Bonita was a small town, there weren't many options for pet owners. As the community Animal Shelter they couldn't ignore animals being surrendered to them because their owners couldn't afford routine procedures. And they certainly couldn't keep mopping up the excess puppies and kittens every summer without providing the surgery to prevent them, at an affordable price.

"That's really great Shane" Dee said. "Seriously, well done."

"Thanks, if only we could do the same for the cats."

"Why can't you?"

"We're not even close to balancing out on cats, you know that. Even if I find fifty more foster homes I'd still have to put some down."

"Not as many," Dee said.

"No, not as many," Shane agreed.

"It'd be a start. And at least a little hope for the really good ones." Dee turned and headed out.

~

Two hours later Shane listened as Kinsey talked with a woman on the phone.

"I'm sorry ma'am," Shane heard Kinsey say for the third time. "We don't adopt out cats if they're going to be declawed. I understand, I wish you luck with that." She hung up the phone with a heavy sigh.

With Dee's comments still circling in her head Shane decided to ask Kinsey something she'd been wondering. Aware of everything going on, Kinsey was in a unique position and could always be counted on to be brutally honest.

"Do you agree with that?" Shane asked from the doorway.

"What declawing?" Kinsey asked, turning toward her.

"Us not adopting out if they're going to declaw them," Shane clarified.

"No. I don't, since you're asking. I mean, I don't believe in declawing, of course. But I also don't think we're in any position to deny an adoption. I mean, look at us," she gestured toward the three large free standing kennels they had rolled out into the lobby a few weeks before. Holding twelve kitten's they were a non-stop hub of activity. "We're overflowing with cats. If someone wants to declaw them, it's not the end of the world."

"Why haven't you said anything before now?" Shane asked, surprised by her strong feelings.

"No one's asked. The policy's been in place forever, I just figured it was a mandate from the Board. But I have thought about it. We could write up an information sheet on what the procedure includes and the side effects. That way we're giving them the information, but the choice is theirs."

"And no qualms if they have them declawed."

"What are we going to do Shane? Beggars can't be choosers and right now we're beggars. I'm pushing a second cat on every adopter. I can't pay people to take them. How can we justify such high standards when we're dealing with such an overload?"

Kinsey hesitated then continued, "You know, we changed the adoption applications, what six, seven months ago? We took out all that unnecessary stuff like how much did the potential adopter make, home visits and all that because we don't need it anymore. People have changed, Shane. And look at how good that's worked out. I'm just saying if we're going to change with the times, we should look at all our policies and not just some of the obvious one's like more lenient adoption procedures."

"Thanks," Shane said turning back toward her office. She couldn't believe it. She had never thought twice about declawing cats.

Considered inhumane in other countries, declawing was a painful procedure with a long recovery period. It involved amputating the last joint of the cats' toes which stopped them from clawing the furniture, but also from being able to scratch any itch they had or use the litter box easily. Shane knew most Veterinarians said it didn't change a cat's behavior, but since so many declawed cats were turned into the shelter for not using their litter boxes, it made her wonder if they were actually right.

~

"Shane, I'm sorry to bother you." Kinsey stuck her head in the office a few minutes later. "No one's answering in the kennel and I have a cat in a trap up here. It's the woman's trap."

Shane nodded. If they had brought the cat in one of the traps the shelter rented out, they could just switch them for a clean one. Cats that had to be trapped were feral, or close to it. It was better to let them relax for a bit before trying to move them. But when the trap was theirs it needed to be emptied immediately. Sighing, Shane stood. These were never fun.

"Page Laura to the back, would you?" She asked Kinsey, taking the trap and walking it through her office. The metal trap was close to three feet long, rectangular and difficult to hold steady. The contraption was a sure-fire way to catch a cat or small raccoon. The spring-release door was triggered when the cat stepped on a small foot pedal. Cheap, smelly cat food or tuna fish was the best to lure the animals into it and Shane could hear an empty can banging around under the debris.

A torn up towel, dried leaves and hunks of dirt were in the trap along with the cat. She tried to hold it level to avoid leaving a trail as she walked. The cat, already pissed off, flipped around in a desperate attempt to free himself. *This is going to be a tough one,* Shane tried to steady the awkward device. Grabbing a towel from her office, Shane covered the end of the trap to give the cat a hiding place.

The cat flipped over and over as she walked through the kennels and into the holding area. By the time she set the trap down, he was panting and had broken a tooth. *Jesus,* Shane thought, *he looked like a feline imitation of Cujo.*

"You looking for me?" Laura asked, coming in through the euthanasia room. "Oh baby, what happened to you?" She asked looking at the skinny, brown tabby who was now bleeding.

"Most feral cats don't live to be this old," Shane said, looking at his matted, greasy hair and the scars across his nose. He was panting and foaming at the mouth. "Yeah, this guy just came in. The woman needs her trap back."

Laura hadn't taken her eyes off the possessed looking cat. "Can't talk her out of it, huh?"

"I wish," Shane said surveying their options. There wasn't an open kennel, and even if there was, they wouldn't be doing him any favors. Feral cats hated being in the shelter. Spending the mandatory three days for them was like spending a lifetime in hell.

Stressed out the entire time, feral cats didn't eat and typically never came out from under their towels. Hissing, spitting and growling, they changed the mood in the holding area and stressed the domestic cats out. It broke Shane's heart to see them so upset and she usually euthanized them before the mandatory holding period was up.

"What are we going to do with him?" Laura asked.

After a minute Shane decided, "We're just going to euthanize him in the trap, no reason to stress him out twice. And we don't have any place for him anyway."

Grabbing a second towel, Shane covered the trap completely and walked it into the euthanasia room. Setting it on the table she turned and grabbed the pole used to inject the cats they couldn't touch. The small dowel acted as a syringe stopper. Shane unlocked the controlled substance cabinet and withdrew the barbiturate. Not able to hit a vein, and sometimes not even a muscle, Shane went heavier than normal on the dosage, just to be sure.

"So, can I ask?" Laura began, "do they know we're euthanizing him? I mean is that why they brought him here?"

"I assume so."

"Okay but I know people that won't use exterminators or pest services because they kill animals. So do we really know they want him euthanized?"

"I can't say I've ever asked any of them, to be honest with you. They want the problem gone. When I first started working up front I'd ask them if we could alter them and bring them back, TNR stuff, but no one wanted it, said it was too much of a problem they wanted them gone."

"Hold the trap," She told Laura as she lined up the needle. Slipping it through the small openings she guided it toward the cat's rear leg. Just as it was about to go through his skin, he jumped. Flipping twice, he ended up on Shane's side of the cage, on top of the wooden pole. Pulling it back, she saw that the syringe was still full but the needle had been bent in half. "Shit."

"Keep the towel on it this time," Shane instructed Laura. The young girl had jumped when the cat jumped but regained her composure and stopped the trap from falling off the table. Shane removed the bent needle and replaced it with a new one. Hoping to have better luck, she tried again.

Shane slipped the needle through the small square openings of the trap and directly into the cat's rear leg. She pushed, but the needle wouldn't go through his tough skin. "Shit," She said, seeing it had bent the needle again.

"Third time's a charm," Shane said wiping a sleeve across her sweaty forehead. She replaced the bent needle with a thicker one and tried again. "God damn it," she swore when the cat did another loop-d-loo, landing with the needle still in him but disconnected from the syringe. The solution was all over the cat, the trap and the table. She thought she got some in him, but didn't know how much.

"Okay, enough of this," Shane said turning on the cold water and splashing it across her soaked face. Grabbing the cat gloves, Shane hoped they wouldn't need to use them. She had one more option. She filled another syringe and capped it with a large eighteen-gauge needle. Pulling the trap off the table, she tipped it on its end, so it stood upright. The cat, in a ball at the bottom was an easy target. "Here, hold these," Shane handed Laura the gloves and knelt down.

Holding the trap against the corner walls she thought she'd be able to do it this time. Inserting the needle, she held the pole close to the trap, hoping the added support would help. The cat turned towards Shane and reached out. His nail dug into her middle finger at the knuckle. Not moving, the cat sat looking at her, his nail slowly sinking deeper into her skin.

Shane continued holding the syringe with one hand and applying pressure with the other. Not having injected all the fluid, there was no way she was going to stop. "Son-of-a-bitch," she said through clenched teeth.

His nail dug its way deeper into her finger. Shane tried to avoid looking in his eyes and kept her focus on the needle. Just as she got the last of the fluid in, the cat jumped with one last burst of adrenaline and flipped over. His nail tore through Shane's finger, splitting it wide open from the knuckle to her nail.

Laura picked the trap up and carried it to the table as Shane walked over to the sink.

Holding her hand to try and catch as much of the blood as possible, Shane wondered if this was the universe's idea of karma.

"Are you okay?" Laura asked as she bagged the cat and emptied the rest of the debris out of the trap.

"Yeah, fine," Shane said holding her hand under the cold water. The water stung, but after seeing how dirty the cat's nails were she knew she needed to flush it out as much as possible. After a minute she dried it and wrapped a paper towel around it. Already stiff from the cold water, Shane knew she was going to have a problem bending it tomorrow.

Laura brought the trap and held it over the sink. Shane sprayed it down as best she could.

"He sure had a will to live," Laura commented before leaving with the trap.

That was a sucky way to look at it, Shane thought noting the additional drug she used and why. Shane checked to be sure the book was staying on track again and closed it up. *Poor thing, coming in here was a death sentence for any feral or even semi-feral cat. God that sucks,* Shane thought. Never realizing before that it was true – and that they were made to carry it out.

It didn't seem right. They were a shelter for companion animals. Feral cats, real feral cats, would never be companion animals. Why should we take them in just to kill them? Shane's finger had bled through the paper towel. She removed it and ran her finger under more cold water.

It was starting to throb but she knew the infection would hurt ten times worse. Bending it a couple of times, she tried to get water into the side areas. *Could we stop taking feral cats? There was a decent TNR programs in town, could we push them there?*

TNR, short for Trap-Neuter-Return was the method of trapping feral or stray cats, neutering them, and returning them back to their environment. The cats were also given a thorough medical exam, received their vaccines, got their ears cleaned and typically had any major dental problems addressed.

Unfortunately, most of the people that brought them feral cats, didn't want them back. Neutered or not they were sick of them harassing their own cats, going to the bathroom in their gardens, or killing the local bird population. *Still,* Shane thought, *they had the medical area, maybe they could give the TNR program free services if they agreed to take all the feral cats off their hands.*

They may not be able to handle thirty at a time, but they should be able to do the one-off's. She sprayed peroxide on her finger then shook it to try and avoid as much of the burning as she could. *There had to be a way,* she thought, hoping the answer would shake off the crappy feeling she'd had since carrying the cat back. Locking the drug cupboard, Shane headed back up front.

Chapter 28

Two hours later Lily, Kinsey, Dee and Shane were sitting in Shane's office. Shane sat on the floor with Chance in her lap, while they discussed possible options for the excess cats they had. Additional foster homes weren't coming available and they were beyond capacity. "We could have another Adopt-a-thon," Shane volunteered.

"Good idea, how quickly can you make it happen?" Dee asked.

"How quickly do you want it?" Shane said then added, "Well to get enough people here to make it worthwhile, we'd need about two weeks. And with the holiday, let's say three." The fourth of July was just around the corner, unfortunately it was one of the shelter's slowest holidays.

"Okay three weeks, what do we do between now and then?" Dee looked at each of them, "If we don't get any more cats in we'd still be overwhelmed, considering how many are coming back from foster in the next two weeks. Not to mention we have two pregnant cats that are going to give birth any day,"

"One," Shane said. "The Tortie had hers last night."

"One," Dee corrected herself. "But we know that's not the reality. We're going to get more and more kittens in over the next few weeks. We need ideas. What else?"

An uncomfortable silence followed. Shane focused on Chance, sitting in her lap. Her creative juices seemed spent on dogs.

"What about with senior citizens?" Lily asked.

"What about them?"

"Well what about a program specifically tailored to seniors? If we find out which of the senior housing allows pets, we could target a campaign directly to them."

"Good idea. Do it. What else?"

"What about the nursing homes?" Kinsey asked.

When no one responded she continued. "I'm in Spruce Hill Senior Center all the time. Paul's mom is there."

"Don't animals already live there?" Shane asked. Volunteers brought shelter dogs to visit the patients on the weekends. Shane knew of a terrier mix and two cats that lived at the home.

"Yeah, one dog and two cats, but I'm thinking something different." Kinsey paused for a minute then continued. "I don't know about you but I could watch kittens for hours. And I see people doing it here. Parents will park their kids in the window of the cat room and if the kittens are up and playing, the kids don't move."

"What are you thinking?" Dee asked, petting June who was making biscuits in her lap.

"Well I was thinking if we got the okay from a couple of the nursing homes and Mitchell could build us a couple of enclosures, we could foster a mom and a litter right in their day rooms. The seniors sit around all day. This way they'd have something to watch. Think about it. They'd love it."

"I'm sure we could get a volunteer to check in on them every day," Shane offered, thinking it was a great idea.

"I like it," Dee said. "Kinsey call around and see who's open to it. I'll check into any insurance issues."

"Mitchell wouldn't have to build anything," Shane said. "We could just buy a couple more of those tall catteries and place them there."

"True," Dee agreed.

"We might be able to do the same thing in the schools." Shane said petting Chances belly. "I mean a lot of them have animals in their classrooms already, so why not a kennel full of kittens."

"Could you imagine the distraction?" Dee said, smiling.

"Yeah, I guess, but I bet there could be a way. And after all it's only for a week or so, when we're over loaded. They wouldn't stay there that long, depending on their age." Needing to be on the adoption floor before they turned twelve weeks old, the kittens would only be in the classrooms for a short time.

"I like it. Check into it, would you Shane?" Dee said, pushing the door to the front desk closed. "Listen, there's something else I'd like to talk with you all about."

Kinsey glanced at Shane who shrugged her shoulders in response.

"It's Kim. I checked with the clinic. She hasn't gone to an appointment in three months. She's left to go to her appointments, and says she's gone, but she hasn't."

Dee paused, but no one spoke.

"I know I don't have to say this to any of you, but for the record, what's said in this room, stays in this room." She looked at each of them, waited until they agreed, then continued. "I'm concerned we have a serious problem here. I'd like to know what you've seen or anything you've heard."

After a minute Shane volunteered to everyone what Dee already knew. "Well, she's way behind. Two weeks in a row now there's been piles of bones in back, waiting to be processed."

"Her temper's also worse than ever," Kinsey added. "Every time she's behind that desk she gets in a fight with someone. She's always been bad, but never this bad."

"Yeah she's definitely got a screw-it attitude," Shane agreed. "She doesn't seem to care about anything, lately."

"I believe she has P.T.S.D.," Dee said.

Everyone was quiet, waiting.

"Looking back," Dee continued, "I think it started with the hoarding house in Montrose. She took it hard. Harder than any of us and I'd even say harder than anyone who quit afterwards. Then I found out she and Walter split six months later. Shortly after, she stopped going to counseling and disconnected from us, even more than usual."

"Dee," said Lily, "I'm sorry I'm not aware of the symptoms of PTSD. Are the things you mention indicative of the disorder?"

"They can be. And of course I'm only guessing here. But think about it. Kim has always been hyper sensitive to the deaths, ever since I've known her. Then two years ago, we stood in the freezing cold and euthanized one animal after another? I think it affected her more than us. I think she's reliving it over and over and feeling guilty for what happened.

"I think you're right," Shane agreed, "but I think it's considered Compassion Fatigue in Animal Shelters, same as what nurses and doctors get. Not that it matters."

"What's the difference?" Lily asked.

"I'm not 100% sure, but I think PTSD is the result of one traumatic situation. Compassion Fatigue is due to a number of situations compounded. It's really common with nurses and people in the social work type situations."

"And that's what you think she has?" Lily looked from Dee to Shane.

"Think about it, her obsessiveness about how the animals are placed in the freezer, her avoidance of the remains, her attitude to everyone at the front desk," Dee paused before continuing, "it seems like it's building to me. I'm worried about her."

"What do we do about it?" Shane asked.

"Well removing her from all activities associated with euthanasia and cremations is a must. Which I think you've already done." Dee said, looking at Shane. "I'll check into the appropriate steps, but I think we've all got to be much more sensitive. I realize she can be difficult to deal with. And I also realize she has no filter and says anything that comes to her mind, which can be troublesome," she smiled at Kinsey. "But I think we need to really try to put ourselves in her shoes."

"She has been a euthanasia technician for fifteen years," Dee gestured to her paperwork, "I looked back through her file, every time she's had an incident, it's been after a significant case - and she's been on all of them. I'm talking about ones before my time and one's that are worse than any we've had to endure."

"I don't know about you," Dee continued, "I know it took me months to get over that house in Montrose. And I don't know how I would have done that without a support system at home. You all know what that one was like. If Kim is replaying it over and over again in her head and dwelling on it, I can't imagine the place she's in."

"Oh the poor girl," Lily said as a knock sounded on the door.

"Excuse me," Laura whispered. "Shane, I'm sorry I have a problem. We don't have any place to put this dog that just came in."

Chapter 29

Two days before the general meeting the shelter was a non-stop flurry of activity. Quarter page ads had run daily in the paper and the phone rang nonstop. People were in looking at the animals, asking questions about the meeting and trying to understand what the change meant.

Judy's followers were in every day handing out fliers and encouraging people to attend. At first Shane didn't know what to make of them, but keeping mainly to the front doors they ended up handling the people that wanted information about the upcoming change, which actually helped. Unfortunately the increased traffic hadn't yet resulted in enough adoptions.

Shane was headed up to Dee's office hoping to get a little inspiration. Last night she made the decision to put Aldo in a crate. They were overflowing, again. And she didn't have an alternative. But it wasn't an acceptable solution. She couldn't sleep all night, she was so worried about him. She'd come in two hours early that morning just to let him out.

It wasn't that he didn't have room, but to be locked in for twelve hours, the first time he'd ever been put in a crate, was more than she was comfortable with. Shane hoped Dee had some good ideas. She'd been so distant lately. Shane didn't understand what was going on or what if anything she could do about it. She knew it was about the meeting but it seemed like there was more going on than she was aware of.

"Hi Shane," Dee said from behind her computer just as she was about to knock.

"Uh, do you have a minute?"

"Of course, what's up?" Setting her glasses down on her desk, Dee looked like she had been deep into something, even this early.

"I'm sorry to bother you," Shane began, "its dogs. I've run out of creative solutions. I had to put Aldo in a crate last night, not to mention the fifteen we have scattered around town, at boarding kennels." Shane took a sip of her coffee, hoping it would give her the burst of energy she needed. She'd felt run down lately and wondered if this was what thirty-six years old was supposed to feel like.

Dee sat for a moment, nodding slightly, "What are you thinking?"

"That we're screwed. We just can't seem to get ahead. I refuse to put a healthy dog down but what am I supposed to do? And there's a couple that need something done ASAP, like Heidi."

Dee's expression showed her sympathy. Heidi had been there for months, too many months. A great dog when she came in, for some reason she didn't get adopted. Now she was bouncing like mad. The weekly runs Brett had organized didn't seem to be enough of an outlet for her energy. She'd be a horrible one to put down though, the staff and volunteers all loved her and Brett had really gotten attached.

"Let's go through what you have." Dee pulled out a pad of paper, made columns then wrote at the top of each; Dog I Breed I Color I Sex I Age I Time In and handed it to Shane. "Write down every dog you have, include everyone in foster and in holding, every dog we're responsible for. Oh and note if the animal isn't on the premises. Throw it in an excel file so we can work with it and send it to me."

It took Shane two hours but she finally had them all; forty adults on the floor, eighteen puppies on the floor, twenty-two in Holding, three in Iso, one in exam, Chance, Snickers, fifteen fostered in businesses throughout community, and thirty-seven fostered in homes in the community. One-hundred-and-thirty-eight, *ohmigod*, she thought looking at the list. *One-hundred-thirty-eight dogs in their care, when did it get so out of control?* She ran her hands through her hair before hitting the send button and calling Dee.

Back upstairs in Dee's office, Dee highlighted the spreadsheet and lined it up to show only the dogs on the adoption floor by how long they had been there.

"Look at this," Dee pointed to the row with the heading Time In. The column started with Snickers, Heidi and Bowser 271 days, 238 days and 202 days respectfully, then it took a sharp decline to fifty-seven days. It continued decreasing and didn't level off until they were under thirty days.

"The majority of the dogs on the adoption floor have been here less than a month."

Shane nodded, there were a couple of exceptions, but Dee was right, only a handful had been there a long time. *At least that was something.*

Highlighting the sheet again, Dee re-sorted the material by breed and color. "Nothing surprising here," Dee said. "Mostly Shepherd mixes. Huh, I think you have more black and tans than black dogs for a change." She scrolled down further. "Look at this, none of the dogs out in foster are Shepherd mixes."

"Impossible," Shane leaned forward for a closer look. Dee was right, Aussie/Lab mixes, Hound mixes, even a couple Boxer/Rotties but no Shepherd mixes. "Amazing."

"Ah, here's our problem," Dee said, re-sorting the data again, this time lining up the list of dogs by age. "Look at this. If you take the puppies out of the mix, we've got a glut of older dogs. Look, these ones are less than four-years-old, and half of those are out in foster.

Lining up all the dogs by age, Shane could easily see that over half of the remaining dogs were over four years old.

"Shane, let's do this." Dee said leaning away from the computer. She grabbed another sheet of paper, "we have forty spots on the adoption floor, right?" She drew a quick grid of the kennel. "Of that, how many should be good, adoptable dogs?"

"Like puppies or bullet-proof dogs?" Shane asked. Bullet-proof was the term they used for a dog that could deal with anything. Golden's and Labs were often bullet-proof, allowing the novice owners to screw up their training and kids to do virtually anything they wanted with them.

"Yeah, but I'd say we count puppies separate," Dee said. "At least those young enough to stay in the end pens. What are the stats? It's been a long time since I looked," Dee asked, referring to the industry research on what animals got adopted the quickest.

"The younger they are the more adoptable. Three years is the top, after that the adoptions drop right off. "

"Alright, let's do this. Let's classify the dogs, for example any that are four months to four years and bullet-proof are Adoptable A. Puppies are Adoptable B. Seniors Adoptable C and those with issues Adoptable D. I guess it's not politically correct, but." She paused then shook her head and continued. "Then let's decide how many of the forty spaces we want to dedicate to each class. Obviously the majority need to go to Adoptable A."

Dee continued, "You know as well as I, without having these dogs turning quickly people won't keep coming in and no one will get adopted. By creating a formula, you'll be able to have a better grasp of what's here, and who should come back from foster or be transferred in."

Shane had been trying to envision what she was talking about and finally got it. She could draw a picture of the kennels and color code them for the different types of dog. She'd need at least two spots for transfers and two for seniors but she could also set up a couple spots for those dogs over four but not yet seniors. Her heart began to race, this could help, she thought letting out her breath.

"The second thing," Dee continued, "is what do we do with all that you have now? We have way too many. The foster network you have set up will only last so long, especially with the upcoming holiday. Plus, it's too stressful for you and for the dogs. People are going to start burning out. You're going to burn out. When was the last time you had a day off?

Shane shrugged, "it's been a while."

"I thought so," Dee said nodding. "Let me make some calls. I told you about my conversation with the Director of Larimer at the last conference. Maybe they can take some off our hands, Boulder and Longmont too. The only thing we can control is transfers so let's not transfer any in for the time being, until we get a handle on this."

"What about the one's here," Shane asked, "the one's that haven't moved? We've done so good over the last year, I don't want to start euthanizing for space now, but pretty soon we're going to have them living in kennels all over the building."

"Shane, it seems to me you have a couple of choices, but they all start with the same thing. Evaluating each dog individually. For example, Bowser, he's been here forever what's up with him?"

"He's a great dog, Shepherd mix of course, big and mostly black, he's just aloof. He spent most of his life outside and doesn't like being in a house." Shane continued with the remaining long-termers, "Snickers, let's just assume he's staying here. Aldo is a dog for a hunter. He wants to do a job and he'd be good at it. And Onyx is just bored. She needs a home that will play Frisbee with her or really run her."

"So back to Bowser," Dee said, "he sounds like a perfect dog for a mechanic, maybe guarding someone's shop. What about doing fliers up just for him and bringing them around to the local garages? Same thing for Aldo and Onyx. We don't get many hunters or agility people through the shelter so why not bring the dogs to them?"

"I like it," Shane said, nodding and feeling her stomach unclench. "Be a little more proactive, it sounds great." Fifteen minutes later they had a plan for every dog, except Heidi and Snickers.

"Have you considered doing another behavior eval on some of the long-termers?" Dee asked. "Those that have been here a while may have changed. It would show us where we need to focus."

"That's a good idea," Shane nodded, debating if she should say what she'd been thinking, then decided to plow right in.

"Dee, can I ask you a question? I mean if you don't mind." Shane didn't wait for her to respond. "I've been working on a lot of grants lately. And it seems like there's organizations that call themselves no-kill but that still have government contracts, so they can't be limited admission. If there really is more grant money to be had, and we didn't have to become limited admission, what difference would going no-kill make? We could certainly use the money."

"You're right we could, but I can't get behind an organization that calls itself no-kill," Dee replied, sitting up straighter. "First of all it's inaccurate second, it leads to long-term incarceration for animals, and third – the law of attraction. I would never say the word "kill" every day, putting the word "no" in front of it doesn't change the power it has or the energy it attracts."

Dee continued, "Animal Shelters aren't about killing, it has never been about killing. Medical laboratories, veterinary hospitals, shoot even cosmetic companies have all gone to less or no killing over the last fifteen to twenty years, just like Animal Shelters, but you don't see any of them putting it in their names. It's short-sighted. It's stupid to draw attention to an old strategy - especially one we're vilified for. This is a kinder and gentler country, our language is getting softer, not harsher."

"You know if there really was such a place as an animal sanctuary," Dee continued, "where the animals could have all the freedom and affection they desired and deserved, then of course no one would ever be put to sleep. But there's no such place. Locking dogs and cats up isn't the answer. I'm a believer in quality over quantity. And if that means I have to carry the burden of taking animals lives, so be it. I've seen how bad it is for those forced to live on the streets, euthanasia is a blessing to many."

"Shane, we'll be debating the quality of life over quantity of life argument forever. I hate seeing dogs go kennel crazy or cats withdraw completely. It very disheartening," Dee sighed. "And it's what happens in so many in no-kill organizations. When they first start, their adoptions are great because they have a lot of adoptable dogs. Then they have a Heidi, a Dalton or a Hogg who don't move quickly. A short time goes by and they get another Heidi, Dalton or Hogg, then another. In a year they have a kennel full of hard-to-adopt or outright unadoptable dogs. People stop coming in because it's always the same animals, all of which need a lot of work. The animals don't get better since they're forced to live in the very environment that caused the issue in the first place. It is not a winning formula."

"So why's it so popular?" Shane asked, frustrated. It would be so much easier if the new no-kill policy helped them.

"I don't know. Maybe it seems cool to say "I only support no-kill." Perhaps people are trying to send a message; they support Animal Shelters but don't support euthanasia for population control. It's one of the only slogan's that's popular. It's not exact, but it was never meant to be a philosophy, just a rally cry."

"Shane, I'm actually glad you came up today." Dee said, abruptly changing the subject. "There's something I wanted to talk to you about."

The change in Dee's tone made Shane sit up straighter.

"You know I think the world of you, Shane. You've done remarkable things through tremendous obstacles and I want to be sure you know that. No matter what happens over the next couple of days, you need to know that you've really done great over the last year, and it's been noticed."

"Thank you," the relief Shane felt a minute ago was gone. "I appreciate it. What's going to happen? Oh shit," she said, finally realizing what Dee meant, "you're leaving? Aren't you?"

"I have no idea what's going to happen, to tell you the truth. I haven't been privy to any of the recent discussions or decisions. But that alone says volumes. The fact that they would reorganize an Animal Shelter without speaking with the Executive Director doesn't bode well for my job. And it's no secret how I feel about the changeover."

Shane didn't know what to say. She had tried not thinking about the meeting or what it would mean, she had enough to keep her busy lately, but now with it so close and with this, Shane was at a loss. She loved her job and though there were times that it sucked more than anything she'd ever done in life, she couldn't imagine doing anything else. She'd made some serious changes around that place and didn't want to stop now. Life was better for the animals, a lot better. "Should I be worried?"

"We all should be. Now get out of here and let me call Larimer and see if I can move some of these dogs."

Heading back downstairs with a plan for the dogs, Shane should have felt better than ever. But she didn't. Seeing Dee so dejected, so defeated scared the shit out of her. *She'd always been a rock, always a glass-is-half-full kind of person.* Dee had gotten Shane through some pretty tough times. *Could I do it without her? Do I want to?*

If they're getting rid of Dee they're definitely getting rid of me, Shane realized. *Unbelievable, I haven't had a life in weeks because of this place. I haven't gone to one of Jeremy's games, hiked my dogs, or even had a day off, and they're going to fire me.* She couldn't believe it.

The front desk was a mad house. *Good,* Shane thought, hoping some of them were adoptions. By the time she talked to Kinsey, Jamie and Laura about their plans it was after lunch.

"I don't understand, are you putting Bowser down?" Jamie asked.

"No, but we're going to make up fliers just for him and bring them around to mechanics and garages and see if anyone there is interested."

"Shit, why don't you just bring him with you? He'll sell himself, he's a handsome, solid dog." Jamie said, obviously relieved.

"You're right, great idea." Shane told them about doing the same things for Aldo and Onyx and asked if they had any connections.

"I know a woman in the agility club. They have a mailing list, I'll email her." Kinsey said. "Can we make up a video of her playing Frisbee?"

"Of course, get Mary on it."

"And let's see if one of the outdoor stores will let Aldo come stay at their place a couple of days a week. I think the best place to find hunters is in Wal-Mart probably, but that doesn't mean some don't come into the tourists shops when they need something."

"Still, it's a good point, Kinsey said. "I wonder if we can post a flier up in that section of Wal-Mart."

"We already have a board in where the pet food is, but if we can put something in the hunting section, that'd be great. What about the fishing shops?" Shane asked.

"What about them?"

"Well obviously still touristy more than anything but I bet a lot of hunters also fish, wouldn't you think?"

"Sure," they agreed. Shane asked them both to think long and hard about Heidi and come up with some options. With a plan in place Shane thought they may find a way through this after all.

The general meeting was two days away. If they were going to fire her, Shane wanted to have the place in the best shape possible before it happened. She picked up the phone to call some of the neighboring shelters.

Chapter 30

"Shane, you're putting down Bowser. You can't." Betty, the long-time volunteer walked into Shane's office. "You can't," she continued shaking her head. "I'll make some calls, I'll get him out of here."

"Who told you I was putting down Bowser?" Shane asked, erasing the line she just wrote. She was trying to find a way to differentiate the dogs that were over four years old but not yet seniors. The term "adults" was too general to use since they used that for most dogs over six months. "Adolescence" was more appropriate for those under two years but it was a mouthful. So far, she had 30-something's and mid-lifer's on the page in front of her. But she wasn't thrilled with either.

"Uh, um I don't know, I heard it in back."

Rolling her eyes, Shane looked up, "gossip, really Betty?"

"Well it's not like it's inconceivable. He's been here forever. No one's looking at him and it's no secret that we're seriously full."

"Yeah, but he's a good dog. He's not having any issues staying here."

"I think he prefers it," Betty agreed.

"Exactly, that's why we're going to bring him around town. He's a guy's dog and a big burly mechanic, might be the perfect home for him."

"Oh Shane, I'm so happy to hear you say that. I was talking to Jackie and we just couldn't believe you'd put him down. I feel so much better. Thank you, Shane." She turned to leave.

"Betty if you know anyone that might be interested in him or anyone else, don't wait until we get to that point, please. Have them come in here now."

"Oh, of course, of course."

What the hell? Shane thought, *if she knows someone who could adopt him, what is she waiting for?* She didn't think Betty got what she said but she was grateful it didn't turn out to be a big drama. Shane looked back down at her paper and crossed off mid-lifer's. It sounded depressing.

"Shane to the kennel, Shane Kennel!" Jamie's voice sounded upset over the loud speaker. Lately with so many strangers hanging around, everyone had been on edge, including Jamie. Shane would be happy once the meeting was over and they could back to a routine. That was if she still had a job.

Even after reading the fliers the no-kill women were handing out, Shane still couldn't see any major differences between what they were doing now and what they would be doing as a no-kill organization. So the staff tried to focus on the increased funding that would be available.

"Donors are much more willing to give to a no-kill establishment than traditional shelters, which we are." Shane said at a recent staff meeting. "I have no idea if it's simply because it sounds better or is just a way to differentiate shelters from Animal Control Facilities. But the fact remains, people and grant funders are much more willing to give to no-kill than traditional shelters."

Day after day they fielded calls on the topic. The callers all seemed to have a similar message; they declared their relief that the shelter wasn't going to kill any more animals. At first the staff tried to explain that they didn't kill animals and how long it'd been since they euthanized a dog for space, but the callers rarely seemed to understand or care. Shane now ignored their comments and instead declared her happiness at the additional grant money they could tap into. But the entire staff was feeling the effects and morale was low.

Shane wondered if the public or the volunteers had any idea what they were talking about. She didn't understand no-kill, so how could they? She couldn't believe the amount of calls, though. It seemed the entire town really believed they killed animals. She thought people knew what they did. Even before she took over it wasn't like they just sat around euthanizing animals. She didn't know about anyone else, but the calls were making her feel like she'd been doing something wrong. And it sounded like people really hated them, or at least hated the place.

Hearing the commotion as soon as she pushed open the kennel doors, Shane realized it wasn't the dogs that had a problem. She walked down the aisle, following the voices to the prep room. Betty and Jackie stood in the doorway. Coming up behind them, Shane saw Jamie in the small room with Chelsea Gardner, MaryAnn the volunteer, and a woman she didn't know.

Shane sighed and looked from Betty to Jackie. "Is this the same misunderstanding?"

"Kinda. It started that way but," Jackie made a face, "but it's gotten worse. I'm sorry."

What's Chelsea doing here? Shane wondered. Chelsea Gardner was one of the original founders of the PHS. She didn't come in very often, typically only to the annual meetings. Unless, of course she heard they were putting dogs down. *Son-of-a-bitch,* Shane thought, *that's what she's doing here.*

"Shane, there you are." Chelsea said, turning towards her. In her late sixties Chelsea, looked fantastic. A die-hard runner she had that lean, sinewy look that complimented her small frame. Wearing three-quarter length black spandex pants, sneakers, and a Leadville 100 running jersey, she looked more like forty years old than almost seventy.

"Hi Chelsea, it's good to see you." Shane said, ducking into the room. "Let's close that door, shall we?" Betty waited until Jackie squeezed into the small space before closing the door. Jamie hopped up on the dryer to sit, out of the way.

Chelsea wasted no time, "I've been told you're putting down dogs. Is it true?" A formidable woman, Chelsea was only 5'3" with long white hair and a rarely seen smile. She was always polite, but Shane couldn't remember a time when she didn't get her way.

"Who are we putting down?" Shane asked, looking back at Betty.

Chelsea followed her gaze then looked back at Shane, "you're not putting dogs down?"

Shane shook her head. *This is ridiculous. I'm standing in a tiny room with six women being accused of killing dogs. No matter what I do, this is the thanks I get. Unfuckingbelievable.* Shane shook her head. *Weeks of moving dogs, begging people and throwing my own house out of whack and this is the appreciation I get. Business as usual; Shane's killing dogs again, unbelievable.*

Just as she was about to fire back she heard Dee's voice in her head reminding her that they were all there for the same reason. Even if they didn't agree on the strategy they all had the same goal. "Someone just needs to remember that we're all on the same team," Dee had said last time they talked.

Shane took a breath before beginning, "Chelsea, I appreciate your concern. Let me give you an update of where we're at. We haven't euthanized a dog for space for over a year. About six weeks ago our intakes picked up and our adoptions dropped off. Now our adoptions are back to where they should be but we're full, really full. I have spent the last three weeks working with local boarding kennels to get them to foster dogs. Chelsea, we have 138 dogs in our care right now." Shane paused knowing Chelsea would understand the implications.

"Now our worlds have been ripped apart here. We have spent weeks racking our brains, driving across the county and inconveniencing our own families just to ensure these dogs stay alive and have a chance. All the while answering one call after another saying "thank god you guys are going no-kill, now I'll finally come in and adopt from you," or worse. I'm sure you can imagine."

Chelsea nodded. She was listening intently and hadn't broken eye contact but she seemed to lean back a bit.

"Now I have to make some decisions. And yes some of them are difficult. Heidi's been here for almost eight months. She's not moving, the public is seeing something in her that is causing them to not adopt her. I can't keep ignoring that. She's a Boxer that looks like a Pit so it's difficult to transfer her. She spends her days jumping non-stop in her run. It's the saddest thing in the world to watch."

"Now if you, or any of you," she looked at each woman, "want to adopt a dog, or want to help one of these dogs, I encourage you to consider her, Bowser or Aldo – dogs that have been here for a while. But you walking in because you heard we were going to euthanize some, pisses me off. Where were you for the last six months those dogs were here?"

"And for the record, I'm not planning on putting down Bowser. If anything, the opposite. We're featuring him, Aldo and Onyx this month, but Heidi," Shane shook her head, "we've tried. Brett has been bringing her out to Dalton ranch and running her three times a week, it's not helping."

"He's not going to take it well," Jamie said quietly.

"Maybe not," Shane knew Jamie was right, "but I can tell you at this point," she said, looking back at Chelsea, "I value his opinion and feelings on this issue much more than yours, Chelsea. Just because he's been here. He's spent hours and hours with these dogs. You got called in over a miscommunication."

Five minutes later Shane left the prep room with the first ever apology from Chelsea Gardner. Her heart was beating as fast as ever but she felt great. She couldn't believe she had just said that. It felt good to stand up to such a strong woman. And to see the look on Chelsea's face. She wasn't pissed, she actually seemed pleasantly surprised. She actually shook Shane's hand before she left, that was the first time she'd ever done that.

Smiling, Shane answered her ringing phone. "Hey Sheila," she said to her sister, "How's your day going?" Shane walked into her office feeling better than she had in days.

"Shane, did you hear?" Sheila sounded upset. "Jeremy's friend Bart got mauled by a dog. A dog that was being fostered by his family. Shane this is serious, is it one of your dogs?"

Shane put her head down on her desk. *Son-of-a-bitch, once this hits the papers, all the fosters would be back.*

Chapter 31

The following day the story hit the paper. Knowing it was coming, Lily, Dee and Shane called every foster home the night before. They explained the situation and why the families didn't have to worry about the animals they were caring for. Most were fine with it. A couple seemed nervous and Shane thought they'd probably return the animals before the end of the day, but most understood.

Her day went a lot better than she had imagined it would. Calling everyone the night before was Dee's idea. And it worked brilliantly. Considering how badly it could have gone, by three o'clock Shane was grateful they were just dealing with the typical calls. Questions about the meeting still dominated so Shane wasn't surprised when she answered a call for Judy.

After explaining that Judy didn't work there but that she could get her a message, the woman hesitated. "I, I suppose. I guess that would be okay. I just don't know, I just –"

"Okay," Shane said before taking a deep, loud breath. It was a trick she used to calm down stressed dogs and she hoped it would work with the woman. "Do you have a message for Judy?"

"Yes, yes" the woman sighed. "Can you please tell her Kathy from Pet Orphans of Central Colorado called?"

Pet Orphans, Shane thought *wasn't that the place that Judy sent Hogg/Harley too?* "Is this about Harley?" Shane asked, she didn't want to upset the woman but now she was curious.

"Yes."

"Well you can tell me. My name's Shane Hillard, I'm the Director here."

"Oh, I uh, oh okay," she hesitated. "I, uh, I just wanted to explain. As you can imagine we've been inundated with calls all day. But before you are, I wanted to let you know how it happened."

Shane had no idea what the woman was talking about but a feeling of unease was growing inside her. Pulling a chair over, she sat down.

"We fostered Harley with one of our volunteers. She's really active and does a good job with the bigger dogs. Well her husband's father passed away and they had to fly west for the funeral. None of us could take him, we're all already full. So she asked her sister. That's why she was back down there near you, she was at her sister's house. We had no idea he would ever bite."

Like a combination lock clicking into place, Shane realized what she was talking about. "Are you talking about Harley? The big, black Shepherd Judy transferred up to you." She couldn't believe it. *Hogg was the dog who mauled Jeremy's friend? Ohmigod.* Shane sat back in the chair hardly noticing anything going on around her.

"Harley mauled that kid?" Shane asked, knowing she should have kept her voice down but unable to.

Kinsey turned and faced her, her mouth hanging open.

"Uh, yeah, that was him. Did you have any idea he could bite? I mean our records don't indicate a bite history."

"Where is he now?" Shane asked. She supposed she should have felt vindicated but she didn't. Instead she felt awful, sick to her stomach. "I'll pass the message on to Judy."

"You have got to be kidding me," Kinsey said after Shane hung up.

Shaking her head, Shane didn't answer as she walked out back. She couldn't believe it. *It was Hogg, Harley. Right here, at Jeremy's friend's house. Unfuckingbelievable. The dog I said would bite, did. And worse, he bit a kid. It could have been Jeremy. Jesus, it could have been way worse.* Her heart was racing and tears welled in her eyes. She couldn't believe it.

~

Four hours later, sitting at the kitchen table, Shane's sister Sheila just kept shaking her head. Jeremy had gone out to play with the dogs and they were finishing off their iced tea's.

"Shane, I'm just saying," Sheila stood, picking up the dirty dishes. "Put yourself in my position. I sat up with Patty all night last night. Her life is never going to be the same. She's going to have to spend the next few years going from hospital to hospital, surgery to surgery. She has to help her son, a boy Jeremy's age, go to the bathroom, take a shower, hell she's got to help him with everything. He's not going to be able to play sports any more. Jesus, Shane I don't know what I'd do if that was Jeremy."

"I know," Shane said, and she did know. It had been on her mind all day and was practically all she could think about. But one dog, one bad dog didn't represent all dogs. Ever since she first heard, Shane had been rolling a similar thought over in her head. How do they defend all the good dogs out there when something like this happens? How will anyone trust her, when they're talking about kids getting bit in the face? How will any of them ever be trusted again when he went through their doors?

"That dog came through our shelter," she said finally.

Sheila turned away from the sink, "What?"

"He was surrendered to us."

"And?"

"And none of us trusted him. We told them not to transfer him."

"You did," Sheila said, sounding relieved.

"I did, and so did Dee, but we were out voted. Tomorrow at the annual meeting we're going no-kill, which in some ways doesn't mean anything but in others it means everything. Anyway, they wanted to use him as an example, a test run they called it, towards implementing their no-kill philosophy."

"And transferring a dog like him would help them do that?"

"No. And the stupid thing is we transfer tons of dogs, just not questionable ones. I don't know, I feel like a puppet. The President of the Board told me I've gotta get the staff promoting the changeover while Dee tells me she's gonna leave if we go no-kill. I don't know, I just –" Shane trailed off, she didn't know what she felt.

After a minute she continued, "We keep bunches of dogs, older dogs, ugly dogs, spazy dogs, some we have to work with for months before they can be adopted. But others," she gestured to the paper sitting on the table, "this dog tolerated humans, that was it. Made to live around them, and worse with kids, it was only a matter of time before he snapped. I think it was a cruel thing to do to him. I think he was probably suffering," Shane pulled the napkin out of her lap and walked over to the counter. "He really didn't like anybody."

And I knew it, I knew he was dangerous. Why didn't they listen to me? Now a kid has been bit and the entire community is nervous about the dogs in their homes. Unbelievable. No one believes Shane, though. What does she know? God damn it, she thought, *I was right about that dog. I read him correctly.*

"You know Shane," Sheila said drying the last of the dishes. "I heard a story on the radio the other day. It was a guy who had worked at ground zero in New York. He was on the clean-up crew and said that he and his co-workers felt horrible about what they were doing. They thought of themselves like ants crawling over the graves of all those people. Then he went to a parent-teacher conference at his daughter's school and read a story she had written about him. She called him a hero and said how proud she was of him for what he was doing. It changed the way the guy thought of himself from then on."

Sheila continued, "I'm just saying, you know Jeremy thinks the world of you. You're the dog whisperer. There's nothing you can't train these dogs to do, when you have the time and energy," she paused, smiling briefly. "And I'd bet there's nothing you can't do at that place, with the right backing and support. Maybe if you look at yourself differently you might just see what the rest of us already do."

"Like I'm helping instead of hurting them?" Shane asked, pouring herself more iced tea.

"Exactly. Shane you don't hurt animals. You'd never hurt an animal. Do you really believe that?"

"No, I guess not. You know," Shane said, picking up a dish towel. "I hear dad's words in my head all the time. No emotions Shane! Suck it up. A strong person is a silent person." She pounded her fist in her hand just like he used to do.

"Oh god Shane, let it go." Sheila put the last plate away and took the dish towel from her. "You spent your entire childhood trying to please a man, impossible to please. I mean listen to that, no emotions, be quiet. Give me a break, it's no wonder he was so dysfunctional. Let it go Shane. Find yourself some new mantras, hell," she said wiping her hands, "my friend Missy's got me saying I'm a strong, confident woman twenty-five times a day. Say that – but don't tell yourself to shut up. Strong people stand up for what they believe in. They don't keep their mouths shut. The people that keep their mouths shut are the followers. And Shane, you're no follower."

Chapter 32

Shane went for a drive after dinner. She needed some time alone and hadn't been able to spend much time with her kids lately. Juice and Henry were in the backseat with their heads out the windows while Chance jumped between them trying to find an open spot. The windows barely went half-way down so the small dog stood on the armrest to reach.

Shane shook her head wondering again why every vehicle she'd ever had had back windows that didn't go all the way down. She could appreciate that some people had kids and not letting the windows go down for them was a good thing, but did everyone have to suffer? Was every car made for kids? Chance barked at Juice, took two steps to her right and tried the same move with Henry. Shane smiled, she really was a good dog. Shane didn't want three dogs, couldn't give three dogs the attention they deserved, but still.

She pulled over next to the river, looking around before opening her door. Neither Henry nor Juice needed leashes, but Chance would. Shane tried to remember where she left her retractables. A runner was coming up the bike path so Shane waited for her to pass. The breeze felt good and she lowered her window all the way to enjoy it.

The runner had a dog with her. He wasn't leashed, just trotting alongside of her, his tongue hanging out. His eyes were focused on his owner, only glancing at the sidewalk from time to time.

It has to be more than just keeping them alive or adopting them out, Shane thought. *Don't we also have a responsibility to the community?* She watched as the runner stopped at the corner, the Lab mix comfortably matching her pace. *If we, the professionals, put adopting the animals over everything else, how can we be considered professionals at all? We'll be helping ourselves at any cost and using the emotion card to justify it.*

Jesus, I'm defending killing. Listen to me, Shane thought shaking her head. The thing she hated most about her job, the thing she wished she never had to do again, and the thing that woke her up most nights, sweating and freezing at the same time. *And they've got me defending it! What the hell?*

Shane would never have guessed this a year ago, when Payton was pleading with her to become a Euthanasia Technician. Shane had put it off as long as she could, but the shelter was short staffed. Only Kim and Jamie were doing euth's at the time. And they were doing a lot; a couple of dogs and triple that in cats each week.

Both Kim and Jamie had been calling in sick a lot and Payton refused the training, saying as Shelter Director she didn't have the time. So Shane had a choice, become a Euthanasia Technician or get fired and they'd hire someone who would.

"I'm sorry Shane I know you want more time, probably need more time, but I can't give it to you. Either you take the training and start performing the procedure or I hire someone who will. It's that simple," Payton Williams, Shelter Director and Shane's boss said to her.

It was anything but simple to Shane. She of course had considered euthanizing animals before taking the job. It was the animal shelter, that's what they did. But was it something she did? In the past few months she'd held the animals while someone else injected the drug. Was there really a difference?

Shane had only planned on staying at the job for a short time but she'd really started to like it. It wasn't like she had much of a choice. She knew she'd be able to do it, be strong enough to do it. Kim, Jamie and Dee all did it. If they could do it and still be fine every day, so could she. But did she want to do it? For years she'd been trying to define herself, trying to find out where she fit into the world. Was Euthanasia Technician that place?

The only way to move up at the shelter, if she was planning on staying, was to become trained. And technically they euthanized a lot more old, sick and mean dogs and cats than anything else. Shane was okay with some of those being euthanized, especially if they were suffering.

"Fine. I'll do it," she told Payton. Not bothering to explain what she was feeling. After all, Shane figured it wouldn't have been a surprise to anyone that she didn't want the training. Why bother saying what everyone already knew. The strong remain silent, her father always said. How stupid she'd been to listen to his advice.

The first dog she put down, Kim assisted and yelled at her the whole time. The dog was older and had only been with them a couple of days. But Ernie, Shane remembered the second she had to do, that was a tough one. Being one of Jamie's favorites she refused to do him and Kim called in sick so it was up to Shane.

Shane had loved that dog. She'd walked him every day her first two weeks there. He was a wonderful old dog that just needed a place to live out his days. An old terrier mix he was shaggy and silly and just a good old boy. Shane considered adopting him but at the time her sister wouldn't allow it.

Shane put him down on Friday afternoon and cried the entire weekend. Every time she closed her eyes she saw his shaggy eyebrows, his wiry goatee and his cute little black nose. Her sister, never having seen her so upset, felt horrible and told Shane she could have the next one. But it didn't matter, by Sunday she couldn't take it anymore – she was going to quit instead.

She couldn't do it again. She would not take a dog that was wonderful and put him down for something as trivial as space. She wouldn't do it, couldn't do it. So she went in Monday morning with her two-week noticed typed and in her hands. She would refuse to euthanize another dog. Jamie said no, she could too. But by the time she had an opportunity to talk to Payton, Payton had been fired and Dee asked Shane if she would take over the Shelter Director job. Thinking this was her opportunity to change things, she tore up her two-week notice and took the job.

Getting out of the truck, Shane opened the hatch and put a leash on Chance while the other two ran full speed into the water. They both loved the water but in different ways. Henry stopped a couple feet in and lowered his head to drink while Juice scrambled for a stick that was quickly floating by.

It was a beautiful evening, in the 70's with just a light breeze. Shane watched as the sun dipped behind the Mountains. As popular for kayaking as it was for fly-fishing, the river was typically crowded during the day. But in the evenings the bugs took over and most people confined their activities to its shores. Shane looked up river to see if anyone was fishing before she began walking.

She wondered if Judy would say Harley was a random incident. But then realized it didn't matter. Shane knew that dog was dangerous. *I told them that dog was dangerous and they ignored it. Acted like my opinion wasn't worth squat. Acted like all dogs are equal, shit she even said so much with Chance.*

Chance pulled Shane down to the water and took a cautious step in. Shane wondered if the dog had ever seen water like this before. Chance put her nose down into the water before taking a second hesitant step. As she stood, looking for a place to put her paw down, Juice ran over, soaking her completely. Chance ran back out of the water and shook off.

And that poor dog. I didn't like him, but he must have been out of his mind being in a house with kids. He barely tolerated other dogs, but kids. Poor thing, making him endure that just so she could feel like she saved one? And why him? Why the worst dog we had in there in months? Because I was against it? Shit, she compared Hogg to Chance, what did she know?

She didn't know, Shane realized suddenly. *Judy had no idea that this was preventable. She has no idea that we know what we're talking about. Holy Shit,* Shane hadn't thought about it before.

She obviously doesn't give us any credit for knowing animal behavior. She doesn't give us credit for much. But was it more than that? Shane wondered. *Could I have done more? Insisted on another opinion?*

The strong remain silent, her sister was right. The strong don't remain silent, the strong speak out. They don't sit idly by while a dangerous dog is sent away. They don't let people tell them they're wrong when they know they're not. They stand up for themselves, they stand up for what's right.

But what about my job? What about it? They should want the Director to be strong, to stand up for what's right. And they should trust me, they should know that I have experience and know what the fuck I'm talking about.

"Hmpf," she had hardly trusted herself over these last few years, was it any wonder no one else trusted her either? She threw the stick for Juice a couple of times while Henry and Chance dug in the bushes, following the smell of some small critter.

The strong remain silent. Now thinking about it, it sounded so stupid. If I heard anyone else say it I'd think they were nuts. The strong may not be the biggest talkers in the room, but they do something when something needs to be done. They may not get all emotional but they don't turn a blind eye on something they know is wrong.

Her sister said she was a leader. Was she a leader? Shane ducked as Juice shook off, but the dog still covered her legs with river water. *I don't like to be a follower, that's for sure. But do I have what I need to be a leader? God I wish Dee wasn't so distant lately, I'd love to talk to her about this.*

Of course, I know what Dee would say. "Don't you worry about having or not having what it takes to be a leader; that's fear showing through. You were born with everything needed to be a leader; otherwise the idea wouldn't be in your mind at all. Trust yourself, trust your gut, and do what's right."

So what is right? Shane thought, knowing the answer already. After a few more minutes of tossing a stick into the water, she loaded the dogs back up in the truck and started the engine. Hoping to get a break from thinking for a minute, she turned on the radio.

Shane switched between channels until she came to a song just starting with a good beat. It sounded familiar so she turned it up. After a few seconds she realized it was the song Jamie had been singing.

"Well you know those times when you feel like there's a sign there on your back, Says I don't mind if ya kick me
Seems like everybody has, Things go from bad to worse, You'd think they can't get worse than that, And then they do"

"Sounds familiar," Shane said aloud.

"Yeah, If you're going through hell Keep on moving, face that fire, Walk right through it You might get out Before the devil even knows you're there."

"Guess that's my answer right there," Shane said shaking her head and pulling out of the parking area.

She drove home slowly. She was going to have to say something at the meeting tomorrow. But she didn't know if she could speak in front of all those people. There was supposed to be a hundred people or more. *Do I have the guts? Maybe, I'll be up all night thinking about it one way or the other. Would it matter?* She didn't know. *Was it worth it? Yeah, it's worth it,* she thought, realizing she'd already made the decision.

"If you're going through hell Keep on going, don't slow down, If you're scared don't show it You might get out, Before the devil even knows you're there."

Chapter 33

By eleven the following morning Shane was both excited and nervous. She had hardly slept the night before and figured it might be her last day working at the shelter, but she knew today was going to be different. The days of her standing in the back of the room and keeping her mouth shut were over. She was going to stand up and be strong.

At least that was the plan, she thought as her stomach churned on her second cup of coffee. Turnout was better than expected, even the seats in the front were filling in. Shane sat with Jamie, Kinsey and Laura in a row toward the back of the large room.

Kim wasn't there. Dee had had a long talk with her after their last meeting. During it, Kim stormed out twice and quit once, then broke down. She told Dee she couldn't do the job anymore but felt trapped because she couldn't afford to quit. She said she didn't have any other skills and that no one would hire an executioner. Dee promised to help her get another job if she'd continue going to the psychiatrist. After her first meeting back with the doctor, Dee introduced Kim to her cousin who owned a landscaping business. "Good hard work, outside where she can get a lot of sun." Dee commented later, happy with the outcome.

"I'd like to thank you all for coming," Paul, the Board President began. "As you know," he paused, waiting while it quieted down, "As you know, today is a very exciting day for us. We are setting sail on a new path today. A path that brings us into the 21st Century. A path that coincides with your beliefs and a path that you can be proud of. Today we are asking you to vote with us to change our by-laws. Times have changed, yesterday's way of doing things is no longer accepted, it's time for us to show our commitment to the animals and to all of you, by pledging from this day forth that we are a no-kill shelter."

The room erupted in applause. Shane remained sitting. She could just barely see Dee between the bodies standing in front of her. Seated up on the stage with the Board of Directors, Dee's chair was pulled off to the side. The only one on stage not standing or clapping, Dee sat looking around the room, her lips pressed tightly together.

There were a lot of people Shane didn't know there, which worked out great for her plan. Halfway through her sleepless night, Shane had an idea on what to do with all the fosters that would be returning over the next few days. The following weekend was 4th of July, the boarding kennels were booked and two-thirds of the foster homes would be going out of town. She needed new foster homes quickly. Getting volunteers, Betty, Brett and Jackie together just before the meeting, Shane told them her plan. All three were happy to help and were now sitting near the doors.

"To spell out exactly what this change means," Paul continued. "I'd like to introduce the driving force behind this ground-breaking referendum; Judy Bishop. Judy has spent an exorbitant amount of time gathering information, researching best practices and realigning our programs to ones matching the best in the nation. I'm also pleased to announce that she has generously agreed to take on the role of Executive Director. We're sorry to be losing Dee Nizhoni, who has been a tremendous leader these last few years. But we know this decision will move us on the right path forward. Please join me in welcoming, the leader in our communities no-kill movement and Pinewood's new Executive Director; Judy Bishop."

Shane sat in stunned silence as the applause sounded around her. *Executive Director? Executive Director? Her boss. Son-of-a-bitch.* Her heart raced. Shane stared at Dee who looked her way and offered a sympathetic smile. The girls next to her tried to get her attention but Shane just shook her head slowly not believing her own ears. *Unfuckingbelievable! Breathe*, she reminded herself as she heard her clenched teeth grinding against each other.

"Thank you all," Judy said, taking the microphone from Paul. "I'm thrilled to be orchestrating such a worthwhile endeavor on behalf of all of you and of course on behalf of the animals. As you'll soon hear, this is the future in Animal Sheltering. No longer are we a country accepting substandard practices and care for the animals we love so much. No longer are we accepting the number one killer of animals in our country – killing for space – as an acceptable practice. And no longer will we accept ignorance or be blamed for outdated practices and ways of doing things."

Substandard practices?! Shane couldn't believe it. *What the hell? Ignorance?! Look who's talking about ignorance. Ohmigod.* Her heart pounded. She couldn't believe it, the bitch was trashing them. And making herself look like she was the hero there to save the day. *Unfuckingbelievable. Breathe,* Shane reminded herself again, though it was getting more and more difficult.

Judy continued, her voice rising, "we're told it's our fault Animal Shelters have to kill. We're told that we're to blame for there being too many animals. When in fact it is Animal Shelters' own bad business practices that cause people to go elsewhere for an animal. By not being open when the majority of the people are off of work, by not having offsite adoption locations, and by being rude, ignorant and generally unpleasing to deal with, Animal Shelters drive people away. Then they kill the animals and blame us for there being too many. This has got to stop, and with your vote today we'll do just that."

Sheila and Jeremy were sitting two rows in front of Shane and off to the right. Sheila turned in her chair and looked directly at Shane, a question raising her eyebrows.

Shane nodded once, her heart pounding. The more she heard the more she wanted to scream. *You're no follower, Shane.* Her sister's words echoed in her ears. *I can't, won't work with that woman, which means this is my last day. Unbelievable.* Tears welled up in her eyes. *Breathe, god damn it,* she thought blinking quickly and biting the inside of her mouth.

"For years shelters have made the rules, have chosen to kill rather than find alternatives. Now, finally we have a voice. A voice that screams, No More! We will not accept the death of so many wonderful animals any longer. An Animal Shelter by its very name implies protection. A shelter – a place of protection. Not a place that you're locked in then killed at, that's not a shelter, and that's not humane.

For years we've accepted the shelters practice of Adopt a Few, Kill the Rest. Well it's time we brought back the humane in our name. It's time to make people responsible for their own animals, to insist upon it. It's time we treated the animals – we share our homes and our hearts with – the way we'd like to be treated. The time of killing is over. We no longer accept it. We are going to be a truly humane Humane Society – a no-kill Animal Shelter."

The crowd erupted. Shane looked down the row at Jamie, Kinsey and Laura. *Did her face mirror the confused looks on theirs?* Not understanding how so many people could be so passionate about this, Shane looked around. She saw a few groups of people really hollering and clapping, but the majority seemed like they were clapping because they were supposed to. *Well at least that was something.*

The applause lasted more than a minute and finally Judy held up her hands to quiet it. "At this time I'd like to open the floor to questions."

Shane watched as Dee's hand flew into the air. Judy looked at her for a couple of seconds before nodding her head. Dee walked over to Judy, who reluctantly passed her the microphone.

"Thank you, Judy for allowing me the chance to speak." Dee waited while it quieted down. "Ladies and gentlemen first of all I'd like to thank you all for coming today and supporting all the animals of our community. It has been my pleasure to serve you for the last five years.

I'm delighted to report that the fundraising drive I've been heading up the last year has been highly successful. We've raised over 1.8 million dollars! Thanks to all of you!" Dee waited until the clapping quieted. "It will of course go with the donations the Board has raised. I believe that amount is $200,000?" She paused, looking at Paul. He nodded once. "I'm sorry that I'm not going to be around to raise the additional three million that's needed to build our new shelter, but I cannot support this change to no-kill."

The room got completely quiet for a moment then a number of people began talking at once.

Dee held up her hand, when they quieted down she continued. "As many of you know I'm not a fan of scare tactics, or generalizations, so let me just take a moment to respond to the points Judy has just made. Let me read them to be sure I have them all," Dee looked down at a napkin she'd carried up with her, "substandard care, outdated practices, ignorant and unpleasing manners, being rude, blaming the public, number one killer of animals," she looked up at the audience. "I'm not sure who she's talking about, there are certainly organizations struggling with a lot of these issues, but PHS isn't one of them."

"I don't want to downplay how important these things are, but I want you to vote for this change because it's good for this organization and this community, not because other shelters, in other areas are still struggling with these issues."

Dee continued, walking around the podium. "There are shelters still so overwhelmed with the number of animals coming to them that they are indeed forced to euthanize many. And there are others who are steeped in yesterday's mindset and culture, but not here. We do not employ substandard care and outdated practices."

"We have more than twelve different programs running at any given time which provide enrichment for the animals in our care. We have multiple options for animals, even after we exceed the space we have available, and we have active and supportive volunteers and foster families. This fact alone should tell you what kind of organization we are. We could not have 400 active volunteers if we employed substandard practices or if we were the number one killer of animals."

Dee paused and walked across the small stage. "We're not broken. We don't need to be fixed. But if this is about evolving and progressing forward I would urge you to consider a couple of things. First, the term no-kill is inaccurate; under no-kill doctrine we will still euthanize animals at the shelter, we just won't be doing it for space. Which is something we've been doing with dogs for a year now. We're still struggling with the number of cats coming in so this change would only affect cats - and to be honest with you, we euthanize more feral cats than we do domestic cats for space."

"Second, making people use the word kill when they say the organizations name is completely against my principles. Have you heard of the Law of Attraction? We draw to us what we focus on. And focusing on an unpopular strategy that is hardly being used any longer is shortsighted. And if part of this decision is an image change then you're even crazier to put the word kill in your name or strategy because it reinforces the old image."

And lastly, but equally as disheartening is the fact that it separates us. It separates us from other shelters that are still struggling and from all the amazing people that worked for decades and made it possible for us to even be having this discussion today."

"The number of homeless animals in our country did not lower by itself. It lowered because of the tremendous work and efforts made by thousands of people in the industry before us. It has gotten better because they insisted on programs in schools and because they made spaying and neutering household terms. When local veterinary clinics wouldn't alter young animals, they worked with Universities and progressive Veterinarians to establish safe and successful early-age spaying and neutering programs and then pushed until they became commonly accepted. They fought to get us where we are today so I'm having trouble understanding why we'd want to separate ourselves from them."

"Judy said our mantra is Adopt a Few – Kill the Rest, but the mantra of the no-kill movement is Adopt a Few – Ignore the Rest. And that's something I cannot do. No one wants to put down wonderful animals, but to turn them away and let them fend for themselves which is what happens with so many no-kills. I just don't see how that's humane."

As Dee was continuing, a thought formed in Shane's head. *If they were no-kill, they would never have taken in that dog in the first place. The Husky from last year or Hogg for that matter. Interesting,* she thought, wondering briefly what they'd be talking about instead.

"For those of you unaware," Dee continued, "we have been in a war for the better part of thirty years. It's been a war against overpopulation. And we're winning the war. In the early 80's we had twenty million animals without homes. Today we have around seven million. That's only three million dogs and four million cats. That's an amazing accomplishment."

She paused, lowered her voice and concluded. "Listen, it's not about my job. Though I loved my job and I love what we've been able to accomplish here over the last year. But I'm one of those people who is committed to all animals, not just the chosen few that we will end up letting into the facility. I can appreciate rescues, after all we're all different and it's great that there's different non-profits to fill our personal needs, but when you live in an area like we do, where there isn't another option for animals, adopting a black and white philosophy like this often leaves many with no resources. We have to maintain open-admission status, for their sakes. Because it's not about me, it's about them and that's why I cannot be a part of the new policy going forward."

The room had grown completely quiet. Even the kids who had been fidgeting earlier seemed to feel the change. Everyone waited as Dee took her seat and Judy stood back up.

"Okay then, thank you Dee." Judy looked around the room, "Now that that's been said, are there any questions, questions about the upcoming change?"

"So is that an issue?" A woman's voice sounded from across the room. "Will we have to close our doors to local animals?"

"Of course not. With all due respect to Dee, our goal is to remain open-admission while of course abiding by the no-kill philosophy."

"And what if you can't?" Another voice called out. "What happens to our animals then?"

"Don't worry," Judy held up her hands at the growing unrest sounding in the room. "If it ever comes to that, we'll ask you to hold onto your animals for a few days or weeks until we have an opening. I assure you we realize there isn't another option for animals locally so it's in our best interest to take in everyone in need."

"And what if we can't wait a week or two?" The same voice called out.

"I'm sure that won't be a problem. With the changes I have in store we'll be able to move animals faster than ever before. You won't have to worry about it."

Chapter 34

Unbelievable, Shane thought. She knew she had to say something. It felt to her like the room could go either way so she raised her arm quickly and asked the woman in front of her if she could borrow the newspaper that was sticking out of her bag. The headline read, Child Mauled by Dog in Own Home.

Shane didn't know if Judy would call on her. She didn't know if she'd even hear her over the sound of her own heartbeat which was filling her ears. *Should I just stand up?*

"Yes, Shane." Judy pointed to her, a questioning look crossing her face.

"Hi everyone," Shane said, standing.

"Louder." Someone hollered.

"Sorry. My name is Shane Hillard, and I've been the Shelter Director for the last year." Her heart thumped so loud she was sure the girls next to her could hear it. "I wanted to talk about the 800-pound gorilla in the room. The incident that happened last year. That's when this no-kill stuff really took hold. It's also the time that the Board stopped trusting us and when you lost faith in us. So I'd like to talk about that just for a minute."

"Shane, now's really not the time." Paul, the Board President, had taken the microphone from Judy.

"Let her talk," Dee called out.

"Yeah, let her talk," Sheila, Shane's sister hollered, smiling.

Shane saw Paul shrug his shoulders so she continued, "We were never allowed to set the record straight about that event. And since we are your community Animal Shelter, you have a right to know what happened. For those of you unaware, last year a dog in our care was put down because of his health. He was a large, ninety-pound Husky. He had lived outside his whole life, and had a tumor on his belly that hung down close to his elbows, which made it difficult for him to stand up, lie down or go up and down stairs. He was ten years old. His owner, a woman brought him to us as a surrender.

Now a dog in his condition, if he couldn't live with his family any longer, should have been put down by his family. But she refused to do that. He stayed at the shelter for four days, in the holding area. On his last day we got six dogs in. That put us over seventy-five adult dogs in the building. We have space for less than seventy. Payton, the Shelter Director at the time, chose to put him and a number of other older dogs down, six total.

The story broke that we had killed a man's dog. That his wife had stolen it and that he had come to the shelter looking for it multiple times. The paper implied that we hid the dog in back then killed it as soon as possible. This was not the case at all. The dog was surrendered by the wife who was worried he would slowly die in the backyard. The man never came looking for his dog. And unfortunately we were not in a position to save elderly, sick dogs who had one maybe two years left of their lives. The Board fired Payton following the story. Now I'm not defending her, I do things a lot different than her, but I can understand what she did and why."

Shane wanted to take a breath but didn't want to lose her train of thought so she plowed forward. "Because you see, something I didn't get until just a little while ago is that she worked here and dealt with things from the mindset that she had to protect animals from you. This must be the blame Judy talked about. You have to understand, we deal with a lot of people that have very little common sense and sometimes zero animal sense. I think we may get lost in that from time to time and assume everyone is that way. It's probably more likely the 80/20 rule. Twenty percent of the people account for eighty percent of our headaches. But you know what this is?" Shane gestured to Judy and the Board sitting at the front of the room, "and this" she said, holding the newspaper up, "this is you protecting the animals from us. And that's what I just realized."

After swallowing, Shane continued, "you know part of this job is taking animals lives. That's our responsibility. It's not fun, believe me. It weighs heavily on all of us when we have to take an animal's life, any animal. But some animals are not safe to be in the public, some animals, like that Husky last year, should have been put down by his owner. And this one," she held up the paper again, "this animal was not safe in a home." Shane paused, feeling all eyes on her. The room was completely quiet except for her heart beating loudly in her ears.

"You see, this dog came to us weeks ago. He was aloof and guarded. I assessed him and came to the conclusion that he was dangerous. He had aggressive tendencies and was very uncomfortable around people. Dee," Shane gestured to the stage, "also assessed the dog and agreed. Judy however, did not. She convinced the Board to transfer the dog. They told Dee and me they were going to use him as a test case for the upcoming no-kill vote. Now here we are on the day of the vote, and this test-case hasn't been brought up, and now another 800-pound gorilla is brewing."

Everyone began talking at once so Shane waited. She wanted to finish but appreciated the moment to regain her thoughts. "The boy in this story. The boy, who will never be the same because of this dog," She said once the room quieted down, "is a good friend of my nephew's." She looked toward him, "his family's life will be scarred forever because of this avoidable incident."

"And it was avoidable. Both Dee and I cautioned that this dog was a ticking time bomb and they didn't listen to us." Shane turned toward Judy. "Both of us advised you against transferring him. And Judy," Shane's voice cracked and she paused briefly, "I told you specifically to make sure that dog didn't end up in a home with children."

Shane paused not sure what she should say next. "You know, I never understood this whole kill, no-kill thing. We've never been about killing. Never. Yes we had to do it when we had tons more animals than we had homes for, but luckily in our area, at least with dogs, we're not there anymore. We use non-euthanasia solutions every day. Right now I have more than 170 animals out in foster. That's more than we even have in the building."

"In the last month we've gotten slammed with dogs. Rather than euthanize them or close our doors I've reached out to the grooming shops, boarding kennels and daycares and they've allowed our animals to board there when we're out of space. I even reached out to the Veterinarian's in town, who have shunned us since we opened our clinic. And one is even helping. We are putting nursing moms and their litters in Senior Centers so seniors can enjoy watching the kittens. The dogs in our care all leave knowing basic commands, including, sit, lie down, and shake hands. Every dog up for adoption is walked three times a day and every afternoon they're provided with enrichment activities."

"I guess what I'm saying is that, Dee's right; we're not broken. We're doing it right. We're doing great things. And I suppose it's my fault for not sending out press releases or a newsletter touting that information. But to stand here and fight for killing; I can't, won't do it. But I will fight against this," Shane gestured to the Board. "I have to fight against ignorance. Maybe we're not the most savvy people to deal with and maybe we curse too much and get pissed when someone brings a dog back after having it only one day, but we know what we're doing." Shane realized it was true and felt herself stand up a little straighter.

"This vote to me isn't about killing or not killing, it's about who you want running your Animal Shelter. Do you want people that know what they're doing, that understand animals and that realize that it's bigger than just getting them adopted? We have a responsibility to you, our community to take in everyone in need but also to not let out any animal that is dangerous."

"You know our hearts may bring us to this job but it's our heads that keep us here. It's knowing that if we don't shoulder the burden, the animals will. This should never have happened." She held up the newspaper again. "This could have and should have been avoided. How many homes did we just loose? Probably all the classmates of this young boy, but what about the rest of the school, the teachers and administrators, the boys neighbors and anyone putting stock in the paper. All for something that didn't have to happen."

"Anyway," Shane said winding down. "I think it's important that you know, that we know, that the days of us protecting the animals from you are long gone. But I think it's also important to know that the days of you, needing to protect the animals from us, are also past. It's time we did this together. We already work in a humane way. Instead of needing to put the humane back in our name I say we put the word community into it. We *are* your community Animal Shelter, we all love animals and we all want what's best for them – let's work together to make it happen."

As Shane sat down she heard the applause and smiled when she saw the girls next to her standing with others in the room. She had no idea what she'd said but hoped it was semi-intelligent. Sheila was smiling broadly and Shane nodded back trying to hide her shaking hands.

Paul, who was still holding the microphone, asked everyone to quiet down and if there were any more questions. A hand went up near the front and a woman stood.

"May I borrow that?" Chelsea asked Paul as she stood near the stage. He handed her the microphone tentatively before walking back to his seat.

"For those of you who don't know me I'm Chelsea Gardner. I'm one of the founders of this fine establishment. If you haven't seen me around, that's because I haven't been around. You see we began this organization in the early 80's when there were packs of animals on every corner. It was a lot of work to set up and by the time we got it done I was pretty burnt out, so I let the others run it."

"Now I check in from time to time but I really have a hard time with it. You see, the first week we opened our doors, with half the space the building now has, we were brought twenty dogs. The next week, thirty. And it just kept going up from there. We didn't deal with cats at the time, there was no way we could have. And no one was adopting the dogs, they were a dime a dozen. If you wanted a dog, chances were your kid was going to bring one home from school or you could get one outside of the grocery store, they were everywhere."

"Well, as I'm sure you can imagine our joy of opening the shelter quickly turned into overwhelm and despair. We closed our doors at the end of the first month to regroup and determine what we were going to do. The dogs were dying slowly on the streets. Fighting was rampant and there wasn't enough food to go around. You've all seen it. Anytime you drive through the reservation. Dogs covered in parasites, suffering from preventable diseases, and of course, starving. The same thing we see every time we drive through northern Arizona, was our reality twenty-five years ago."

"We never set out to hurt animals and we certainly never set out to take their lives. But we did set out to be a voice for them." Chelsea paced back and forth across the front of the room as she spoke. "To be a resource and an entity devoted to those we love so much. I may not agree with everything they do here. But I respect them and I respect the knowledge they have and the burden they carry. I cannot possibly understand their world without walking it and living it. But I can put my faith in the hands of the people that truly have not only the animal's best interests at heart, but ours as well. And as a business owner I can respect the point that the people who hold the top positions at this organization, namely the Executive Director and the Shelter Director, are people who balance the needs of the many with the needs of the few. I respect people that balance their hearts and heads both for the animals and for our community."

"When I think about the shelter I helped create, people like Dee Nizhoni and Shane Hillard, are the people I want to see running it. People that have proven themselves through some really difficult challenges. Did you hear what the two of them just said? They have already, on their own, employed this no-kill concept for the last year – successfully. Without tooting their own horn, without asking for more, they've been doing it. And isn't that what we want? Shane shared with us an example of their skills - their ability to read animals. Wouldn't we be smart to trust the horses with a proven record through all types of obstacles than the one who failed significantly the first time out of the gate?"

"Mr. President I vote No! To your no-kill proposal and I offer a rebuttal vote, reinstating Dee Nizhoni as Executive Director and letting the by-laws stand as they are!"

Everyone started speaking at once and the room erupted in a mixture of clapping, accusations, and shouting.

Paul pounded his hand on the table trying to gain control but it was no use until a loud, piercing whistle sounded. Slowly everyone began taking their seats and lowering their voices.

"Um," Shane stood and started speaking as soon as it was quiet enough to. She figured there was no way Paul or Judy would let her speak again and she forgot something she wanted to say. "Um, everyone. One thing I forgot to mention." The room got quiet and all eyes turned towards her again. "As I said, we have quite a few animals out in foster. And looking around the room I see a lot of you who are already fostering. Thank you for that. But as you know Fourth of July is next weekend. Many of the places our animals are staying at are either closed, full or going away and we need your help."

"No matter what happens with the vote in a few minutes I have volunteers who will be standing at the door on your way out today. They have foster-home sign up forms. Please, the only way we can succeed, is with your help. From time to time, like right now we have way more animals than we have space for. If you could just foster them until space opens up in the building," she took one last look around the room. "We can only succeed if we work together. So please, whatever your vote today, consider fostering an animal even if it's just for this weekend and you'll help us, and them, a ton."

Shane's plea was just what Paul and Judy needed to regroup. Paul asked if anyone else had any questions. When no one spoke he indicated the vote was about to begin. "So I'd like to do this by a verbal vote, but if it's at all close, we'll do a paper ballot, just to be sure. All those in favor of changing the by-laws and going no-kill please raise your hands."

Judy's hand was the first to go up, followed by two other people on the Board. Shane was surprised to only see three hands raised on stage. In the crowd a number of hands went up from different sections around the room.

Whispering began again and Paul than asked for a show of hands of people wanting to stay under the current by-laws and vote no to the change. Dee's hand went up followed by the rest of the Board. Shane stared in shock as Paul raised his hand. Shane's was already up, so was Sheila's and both of Jeremy's. Shane smiled at her nephew when he turned to show her. More than half the room had raised their hands.

Paul called for order again, "By a vote of two to one we are voting to keep our by-laws as they stand and will not be changing to a no-kill policy."

The room erupted in applause. Shane was quickly overtaken by slaps on the back and congratulations. It was a few minutes before she could get to the front of the room to find Dee. She hoped this meant Dee would keep her job, but she didn't want to get her hopes up. She finally found Dee off in a corner talking to Chelsea.

"So?" Shane asked, once they were alone.

Dee smiled, "Chelsea has just promised $500,000 for the capital campaign."

"Oh yeah?" Shane asked, smiling as the weight lifted from her shoulders. "You're gonna stay?"

"Of course Yahzi, Ripples, right?" Dee smiled and gave her a hug. "You were great Shane, we're going to make a public speaker out of you yet."

Laughing a few minutes later, Shane led Sheila and Jeremy out of the room. She had promised him lunch at his favorite restaurant and was finally in the mood to actually enjoy it.

Shane stopped at the door to check the foster-home sign-up forms. Two pages of email addresses had been collected of people offering to open up their homes to an animal this weekend. A odd but comfortable thought struck Shane as she left, *what if it all happened just as it was supposed to?*

Epilogue

Two weeks after the annual meeting Shane found herself sitting in a kennel again. This time it was on the adoption floor instead of Holding. And instead of trying to get a dog to eat, she was saying good-bye. Bowser was leaving, to go live in a perfect home.

A mechanic, who owned a garage in town, adopted him. The man lived in an apartment above the shop and had doggie doors to the connecting apartment and the yard. Bowser had been by three times so far and seemed to love the place. And the guy was great. It was the perfect scenario for the large, stately dog, but Shane was going to miss him. Lying with his body up against her outstretched legs, the large dog sighed and put his head down.

It had been crazy at the shelter the week following the meeting. They were only just now beginning to settle back into a routine. Judy resigned following the meeting. She said that she had been blindsided and was never given the support needed to win over the community. Dee rescinded her resignation the following Monday with full Board support and got Shane a dollar-an-hour raise.

Over a hundred families had signed up to foster animals but amazingly they weren't needed. The three days following the meeting ended up being the biggest adoption days on record. Adopting close to ninety animals, they were able to bring all the dogs and many of the cats from foster, back in.

The biggest change however, had been with the community. It felt to Shane like the always present but never declared - us vs. them - undercurrent had disappeared. Normal people were coming in just to thank them, sharing stories about their pets, and asking behavior and training questions. The building had never been busier and everyone was in good spirits.

As for Shane, the day before she'd made it official. Chance was now hers. She knew she could have adopted the sweet girl out from behind the front desk but the small dog had carved a niche in her heart. Every time Shane looked at Chance, the happy dog thumped her tail on the floor.

Sighing, she leaned her head back against the wall. Since the meeting she'd been feeling better about herself than ever before. It was as if for the first time, she knew she was exactly where she was supposed to be. A feeling of complete contentment had been growing inside her. And for the first time ever she felt completely at ease.

Acknowledgements

There have been so many people who have come into my life and supported me on this project. First I need to thank my family, who have been ultimately patient with me through this journey: Chris, Cooper, Oliver, Shunka, Ziva, Kele, Bill and Stripe. A sincere and heartfelt thank you to Chris Nelson, for his love, support and never-ending supply of stories and adventures. A big thank you to Rochelle Smith, Sandy Jones, Jan Koch, Mark Ready, Sue Sternberg and Denis Masella for taking the time to read early versions of this book and providing crucial changes and feedback. Thanks also to Michael Thunder and Lesha Powell for their skilled editorial and proofreading skills.

I would not be where I am at today without the many wonderful canines that have taken the journey with me: Cody, a special Airedale mix and my first true love; TJ, a neurotic Shepherd mix adopted in Minot, N. Dakota; D.O.Gee the hairy Australian Shepherd who left me for my mom; Bowser a giant teddy-bear whose life was taken too early; Oliver, a beautiful black Lab mix who taught me that it is more about them than us; Cooper a devoted Hound mix found in the middle of a highway and my second kindred spirit; Shunka a beautiful Coonhound mix full of attitude, Ziva, a gorgeous but insecure German Shepherd and Kele, a Navajo Terrier – adopted from a Burger King parking lot on the Navajo Nation and featured on the front cover.

A very special thank you needs to go out to all my local sources, resources and contributing organizations. Thank You to the La Plata County Humane Society and everyone who works with and for them, Dr. Patrick Goddard for always giving so much, Foundation for Protection of Animals, La Plata County Animal Protection, Dogster's Spay and Neuter Program, Soul Dog Rescue, Ute Mountain Ute Indian Tribe and the Navajo Nation.

I am also grateful to Sue Sternberg, for her years of guidance and support to Animal Shelters nationwide. To the Humane Society of the United States for providing high-quality publications so vital to those working in the field. To PetSmart Charities for the national transfer program and the many resources they provide to Animal Shelters. I'm grateful to so many groups and organizations that share their resources and knowledge, including: Alley Cat Allies, AHA, ASPCA, Austin's Pets Alive, Boulder Valley Humane Society, Helen Woodward Animal Center, Humane Alliance, Humane Strategies, Maddie's Fund, Wisconsin Humane Society and Longmont Humane Society. Through their efforts and the efforts of many, many others, the Animal Sheltering Industry is evolving into a new era, one that we can all be proud of.

Made in the USA
San Bernardino, CA
21 August 2013